D0581693

Roads and Trackways of the Yorkshire Dales

Roads and Trackways of
The
Yorkshire Dales

Geoffrey N Wright

British Library Cataloguing in Publication Data

Wright, Geoffrey N.
    Roads and trackways of the Yorkshire Dales.
    1. Roads — England — Yorkshire Dales
    National Park — History
    2. Roads, Prehistoric — England — Yorkshire
    Dales National Park — History
    3. Yorkshire Dales National Park (England) —
    History
    I. Title
    388.1′09428′4   HE363.G74Y6
    ISBN 0 86190 123 1

ISBN 0 86190 123 1

Printed in Great Britain by
Billings & Sons Ltd,
Worcester
for Moorland Publishing Co Ltd,
Station Street,
Ashbourne, Derbyshire,
DE6 1DE England.

Contents

Acknowledgements

Many people have helped in the making of this book. The staff of the County Record Offices at Northallerton, Leeds and Wakefield, and of the reference departments of local history sections of libraries at Harrogate, Leyburn, Northallerton, Richmond, Settle, Skipton and Lancaster, have all shown the kindness and patience I have come to expect at such storehouses of knowledge. Special thanks are due to Mr R. Ellis, Head of History Department of Wensleydale School, Leyburn, for allowing me access to the remarkable collection of local history material in the MacFie Library at that school. Members of the staff at the Bainbridge and Grassington offices of the Yorkshire Dales National Park have kindly allowed me to browse through some of their maps and photographs, and I am particularly grateful to Mr Lawrence Barker, of Swaledale, Area Warden in the National Park, whose willingness to share his knowledge of Swaledale local history and lead mining is deeply appreciated. He has kindly allowed me to study and use some of the maps and documents in his collection of Swaledale material. The County Councils of North Yorkshire and West Yorkshire have generously allowed me to reproduce sections of maps and documents from their Record Offices.

The Rev James Alderson, Laurie Fallows and David Hall have all made thoughtful suggestions about tracks in Wensleydale, while Colin Speakman's knowledge of, and enthusiasm for, walkers' tracks throughout the dales, is always stimulating. Mary Mauchline has guided me along the right lines so far as monastic influence in general, and of Fountains Abbey in particular, has been concerned. Various friends in the Dales Centre of the National Trust have — perhaps without realising it —been a constant source of encouragement, especially Roy, Cynthia and Ann Irish, who shared a memorable day on Rombald's Way; Martin and Jacqueline Rae, and Nan Purvis.

The use of two cars has made easier the walking of many miles of tracks, and in this respect I must express my warmest thanks to my Sussex friends

Pat and Pearl Mitchell, of Chichester. Their companionship over dozens of Yorkshire miles has always been a delight to share, and they, like my Stratford friend Lesley Nickell, have been sounding-board for some of my ideas and thoughts, and a source of encouragement on the project.

My wife Jean's contribution to this book is incalculable. She has undertaken not only almost all the research and planning, accompanied me on most of the fieldwork trips, prepared the maps and diagrams, and coped with the problem of typing from a rough and sometimes illegible manuscript, but at all times has been a constant source of help and encouragement.

No writer on such a subject as that covered in this book can fail to appreciate the contribution made by previous authors. Dr Arthur Raistrick, of Linton-in-Craven, wrote what has become my 'bible', and I freely acknowledge my debt to his scholarly research, as I do to that of my fellow-villagers, Marie Hartley and Joan Ingilby. The Yorkshire Dales are fortunate in having such a trio of luminaries whose books will be standard works for years to come. My deepest thanks are due to them and to all who have helped in any way. All the photographs, like any errors or omissions, are the author's own.

Askrigg,
North Yorkshire

Introduction

Many books have been written, and undoubtedly will continue to be written, about the Yorkshire Dales. They cover almost every aspect of this distinctive part of the mid-Pennines, particularly history, topography, land use, natural history and industrial archaeology. Special subjects such as abbeys and castles, and studies of local areas, are plentiful, but apart from Dr Arthur Raistrick's pioneering *Green Tracks on the Pennines*, first published in 1962 and reissued as *Green Roads in the Mid-Pennines* by Moorland Publishing Co in 1978, which deals with the subject geographically, nobody has attempted a chronological history of roads and trackways in the Yorkshire Dales.

One obvious reason for this is that, apart from the few Roman roads in the area, and those deliberately engineered from about the middle of the eighteenth century, most visible roads and tracks in the landscape are not only undated but are undatable. In archaeological terms it is extremely difficult to date a road or to prove when it was, or was not, in use. Written evidence as maps, itineraries, or travellers' diaries, though giving some information about some routes, often throws up more problems than it solves. Yet roads and tracks must have been used, as the backbone of local trade, during the thousand years between the Anglian and Danish settlement of the Dales and the beginning of the turnpike system of 1750-1830, and the enclosure roads of the same period.

Although the approach adopted here tries to be chronological this almost inevitably breaks down at medieval times, when the evidence for various types of road becomes greater, and, though there was then no road-building as we understand it, new roads did evolve — in C.T. Flower's phrase of 1923, they 'made and maintained themselves'. Many of these are still in use today, thus illustrating the continuity of use which makes it impossible to look at them in isolation, either through time or space. Roads must be studied as a network, and one which changed to suit changing needs of population, industry and trade. Only with the Roman

9

and turnpike roads can individual routes be studied.

The geographical area covered here is slightly greater than that of the National Park itself, which, for various reasons when its boundaries were drawn in 1954 did not include Nidderdale. This valley, and the surrounding moors, were of particular importance in medieval times, with a resultant network of long-established tracks. Similarly, the rather arbitrary boundary of the National Park excludes most of the peripheral market towns on which so many roads and tracks converged. This survey embraces them, using Stainmore and the A66 as its northern limit, Wharfedale its southern boundary, the Lune valley on the west, and a line Richmond-Masham-Ripon-Knaresborough-Ilkley on the east and south-east, but concentrates on the main area of the dales themselves.

The 1:50,000 Landranger maps of the Ordnance Survey form the basis for all explorations, both in the field or in the comfort of home. Sheet 98 covers the greater part of the area, with sheets 91, 92, 97, 99, 103 and 104 filling in the important bits round the edges. Three Outdoor Leisure Maps at 1:25,000 covering most of the Yorkshire Dales are now available: 'The Three Peaks', 'Malham and Upper Wharfedale', and 'Wensleydale and Swaledale', which are ideal for detailed study. Throughout the book grid references are given to places not instantly apparent, although the prefix letters are omitted (see note at end of book).

The aims of the book are threefold. First, to try to present a picture of one particular aspect of man's activities in the Yorkshire Dales; second, to stimulate local research from the wide range of source materials in county record offices, and the local history section of libraries; thirdly, to encourage exploration in the field with an inquiring mind and an objective view. Although this can be done by car, a pair of walking boots are a great help. There are few countryside pleasures more rewarding than trying to discover for oneself why our forebears of Roman, medieval, or turnpike days followed a particular route. We may not find the answers, but in the search we shall undoubtedly extend our awareness of the landscape history of the dales.

Prehistoric Trackways

A time-traveller journeying into the past and aiming, perhaps, for around 10,000BC, would find some aspects of life comparable with those of today. By then Ice Age glaciers had retreated northwards and a tundra vegetation was beginning to colonise the land. Primeval wildness can be experienced today on the high cotton-grass mosses (above about 1,400ft) which separate the main valleys and also form the Pennine watershed. Moss, grass and sedge on the uplands were soon followed by birch and willow, and so in turn came animals — mainly herds of reindeer — and with them came occasional hunting tribes. Their nomadic lives, influenced by large-scale movements of animals, created the earliest trackways, the 'best' routes along ridgeways, through passes between the hills, and crossing rivers and streams at the easiest places.

Tracks thus created were more likely broad 'zones of movement' rather than narrow routes, and it seems probable that Palaeolithic and Mesolithic man (10,000-5,000BC) followed similar zones of communication. However, from about 4,000BC there arrived from Europe new people with new ideas, bringing with them a much more advanced technology which included the ability to make pottery and use better tools which included stone and flint axes. More importantly these Neolithic folk were farmers rather than hunters. They had learned how to domesticate herds of animals — sheep and cattle — as well as how to grow a primitive type of cereals and certain other crops. Extensive forest-clearance was necessary, for which stone axes and fire were used. High up on Pike o'Stickle, one of the Langdale Pikes in the Lake District, is the site of one of the most famous of the 'stone axe factories' of Neolithic times, in which a particularly localised hard volcanic tuff, grey-green in colour, was used. Archaeological evidence shows how widespread was the use of these axes, and a series of trade routes spread across northern England from Langdale. One of these kept to the southern edge of the limestone uplands of Craven, a route adopted by successive settlers and used today by the

A65 trunk road. Flint tools found at Trenhouse, above Malham, and in Crummackdale, have their source in the chalklands of eastern England, further evidence of trading over large distances in prehistoric times.

Livestock husbandry and the growth of crops means settled life rather than nomadism. In turn, settled life implies permanent tracks of a purely local and functional nature, from farmstead to field and pasture and from one farmstead to another. By 2,000BC much of Britain was a well-organised farming society, far removed in reality from the primitive picture so commonly painted. But it is almost impossible to pinpoint and prove the existence of specific tracks of those times, although we can reasonably assume that they would be restricted to the better-drained areas. In the Yorkshire Dales this means the limestone country of Craven, Wharfedale and parts of Wensleydale.

These areas continued to be favoured by subsequent settlers in the Yorkshire Dales, evidence of whom is most prominently shown in a number of large circular sites called 'henges'. The purpose of these Early Bronze Age structures is not known. Castle Dykes, Aysgarth (982873) and Yarnbury, (013654) above Grassington are two smaller henges, but by far the most spectacular, although largely flattened by ploughing, are at the eastern margin of the area. Thornborough Circles (285795), about a mile north-east of West Tanfield, are three large henges each about 800ft across, and standing in a line. Air photography has revealed a long parallel earthwork, or cursus, extending over a mile in a NE-SW direction and passing beneath the middle circle. There is little doubt that the circles formed an important religious centre but there is no evidence of any tracks associated with them.

Stone circles of Middle Bronze Age date (1,600-1,000BC) exist at Yockenthwaite (900794) in Wharfedale, where twenty stones are set in a circle about 25ft in diameter, and on Ox Close (990902) near Carperby, in Wensleydale, where sixteen fallen stones form a large oval, 92ft by 78ft. There are smaller circles at Appletreewick (063631) a few miles east of Hebden, and at Bordley (949653) west of Grassington. Archaeologists describe stone circles as 'ritual monuments', a suitably vague term since it is obviously impossible to prove what they were used for. There seems little doubt, however, that they were not built for defensive purposes since any earthworks associated with them have banks outside their ditches. Far more likely is the notion that stone circles manifested some sort of religious belief of their builders, but could equally have fulfilled the role of meeting-place for social or trading purposes. What is important is that they were probably constructed by and for communities of people who lived nearby. The farmsteads and fields of these people have vanished but the tracks which they used may still, though sketchily, be traceable, particularly in upland areas where subsequent land-use has not wholly obscured them.

There is not firm evidence for any roads or tracks in the Yorkshire Dales before Roman times. The population was very small, and any routes people may have used are unlikely to have had any effect on later roads.

To adduce the presence of definite routes from the meagre evidence on the ground would be a fatuous exercise. Nevertheless it can be pointed out that the major prehistoric sites in the area do have well-defined tracks passing very close to them.

The Bordley stone circle is within a few hundred yards of the junction of many tracks near the western end of Malham Moor Lane; that near Yockenthwaite in upper Wharfdale lies on a very good green track, now a popular footpath, on the north bank of the river whose valley here would have afforded a relatively easy east-west route across the Pennine watershed. The stone circle on Ox Close, above Carperby in Wensleydale,

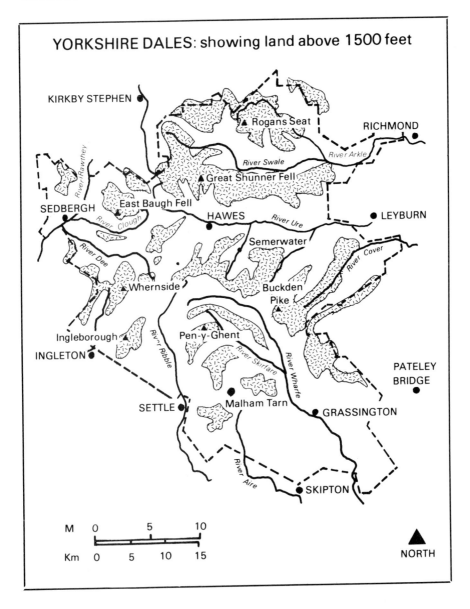

YORKSHIRE DALES: showing land above 1500 feet

is on a trackway along the northern side of the valley known to have been used in medieval times, and could probably be far older again. The Garsdale-Wensleydale route is the most direct east-west way through the Yorkshire Dales, with Mallerstang and the Lune valley convenient branches to the north. Prehistoric sites proliferate in the limestone country south-west of Appleby, and there are more Bronze Age stone circles in northern and eastern Lakeland.

Maiden Castle, on the northern flanks of Harkerside near Grinton in Swaledale, has an old road running along the hillside below it. There may be no significance at all in the juxtaposition of these factors; nor is there likely to be in the other examples quoted. One can merely conjecture, and wonder by what routes prehistoric man moved through the Yorkshire Dales.

Bronze Age stone circle near Yockenthwaite, Wharfedale. The public path which passes close to it may be on a prehistoric route through Wharfedale.

Roman Roads

There was no Yorkshire when Julius Caesar landed on the south coast of Britain in 55BC and again the following year. Those landings were little more than reconnaissances in which the invaders gained no foothold north of the Thames. Almost a century passed before the Romans attempted a deliberate conquest but it is likely that during the intervening time Roman traders made economic contact with Britain, even as far north as Brigantia, a tribal territory covering much of northern England including the area of the former North and West Ridings. The name 'Yorkshire' first appears in writing in AD1055 although the area it embraced was probably marked out in Saxon times two centuries earlier. The Brigantes of the first century were largely hilltribes, who practised primitive arable farming and livestock rearing, a bronze-using peasantry who could make pottery yet still used flint arrow-heads. They were ruled by kings and queens of an iron-using military aristocracy. Brigantian towns were no more than large villages, but some subsequently became the sites of Roman forts: *Cataractonium* (Catterick), and *Olicana* (Ilkley), with *Isurium* (Aldborough) probably a tribal capital.

In the Roman campaign to conquer Britain the south and south-east were quickly subdued so that by AD47 a frontier was established roughly separating lowland Britain from the highland zone, along a line from the Severn estuary to north of the Wash. Subsequently this frontier was protected by a number of forts linked later by a military road, the Fosse Way, which finally ran from the East Devon coast to Lincoln. Near its mid-point it was linked to London by Watling Street, the importance of the crossroads being recognised in the eighteenth century by the erection of a monument which can still be seen today at High Cross in Leicestershire. Other important Roman roads linked London to Cirencester and to Lincoln.

Watling Street was extended westwards beyond the Fosse Way, and near what is now Shrewsbury the Romans built an important fortified town, *Viroconium* (now Wroxeter), to give protection to their western flank against the Silures of South Wales and to provide a base for the legions attempting to subdue the Ordovices of Central and North Wales. This was accomplished by AD51, and Caratacus, the Ordovician leader, fled to Cartimandua, Brigantian Queen, but she surrendered him to the Romans. Internecine strife ensued among the Brigantes, and in the years of treachery which followed Cartimandua divorced her husband Venutius, a native Brigantian leader. She subsequently sought protection at the Romanised town of Aldborough while Venutius assembled tribes in the western dales, the hillfort summit of Ingleborough becoming their focal rallying-point. Within its massive encircling wall enclosing an area 490ft by 450ft, are the foundations of many hut circles which date from this first century occupation, and there seems little doubt that the abundance of roughly-built and probably temporary huts and enclosures of the limestone uplands around Ingleborough and the western part of Craven are of contemporary date.

Venutius realised that eventually there would be a large-scale Roman attack on his Brigantian followers, probably by the usual tactic of driving a wedge through them. Aided by other tribesmen from the north he chose as his defensive centre a site at Stanwick (175113), six miles north of Richmond, and three miles from an important ancient trading route from the Lake District across Stainmore. Any possible Roman advance from York could use this route to the Vale of Eden and Carlisle, while a northward thrust from York along the eastern side of the Pennines would probably need to cross the Tees within a few miles of Stanwick, so a defensive site here would be strategically placed.

Today the Brigantian fort at Stanwick still shows six miles of earthen ramparts and ditches enclosing a total area of 850 acres. In some places the banks are 20ft high, while the defensive centre on Tofts Hill, covering seventeen acres, has a 24ft bank on its western side. But it was all to no avail. Before all the defences were finished the Roman legions under Petillius Cerialis advanced on Stanwick and defeated Venutius in one of the most decisive events of the Roman occupation of Britain. Although many of Venutius's men fled westwards into the hills and dales some were taken prisoner and it is likely they were used as slave labour in the lead mines at Hurst, in Swaledale, and on Greenhow Hill above Pateley Bridge. Evidence of Roman lead mining comes from the fact that the names of Roman emperors were inscribed on two pigs of smelted lead found by a track on Hayshaw Bank, on another pig discovered west of Greenhow, and one in Swaledale. The mere fact of constructing the Brigantian fort at Stanwick on such a huge scale would have needed a large labour force employed over a long time, implying strong qualities of leadership and a sophisticated organisation of equipment, materials, food supplies and transport.

Once the Brigantes were subjugated the lines of communication were safeguarded for Agricola to move northwards. Roads were constructed along the Pennines' eastern margin from York via Aldborough, Catterick,

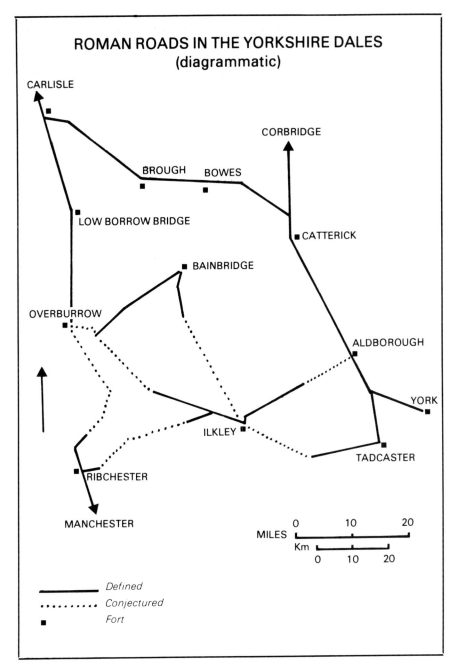

ROMAN ROADS IN THE YORKSHIRE DALES
(diagrammatic)

CARLISLE

CORBRIDGE

BROUGH   BOWES

LOW BORROW BRIDGE

CATTERICK

BAINBRIDGE

OVERBURROW

ALDBOROUGH

YORK

ILKLEY

TADCASTER

RIBCHESTER

MANCHESTER

| | 0 | 10 | 20 |
MILES

Km

0   10   20

—————— Defined

· · · · · · · · Conjectured

■ Fort

Piercebridge, and Auckland to the Tyne at Corbridge, while on the west the main route was through Manchester to Ribchester, Overborrow, Penrith and Carlisle. By AD80 Agricola completed the conquest of Northern England and established, along the Tyne valley, a secure frontier with Scotland, strengthened and fortified early in the next century by the building of the Roman Wall under Hadrian.

17

Roman road above Bainbridge, Wensleydale. Aligned precisely on the Roman fort at Bainbridge, this section strikes south-westwardly towards Wether Fell. Its course was adopted as the Richmond to Lancaster Turnpike in 1751.

Thus, within forty years from the AD43 invasion England had become a province of the Roman Empire. At the peak of its power Rome's communications network covered 180,000 miles of paved roads, a third of these major routes up to 40ft wide, but Roman roads in Britain rarely exceeded 16ft. Even with this width they were built well, and where they crossed marshy and peaty ground drainage ditches were dug along each side, with the space between excavated to a firm base on which stones were laid, with smaller stones and gravel on top of these. Although the reasons for Roman road construction were primarily military, economic and administrative considerations were not overlooked. However, in the uplands of northern England military factors prevailed and roads were necessary to permit troops to move quickly to quell outbreaks of unrest among the unruly elements of surviving Brigantes. Agricola built forts at Catterick and Piercebridge on his eastern route to the north, and at Ribchester, Elslack and Overborrow on the western road. The Aire gap and Stainmore were long-established trans-Pennine trading ways adopted by the Romans for military roads between east and west, and it is reasonable to suppose that these roads continued as important trade routes. A fort was built in the heart of the Yorkshire Dales, at Bainbridge in Wensleydale, and a system of roads developed linking most of the forts in the upland areas with Roman towns on the periphery.

This Roman road network was superimposed upon, and in its authoritarian way complemented, the essential network of existing tracks of humbler and more practical origins. While Roman surveyors doubtless appreciated that the shortest distance between two points was a straight line they were too sensible to follow this precept in constructing roads in upland country like the Pennines. They merely minimised departures from it, constructed long straight stretches wherever possible, taking advantage of river gaps and existing fords, and obviously avoiding major obstacles. Several miles of known Roman roads can be enjoyably followed within the area of the Yorkshire Dales along routes of known provenance, and while there are obvious gaps awaiting archaeological investigation, reasonable conjectures may be made. Some roads of Roman, or prehistoric, origin are now followed by major trunk roads.

Indeed, the Stainmore and Aire gap routes form convenient northern and southern boundaries to the survey which follows.

Ilkley to Elslack

The road connecting the Roman fort of *Olicana* (117478) at Ilkley with Elslack (925495) a few miles west of Skipton, lies outside the area surveyed and will therefore not be dealt with in detail. For a mile and a half to the west of Ilkley it coincides with the main road to Skipton south of the Wharfe, but where the river takes a northward turn by the golf course the Roman road, significantly called 'The Street' (from the Latin *Strata*), takes a direct line north-westwards passing Street Farm (077491) and later crossing Addingham Beck at Street House south of the village. Beyond the main road its course is lost in fields to be picked up again on Addingham Low Moor as a walled lane, continuing as a well-defined terrace over open moor orientated more westwards along the northern slope of Skipton Moor, where some paving has been found. The route descends by Shortbank Road into Skipton, joining the present A65 along Newmarket Street and Swadford Street, and leaving the town along Broughton Road. West of Skipton all traces of the route are lost, first in the alluvial plain of the River Aire and later by the track of the former railway line. However, half-a-mile north-east of Elslack, Eller Gill Lane follows the Roman road for almost a mile beyond Low Ground Farm (940501), and it enters the fort, now called Burwen Castle, along the line of an agger and a ditch, at the eastern gate.

Skipton to Ingleton

Although there is only the evidence of coins to suggest a possible Roman occupation of Skipton the place may have been at the junction of roads, with one coming in from the north-east across Beamsley Moor, a link with the more important road from Ilkley to Aldborough; another conjectured route follows the course of the Aire north-westwards through Gargrave, Long Preston and Settle to Ingleton. The whole has not yet been established but it is thought to have left Skipton to the north-west by what is now Raikes Road, leading to White Hills and the hamlet of Stirton. The route probably turned westwards here towards Thorlby. Although there is the known site of a Roman villa near Gargrave (940535) this lies south of the river and there is no evidence that the road crossed the river. It is more likely that its alignment to Gargrave was that of the present main road, although at a point midway between Skipton and Gargrave a green track over the shoulder of a hill suggests an older route, the section being called 'Stoney Bitts' could refer to old Roman paving.

Further west beyond Coniston Cold and on the edge of the parkland of Coniston Hall there is a straight length of old road marked by fences subsequently picked up at Switchers (875559), after which the line of the A65 is continued north-westwards to Hellifield and Long Preston. Excavations east of Long Preston churchyard (836581) have revealed the probable site of a temporary fort on a plateau where the ground falls steeply to a beck. Beyond Long Preston the course of the Roman road is very doubtful.

An alternative route from Gargrave has been suggested to the east of, and at a higher level than, the one described. This follows an alignment of lanes north-west of Gargrave through Bell Busk (905565) and Otterburn (883576), then climbing to Hellifield Moor by a series of straight sections which are sometimes terraced and look as though they have been engineered. The track is later walled, swinging slightly on a more northerly orientation as Langber Lane, to join the metalled road coming across the moor from Kirkby Malham near Scaleber Bridge (842625). This descends steeply into Upper Settle by High Hill Lane, picking up the line of the old Keighley-Kendal Turnpike at the top of Albert Hill (see Chapter 7), and crossing the river to Giggleswick, beyond which all traces of the road are lost, although the alignment suggests that it may have continued to the important fort at Overborrow (615757) two miles south of Kirkby Lonsdale.

Ingleton to Bainbridge

One of the most direct and best-preserved of the Roman roads in the Yorkshire Dales runs almost continuously from Ingleton north-eastwards to the Roman fort so commandingly situated at Bainbridge, in Wensleydale (937901) nineteen miles away. On Warburton's map of Yorkshire published in 1720 this route appears under the name 'The Devil's Causeway', and is depicted as running from the fort of Overborrow (615758) in the Lune valley to Bainbridge. On the ground all traces of it have vanished south-westwards from Ingleton although its orientation suggests that it may have come from the more important fort at Lancaster, along the valleys of the Lune and Greta — the latter river not to be confused with that in the far north of Yorkshire. The Greta we are now concerned with is a tributary of the Lune below Ingleton where it is formed by the mingling of two smaller rivers, the Doe which comes down from Chapel-le-Dale to the north-east, and the Twiss, flowing southwards down Kingsdale before entering 'Ingleton Glen' and its fine series of waterfalls.

The Roman road leaves Ingleton by a cleverly-designed route on a spur between the two rivers, climbing Meal Bank before turning through about 45 degrees to take a direct course north-eastwards along the western side of the valley of the River Doe. It follows all the way a narrow, metalled road, walled as far as Dale Barn (712754), but unenclosed through the succeeding fields almost to Chapel-le-Dale (738772), maintaining a remarkably level course throughout this length. At Chapel it crosses the river north-east of the church, probably by a ford beyond a small wood, and its course is there identified as a slight hollow across a field before it joins the present main road, the B6255, which has kept to the east of the valley from Ingleton. This road now marks the Roman route for the next three miles until the modern road turns more northwards 200yd beyond the first milestone past Gearstones. At this junction (785803) the Roman

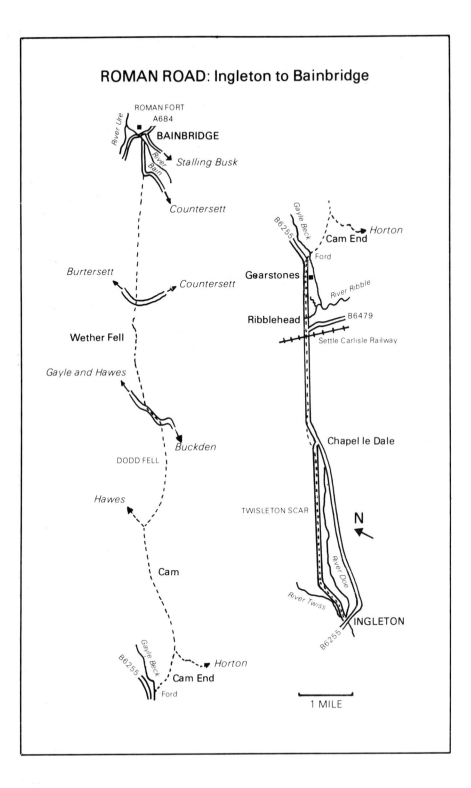

ROMAN ROAD: Ingleton to Bainbridge

ROMAN FORT
A684

BAINBRIDGE

Stalling Busk

Countersett

Burtersett

Countersett

Wether Fell

Gayle and Hawes

Buckden

DODD FELL

Hawes

Cam

Cam End

Horton

Ford

River Ure

River Bain

Gayle Beck

B6255

Cam End

Horton

Ford

Gearstones

River Ribble

Ribblehead

B6479

Settle Carlisle Railway

Chapel le Dale

TWISLETON SCAR

N

River Doe

River Twiss

INGLETON

B6255

1 MILE

Bainbridge to Ingleton Roman road, on Cam End. Ingleborough is ahead.

road keeps to an eastwards orientation, passes immediately through a gate, descends slightly to ford Gayle Beck near a new footbridge, and starts a long climb up Broad Ray to Cam End. Its course will have already been apparent in the view from the main road, and it keeps a consistent gradient for about a mile. About 15 ft wide and slightly raised above the surrounding moor, it reveals in places a stony foundation most likely dating from its use as part of the Richmond-Lancaster Turnpike.

At 1,500 ft on the southern shoulder of Cam End it is joined at a wooden guidepost (802805) by another old road coming up from Horton-in-Ribblesdale, now the route of the Pennine Way, and for the next two miles Roman road, eighteenth-century turnpike, and the Pennine Way of 1960, share the same green highway as it heads north-eastwards, still rising, but only slightly, along the edge of Cam Pasture, with the recent afforestation of Langstrothdale and Oughtershaw to the east. Above Cam Houses the route becomes metalled and at Kidhow Gate (830834) the Roman road, still metalled, swings eastwards round the southern shoulder of Dodd Fell, leaving the Pennine Way to continue its course north-north-east towards Hawes. On Green Side (853842), still keeping to the edge of the limestone, it reaches 1,911 ft and is known as the Cam High Road, soon joining the motor road from Buckden to Hawes, and aligned on it for a half-mile north.

At Howgate Head the motor road descends steeply but the Roman road returns to its north-eastern alignment, as a stony track at first then a grassy one, with a wall on its eastern side all the way. Where the route is double-walled it is about 20ft wide, with a stony foundation about 12ft wide. On the southern flank of Wether Fell (874867) it reaches 2,014ft, is terraced wherever necessary, and in a few short stretches is on a bare limestone pavement. From Wether Fell to Bainbridge is a completely straight alignment of about four miles along a convenient spur of the fell, descending steadily past the Common Allotments, with walls on each side. For much of this part of its course an agger can be identified about 15ft wide, and where it crosses a beck at New Bridge (899880) it makes a slight kink and there is a particularly well-constructed stone culvert. A mile from Bainbridge the Roman road joins a metalled road from Countersett and curves slightly to pass some hillocks, possibly of glacial origin, to enter the village and the southern entrance of the fort (936902).

Bainbridge to Ilkley

The Roman fort at Bainbridge occupies a 2½ acre natural hillock possibly of glacier-formed drumlin, on the north-east corner of Bainbridge village in the angle between the confluence of the River Ure with its short tributary, the River Bain. Its isolated situation may explain the almost complete survival of the fort's foundations, and although all stones of the later, fourth-century buildings have gone some flagged floors of the fort survive about 3ft below the soil surface. In the sixteenth century Camden recorded that two inscriptions had been found here, but one of these has since disappeared. The other caused Camden to infer that the fort was called *Bracchium*, although the name *Virosidum* has subsequently been given to it. Serious excavation started in 1925 but since 1950 Leeds University have used it as a site for archaeological training. It seems probable that the first fort may have been established here by Agricola during his northern campaign, to be followed by a succession of stone forts in use until the end of the fourth century. Isolated in possibly hostile Brigantian territory in the heart of the Pennines, Bainbridge almost certainly needed some road communications with other Roman forts, but there is clear evidence of only two roads, the one from Ingleton and Lancaster or Overborrow, already described, and another crossing the watershed to the south and following Wharfedale down to Ilkley. This is the road we now consider.

Its route can be traced fairly easily from Bainbridge to Buckden (942775), eight miles south, but beyond that its course is only fragmented. Leaving the south side of the fort the course for three miles to just above the hamlet of Stalling Busk follows that of the present metalled motor road along the eastern hillside of the valley of the Bain. However, after 300yd, where the present road swings southwards, a field path on the west, crossing Bracka Hill (933892), and never more than 200yd from the road, rejoins it at a gate in another half-mile. This field path probably represents the Roman route, its early stages showing signs of having been engineered, with some metalling of the surface later on. After the junction

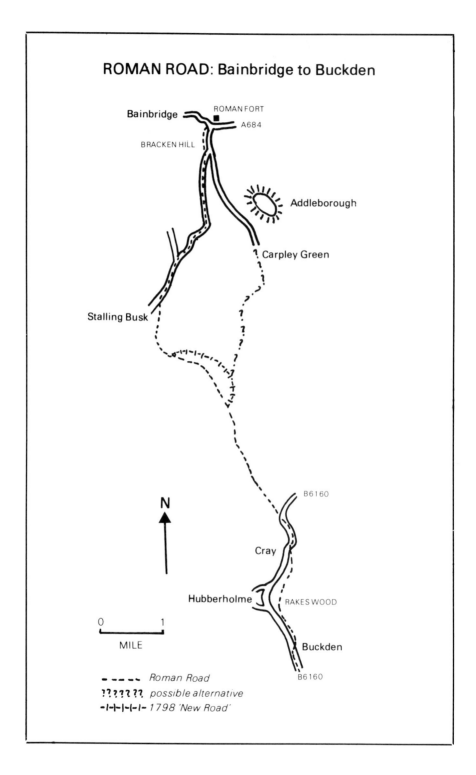

ROMAN ROAD: Bainbridge to Buckden

Bainbridge — ROMAN FORT
A684
BRACKEN HILL
Addleborough
Carpley Green
Stalling Busk
N
B6160
Cray
Hubberholme — RAKES WOOD
Buckden
B6160

0   1
MILE

- - - - Roman Road
?????? possible alternative
-l-l-l-l- 1798 'New Road'

Bainbridge to Ilkley Roman road, crossing Buckden Rakes, Wharfedale. Coming from the right, its course can be seen crossing pastures just above the trees. It continues at this height by the walls above limestone scars before descending to Buckden.

of path and road the motor road makes a 'kink' to cross a steep little ravine and continues south-westwards past High Blean and along Birk Rigg, two miles of fairly straight alignment in good Roman fashion.

Above Stalling Busk (919861) the Roman road diverges southwards to climb steadily as a walled lane nearly 30ft wide, roughly surfaced between wide grass verges. In one mile it curves eastwards above Cragdale, and, with Bank Wood far below, the Roman route leaves the walled lane at a

Roman road descending The Stake, towards Kidstones Causeway. Here it is shown crossing bare limestone at about 1,700ft. Snow in the distance.

field gate (920846), contouring Shaw Side as an easily-identified green track along a limestone shelf. After crossing Shaw Gate Gill above an engineered embankment it swings south-south-east, climbs very rough pasture, its course crossing two field walls, and rejoins the original lane at a stile by a gate and a short cross-wall in the lane itself (933833). Across Cragdale Allotment, although it is rough ground, the Roman road is easily seen, up to 20ft wide and with a distinct agger, occasionally revealing stones on its crest and at the kerbs.

The walled lane, which has kept well above the Roman route and followed an easier gradient, is not shown on Jefferys's map of 1770, or Tuke's of 1787, which both indicate the Roman line. However, Greenwood's map of 1817 does show it, and the Bainbridge Constable's Accounts reveal that in 1798 the sum of £20 0s 7d was paid to John Thwaites for making a road in Cragdale, so it seems likely this was the newer road with the easier gradient.

On Stake Moss (934825) the present track, initially a walled lane 30ft wide, and subsequently an open road, rough-metalled on the only firm limestone ground amid peaty moorland terrain, follows the Roman route south-south-eastwards, crossing the watershed (and the former North Riding/West Riding boundary) at 1,836ft (936818). Soon after it starts to descend it passes a small, unmarked boundary stone at the foot of a wall on the eastern side. A few yards further on a large sandstone boulder by the road bears the inscription 'B4M'. At this point the road is four miles from Buckden, so presumably the information was for the guidance of drovers who used this route in later centuries.

Just beyond the boulder the road surface is on bare limestone and for a few yards distinct parallel ruts, about an inch deep and 4ft apart, are visible. Soon afterwards the road descends, through a series of bends separated by short straights, with the steepest gradient about 1 in 4, and marked evidence of stone paving in places, some of the stones laid edge upwards. Broken walls down each side, as far as the motor road B6160, are 30-40ft apart, with a wide verge on each side of the stony road surface. The Roman road follows the metalled road for about ½ mile before branching off as a signposted footpath above Cray High Bridge (944797), its course easily identifiable beyond the first rough pasture for it is aligned very straight along a slightly-descending limestone terrace across Cow Close, and showing in some sections a well-defined agger. At the northern corner of Rakes Wood (940782) the Roman road turns south-eastwards, narrows to about 12ft and drops steeply into the wood by a terrace partly of natural limestone outcrops and partly cut out of the rock with its lower edge supported on an embankment. The gradient gradually eases through the wood, and emerging from it the Roman road passes through a field-gate above a National Park car park whose entrance road follows a short stretch of medieval hollowway on the Roman line (942775).

Beyond Buckden proven sections of the road are short and fragmented but it is likely that the present road down the eastern side of Wharfedale is on or very close to the Roman alignment to a mile beyond Conistone village. At Starbotton the lie of the land suggests that the Roman road climbed slightly before the site of the village and rejoined the present road about ¼ mile to the east.

Ilkley to Aldborough

The Roman fort at Ilkley (*Olicana*) was at the junction of two important Roman roads, one from York to Ribchester, and the other from Manchester to Aldborough. The east-west Aire Gap route has long been know as the York Gate (ie a way from the Norse *gata*), and on Warburton's 1720 map is a note, 'This Roman road goes to York, and for the most part is visible, being paved with stone throughout.' Part of its course west of Ilkley has been described. We are now concerned with the relevant section of the other road linking Ilkley with Aldborough, 23 miles to the north-east.

The site of the fort at Ilkley is on the south bank of the Wharfe close to the position of the Parish church. Indeed the north wall of the churchyard adjoins the headquarters building of the fort so that it is quite likely that the earliest Christian church at Ilkley occupied the site of a pagan temple — a not uncommon event in Britain. The road passed the western side of the fort, probably following the line of the Old Bridge Lane to a ford about 100yd west of the present Old Bridge, then climbing northwards from the river probably along the present course of Harding Lane and Parks Lane, this latter a walled lane with a rough metalled surface, joining the Hunger Hill road from the east at Moor Gate (115506). This must subsequently have become an important junction of several moorland tracks for there is a tall stone stoop situated so close to a wall at the junction that it almost certainly predates the wall. Its eastern face shows two hands and the inscription '12 miles to Rippon', the south face '3 miles to Ilkley', and the north-west face '6 miles to Skipton, Otley to 7 miles'.

From Moor Gate the Roman road is aligned NNE by the side of a wall

Former Roman road, later the pre-turnpike road, on Addingham Moor between Ilkley and Skipton.

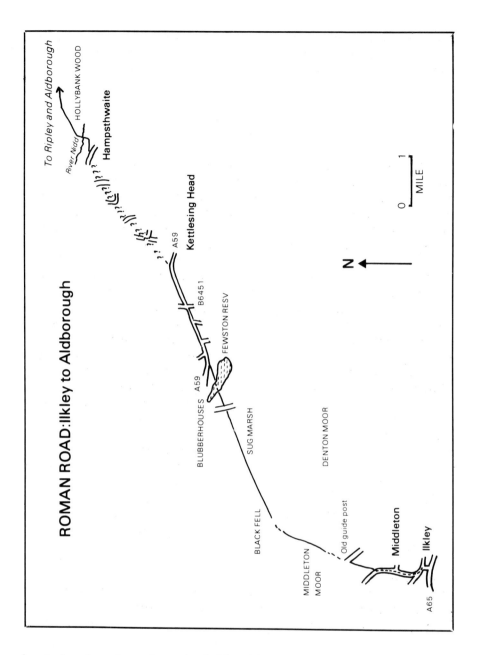

ROMAN ROAD:Ilkley to Aldborough

To Ripley and Aldborough

HOLLYBANK WOOD

Hampsthwaite

River Nidd

Kettlesing Head

A59

B6451

FEWSTON RESV

BLUBERHOUSES   A59

SUG MARSH

DENTON MOOR

BLACK FELL

Old guide post

MIDDLETON MOOR

Middleton

Ilkley

A65

N

0   1
MILE

but is then lost through intake fields, although its course can be picked up again on Middleton Moor ¾ mile away as a sketchy green track through dark heather to the west of Marsh Gill Reservoir. Its course is lost in Clifford's Bog, but is regained at the boundary wall between Denton and Middleton Moors on the eastern shoulder of Black Fell. From Gawk Hill Gill (128533) the road turns sharply to an ENE orientation which is then maintained with remarkable straightness until within two miles of Hampsthwaite. Initially its course is hard to identify but as it starts gradually to descend Sug Marsh it becomes a more distinct causeway, grassy between surrounds of dark heather moor, with occasional bare metalling visible on a well-preserved agger before crossing Sun Bank Gill (146538). Three miles eastwards it is easily distinguished as the A59 trunk road cutting through coniferous forest beyond Fewston Reservoir. Meanwhile the route continues across Blubberhouses Moor towards the low rise of Cote Hill (159543) where dense bracken and heather hide its course. East of Cote Hill it can be identified for a short stretch and then is lost in a series of enclosed fields before crossing the Blubberhouses-Otley road and vanishing beneath Fewston Reservoir, to reappear a mile east of Blubberhouses and pick up the main road at the top of a hill near Meargill Corner (185553), following it for two miles. Where the A59 bends south-eastwards to Kettlesing Head the Roman road continues straight ahead identified as a slight agger intermittently across fields south of Kettlesing village where a footpath follows it course to Crag Lane Farm (234569). As an overgrown path it aims for Horseman's Well Farm but its trace is lost before reaching the farm.

Dr Richard Muir believes that the tangled mesh of minor roads and lanes in the triangle between Kettlesing, Birstwith and Hampsthwaite results from the surfacing of old tracks between hamlets and farms in a settlement pattern characteristic of a Dark Ages landscape, but dominated by the major road in this area, the Roman one, which was probably aiming at a ford on the River Nidd near Hampsthwaite. Beyond Horseman's Well Farm the Roman route is uncertain. It may have continued to Swincliffe and along the axis of Hampsthwaite village to the site of the present bridge across the Nidd, (261592) a seventeenth-century replacement in stone of an older wooden structure. An alternative route lay parallel to this one but a hundred yards to the west, crossing the main valley road west of Hampsthwaite and following an overgrown but paved and embanked causeway leading to Hampsthwaite churchyard. Years ago this causeway was referred to locally as 'our Roman Road'. Its route appears to cross the

Line of Roman road, Blubberhouses Moor.

churchyard diagonally to become a short length of holloway to the bridge. The paving suggests medieval or Roman origins, and a similarly paved stretch of road exists in Hollybank Wood north of the river (273599).

The present motor road north of the river bends sharply to tackle the hill up to Clint, and where it takes a sharp left turn a track continues ahead north-eastwards to the corner of Hollybank Wood, then eastwards through the wood and beyond it as a hollow lane heading towards Ripley. This is the old York to Lancaster road marked on Ogilby's map of 1675, and is probably a right-of-way granted in an 1160 charter to the monks of Fountains Abbey. It seems reasonable to conjecture a much older usage, possibly Roman. Ripley's village plan suggests that the original village was aligned on an east-west axis between the castle and church, this area representing an elongated marketplace — a charter was granted in 1357. The western end of the marketplace terminates as a bridleway aligned on our Roman road (283605).

Ribchester to Low Borrow Bridge

Although this route lies outside our area, the section from Overborrow, south of Kirby Lonsdale, which crosses the A65 near Cowan Bridge (630770) and follows a northerly alignment up the Lune valley, and along the western foot of the Howgills, is actually within the National Park area. So it deserves some mention in this survey, but will not be dealt with in detail. From the A65 near Cowan Bridge the Roman route follows the narrow Wandles Lane very straight for 1½ miles to Casterton, and beyond the village, where the metalled lane bears slightly westwards, the Roman line continues forward, passing close to an old standing stone, into a plantation where a slight agger is visible, before swinging slightly westwards to join the main A683 west of Barbon village. Over the next 4 miles the alignment is on, or close to, the main road. Near Hawking Hall a Roman milestone with the inscription MP LIII was found in 1836 and re-erected nearby (622857), 300yd south of Middleton church, on private land. 2 miles further north the main road swings north-westwards (630891) but the Roman road continues as a narrow lane to Holme (636907). For 200yd beyond the farms a straight lane, 12ft wide between one wall and the footings of another, and all overgrown, marks the course of the road to a deep ford, called Lords Dub, on the River Rawthey, impassable in all but low-water conditions. Beyond, Ingmire Back Lane continues its course to the east of Ingmire Hall, where it crosses enclosed fields, and the A684, eventually joining an old road from Sedbergh, Howgill Lane, near Height of Winder Farm (639932).

Except where it bends to make more convenient crossings of the becks which rush down the western flank of the hills Howgill Lane follows a straight course along the contours. Walled as far as Fairmile Gate (978629) and again beyond Carlingill, 1½ miles to the north, where it bends slightly north-westwards, it is embanked in places, and a section near Carlingill showed the Roman road to be 18ft wide with a foundation of large stones, with yellow clay beneath and a closely-packed surface layer up to 4in thick. A quarter of a mile before reaching the fort at Low Borrow Bridge the Roman road crossed the Lune at Salterwath Bridge, another significant name meaning 'salters' ford', and passed the east side of the fort (610013). At this point the Roman road (still Howgill Lane), the A685 Kendal-Kirkby Stephen turnpike, the main London-Glasgow railway line, and the M6 motorway are parallel to one another all within ¼ mile, an illustration of the importance of the Lune valley as a north-south communications corridor. Engineering works have obscured the Roman route to Tebay and beyond. Before the crossing of the Shap-Orton road, B6261, near Howe Nook (601092) the Roman road continues northwards as a bridleway across the moorland of Crosby Ravensworth Fell to Coalpit Hill where it leaves the bridleway and heads NNE to the remarkable Romano-British settlement at Ewe Close (608134). Beyond there its course becomes fragmented in fields and lanes, passing through Wickerslack, Reagill and Sleagill towards Newby, and 2 miles to the north-west, on a straight alignment along a modern lane, it passes Street House (576236). Swinging more to the north-west it aims for Brougham, the Roman fort of *Brocavum* (538289) by the River Eamont, approaching it probably along the present road from Cliburn. Beyond Brougham the Roman road would continue to the important fort at Carlisle, on the line of the Roman Wall.

Scotch Corner to Penrith (*Brougham*)

For part of its length this road forms the northern boundary of our survey and therefore needs to be considered. Scotch Corner today is an important junction for north-bound traffic since from it you can continue northwards to eastern Scotland or north-westwards to central and western Scotland. Thus it was, too, in Roman times, but the Roman junction lay about 300yd north of the present one, and the Roman road crossed enclosed fields to join the present road near Kirklands (202061). Except for a few short stretches the Roman road follows the line of the trunk road for most of the way to Brough, in a series of long straight sections.

The Roman road bends slightly at Greta Bridge to cross the river, where the Romans built a fort on the west bank (085133), and the road turns westwards by Rokeby Park, continuing an alignment over Bowes Moor to the summit of Stainmore Pass. At Bowes the road passes the northern side of the Roman fort *Lavatrae* (989135) above the north bank of the River Greta. Its ditches are still visible but all the masonry has gone, used for building Bowes Castle about 1180, and the parish church, both structures within the ramparts of the fort. Six miles to the west, on the south of the road, is the stumpy shaft of Rey Cross, called in 1280 Rair Croiz de Staynmore, thought to have been erected in the first half of the tenth century as a boundary mark between Northumbria and the Scottish Kingdom of Strathclyde. The road passes through the banks of a Roman marching camp, and shortly crosses the new county boundary between Durham and Cumbria. In ½ mile the modern road deviates southwards from the Roman line which is easily seen continuing to climb slightly to Maiden Castle, site of a Roman signalling post (872132) before descending as a green track to rejoin the main road near Palliard Farm. Near Maiden Castle the Roman road is almost 30ft wide with occasional kerbstones visible.

In 1½ miles, at Banks Gate, the Roman road turns south-westwards across broken country, while the modern road keeps a better route to the north. The Roman route probably goes by Leonard's Cragg and Augill Castle to the fort of *Verterae* at Church Brough (792141) whose site was subsequently used for an early Norman castle rebuilt in the late twelfth century. The Roman road probably rejoins the main road 2½ miles to the west, follows it to Coupland, and then continues to the north-east of Appleby, picking up the A66 again near Kirkby Thore, and adhering to it as far as Brougham.

Sedbergh to Kirkby Stephen to Brough

In the Rawthey valley north-east of Sedbergh the course of a Roman road has been postulated if not proved, although place-name evidence tends to support the possibility of a link between the fort at Brough, on the western edge of Stainmore, and the important highway from Ribchester to Borrow Bridge. Its course through Sedbergh is not known, but beyond the town it probably kept to the eastern side of the Rawthey valley, on or close to the present main road, A683. At Beck Side (695955) near Cautley its conjectured course is represented by a lane running north-eastwards across Bluecaster Side, where it becomes a green track through rough pasture descending by a definite zigzag to Rawthey Bridge (713978). From there it takes the line of a narrow, surfaced lane passing Street Side and joining the main road in about three miles. Immediately it branches off again, as a green lane to Street Farm (738013), becoming a bridleway to Low Stennerskeugh and Flass, beyond which its course is lost.

The Dark and Middle Ages

Roman colonial rule in Britain came to an end in AD410. For years previously the Roman armies had steadily been withdrawn and even before then occasions had occurred when the native Britons had elected their own emperors, but AD410 represents the time when the Romans abandoned any responsibility for defence. However, 350 years of Roman occupation and rule ensured that Roman influence would continue for some time, although for how long is a subject for historical argument. It is known that by about the middle of the fifth century there was an increasing Anglo-Saxon infiltration from the continent which by the end of the century had become strong enough, certainly in the southern part of Britain, to defeat any organised resistance from squabbling British factions. But in Yorkshire the native British kept some degree of independence until early in the seventh century when Anglian settlers, penetrating westwards from the old British kingdom of Elmet, followed the valleys of the Aire and Wharfe into Craven and beyond to the Ribble valley. During the century these settlements spread into all the lower dales of Yorkshire clearing the woodlands which prevailed on the gritstone soils.

Place-names provide the clue to this expansion. The suffix -leah, now identified as -ley, points to such woodland clearance, and shows Nidderdale to be particularly favoured with Ripley, Pateley, Bewerley, and Darley, Stainley and Grantley between the Nidd and the Ure. Wensley seems to have been a lonelier settlement higher up the Ure; Drebley in Wharfedale, Bordley near Grassington, and Bradley in Coverdale represent settlements by real pioneers in what must have been wild country, although Bordley is on the limestone, and had been an area of prehistoric occupation.

Recent archaeological research has caused us to revise our thoughts about the form of settlement. It now seems that the nucleated village as we know it, strung along a street or surrounding a green, was a product of later Saxon settlement, and that the early pattern is more likely to have been one of small farmsteads and scattered hamlets, usually unrelated to any present village and the roads and tracks associated with it. All of this makes it almost impossible to understand or identify early Saxon tracks, since there is simply no evidence for them. We can reasonably assume that Roman routes had survived to provide the Saxons with a national network, and that short and medium-distance journeys would have used Roman rural tracks where these existed, but a local network of tracks in the area of the dales probably did not develop until nucleated settlements as we know them had become established during the eighth, ninth and tenth centuries. Writing about rural Devon in the eleventh century Professor Hoskins has ventured the belief that 'Practically all the thousands of farm names printed on the modern map would have been on the earlier map, could it have been drawn; and nearly all the thousands of miles of lanes and by-roads would have existed also.' Christopher Taylor asserts that the same is probably true of large areas of Cornwall, Wales and the Marches, and much of northern England and Scotland. All these are upland areas, and although settlement pattern is different and road mileages far less, the inter-village basic network of roads and lanes in the Yorkshire Dales is probably at least a thousand years old. But we do not know for certain, nor can we prove this. Of course there have been changes in detail since then, and monastic, packhorse and drove roads have been added to the palimpsest, but in the valleys and around the edges of the area hundreds of miles of roads and lanes we use today were likely to have been in use by the time of the Norman Conquest.

Occasionally, roads are referred to in Saxon charters, as *haehstraet*, rather like our 'High Street', meaning a main road, and *heiweg*, a highway; the Old Norse *gata* or gate, has the same meaning, and throughout the dales this name is commonly found. But the nature of Saxon ways and gates is vastly different from the roads of Roman origin which were deliberately created and the more important ones paved with stones. Dark Age and Saxon tracks evolved through human use, not as physical entities — thin strips of land with defined boundaries — but as customary rights of way, having legal status, and linking one village with another. Such ways are generally of short distance, but it must be realised that not all modern roads called 'ways' have Saxon origins. However a number of 'ways' developed as boundaries between parishes and where 'ways' follow these boundaries such a road or track is probably a Saxon *weg*.

With the coming of the Normans and during the following two centuries there was a resurgence of urban life. Towns developed where Norman aristocracy established castles, at Richmond, Kirkby Malzeard, Knaresborough, Skipton and Middleham. The natural garrison need for food and other goods stimulated local trade, while the security provided by the castle encouraged visiting merchants. Craftsmen settled beneath the protection of the castle defences so that altogether it would not be long before a small but flourishing market town had developed. Parallel with this urban growth was the founding of many monasteries, and in the

Yorkshire Dales it was mainly the Cistercians who had such a profound and lasting influence, particularly in the pattern of roads and tracks which evolved during medieval times.

Markets

Although life for most people in the Middle Ages was very localised, centred on manor and village, monastery and castle-town, recent research suggests that by the thirteenth century there was an increasing mobility among the rural population. Exchanges and the trading of excess farm produce and simple manufactured goods, and the carriage of these over short distances, were factors encouraging the establishment and growth of markets. Some commodities such as salt, wool, metals and grain were transported over longer distances, while imported wine, clothes and furs were similarly carried many miles from coastal and river ports. Rural communities, then, were rarely entirely self-sufficient and for certain things they were dependent on markets, so that a visit to the weekly market was an essential day-trip for a peasant.

A thirteenth-century English lawyer, Henry Bracton, in his treatise *On English Laws and Customs*, considered that markets, to justify themselves, should not be closer to one another than the distance that could be travelled in a day, and at that time this distance would be 20 miles. But Bracton sensibly realised that it would be necessary to spend some part of the day at the market, and of course to return home afterwards. He therefore concluded that

> The day's journey is divided into three parts; the first part, that of the morning, is to be given to those who are going to the market, the second is to be given to buying and selling, and the third part is left for those returning from market to their own homes, and for doing all those things that must be done by day and not by night....

Thus, the maximum range for a market journey would be one-third of 20 miles, or, as Bracton precisely put it, 'six miles and a half and the third part of a half.' If this is placed into the geographical context of the Yorkshire Dales, taken in conjunction with the known markets, we see that there are very few places outside this seven-mile radius from a market.

Markets could be established only by charter and can therefore be dated exactly, or at least to within a few years of their official recognition. A few surviving charters merely regularised older ones that had grown through custom. Most Yorkshire dales were served by market towns at their periphery, where stock-rearing upland farming met the arable farming of the lowlands, while in the dales themselves a number of places which today are pleasant and popular villages were important market centres in the Middle Ages. Early charters for dales' markets include that for Richmond in 1144, Skipton about the same time, regularised in 1203, Clapham 1201, Wensley 1202, Otley 1227, Bowes 1245, Settle 1249, while in 1251 Bedale, Masham and Sedbergh received their market charters, followed by Ilkley in 1253, Gisburn 1260 and Grassington in 1281.

The pace of charter-granting showed no abatement during the next century, when markets were established at Carperby in 1305, East Witton and Kirkby Malzeard in 1307, with Wensley's charter being renewed then. Appletreewick, Boroughbridge and Knaresborough had markets in 1310, Pateley Bridge in 1320, Studley (near Ripon) 1344, Ripley 1357 and Middleham in 1389. Such proliferation was bound to lead to some failures. Generally, those markets at the hub of local communications succeeded while the more remote ones declined, sometimes to be succeeded two centuries later by new ones nearby. In Wensleydale Carperby's market declined but Askrigg, three miles away, received its charter in 1587, while little more than a century later, in 1700, Hawes, near the head of the dale, was granted its charter. While they flourished the markets themselves were bound to one another and to the hinterland they served by a network of roads and lanes. Many of these have grown into motor roads, others are quiet green lanes, and some have apparently vanished, waiting to be re-discovered.

Monasteries
For four centuries monastic ownership transformed huge areas of the landscape of the Yorkshire Dales. The Cistercians founded Fountains Abbey near Ripon in 1132 and Jervaulx in lower Wensleydale in 1145. Augustinian canons settled at Bolton, in Wharfedale in 1155, while smaller foundations were established at Coverham, Easby, Marrick and Ellerton during the next fifty years. Additionally, monasteries beyond the dales area played their part. Bridlington Priory and the abbeys of Byland, Furness, Rievaulx and Sawley all owned large tracts of upland country. Fountains, Furness, Byland and Sawley were granted most of the rich limestone pastures of Craven Ribblesdale; Fountains and Byland shared much of Nidderdale; Jervaulx had large holdings in upper Wensleydale, Bridlington Priory had estates in Swaledale while Bolton Priory owned the Airedale country around Skipton together with part of the manor of Malham.

The Cistercian monasteries organised their pastoral economy through a system of granges, working farms under lay-brothers regularly supervised by monastic officials who checked the state of the buildings and arranged the transport of stores, fleeces and hides. Kilnsey Grange (973678) sent huge amounts of wool to Fountains Abbey; Newby Cote (733706) and Colt Park (773779), at opposite ends of Ingleborough, sent their fleeces to Furness Abbey in the south-west corner of the Lake District. As a result regular trackways evolved between the various outlying granges and their parent monasteries. Some of these, like Mastiles Lane across Malham Moor, followed older routes used in Roman and prehistoric times, and are now splendid examples of green lanes much loved by walkers.

Monasteries influenced the development of other roads and tracks in the landscape by establishing industries. Bridlington Priory owned lead mines in Swaledale, Jervaulx Abbey in Wensleydale, Fountains and Byland in Nidderdale. Smelted lead had to be transported from remotely-

Fountains Abbey near Rippon, one of the greatest Cistercian monasteries, owned vast estates in the Craven area of the Yorkshire Dales, operated through a series of granges. Many miles of tracks linked the outlying granges to the abbey.

placed mines and smelthouses, for which packhorses were needed; hence packhorse tracks evolved, leading generally eastwards to the main marketing centres. The terrain of the dales is such that journeys of more than a few miles, usually much less, must have involved crossing one or more of the main rivers, as well as numerous streams or becks. Fords were commonplace, their positions often indicated today by the name *wath*, a word of Old Norse origin meaning 'ford'. Indeed, Nidderdale has a village just north of Pateley Bridge called Wath, where the former ford across the River Nidd was superseded by a packhorse bridge (145677).

It is likely that the monasteries were the first bridge-builders in the dales. A Fountains Abbey charter of 1184 refers to an

Agreement between the Abbeys of Fountains and Byland representing a certain island and lands in Malessart, Wynkesleia and Stodleia [Kirkby Malzeard, Winksley and Studley]....In the territory of Malessart Byland is to have thirty-five acres of cultivated land where the monks may have provender for their packhorses....Byland is also to have full right of road for cattle and waggons and horse-loads through Wacaldesheng [Kettlestang] towards Sixford [Sigsworth: 148686] as far as the Nid, and another road which Fountains has through the moor and wood towards Burtheit [Bouthwaite: 124712] as far as the water.... Byland may have a bridge across the Nid between Rasegile [Ramsgill] and Burtheit [118712].

Another charter of about the same date, defining the boundaries of Fountains Abbey lands in the Forest of Nidderdale, refers to a number of roads including, 'the road towards Thorescross [Thrushcross, now beneath Thrushcross Reservoir in the Washburn valley] and afterwards by the high road as far as Salterkelde [Saltergate Hill: 264573], and thence to the causeway of Roudunscaha [Rowden: 257575], and afterwards until again it descends to the Nid.' The high road referred to was almost certainly the Roman road from Ilkley to Aldborough, across Blubber-houses Moor, now largely followed east of the Washburn valley by the A59.

The name Saltergate Hill is a sure indication of the commodity once transported along it. Salt is essential to life, and routeways from coastal salt-pans and later from salt-making centres such as Droitwich in the Midlands, and the Cheshire plain, may have been pioneered by salt-

Windgate Nick, near Ilkley, a packhorse route, possibly of monastic origin, from Bolton Priory to Baildon.

traders. One main route into Yorkshire came through Skipton and then continued to Bolton Bridge, Blubberhouses and Knaresborough. A branch coming up from Otley to Blubberhouses is remembered in the name Psalter Gate on Snowden Bank (174514), a strange corruption of the old name Salter Gate. The north-eastern part of the dales received its salt from coastal salt-pans around the mouth of the Tees, and later at Sunderland. Although 'salt' is not shown either in place-names or the names of old roads in the Richmond area it is likely that a number of old tracks were used for the carriage of salt and coal. For transport of most commodities, over long distances and to meet purely local needs, packhorses and pack-mules were predominantly used for almost six centuries, and packhorse tracks are dealt with in detail in a later chapter.

Little documentary evidence survives to throw much light on the state and appearance of roads through the Middle Ages. Rights of way they may have been but they were little more. In 1285 the Statute of Winchester established the responsibility for maintaining the highways on manorial landowners, and also decreed that a zone on each side of a highway should be cleared of any form of cover except for large trees of commercial value. Removal of bushy cover was intended to reduce threats posed by highwaymen and outlaws, and it would also make more practical another stipulation of the Statute, that if a track or bridleway became impassable another should be made alongside the original. As a result the most-used medieval roads and tracks tended to become broad zones or corridors of communication, unbordered by hedges or walls. Sometimes even this failed to prevent some medieval roads from becoming eroded deeply into the ground, a process accelerated in prolonged wet weather, forming the many 'holloways' which signify long-abandoned routes between villages, or leading to villages deserted since medieval times. The state of a medieval road depended on its importance and the extent to which it was used, as well as on the powers of manorial courts to persuade the local population to accept responsibility for repairs, always providing the necessary materials for this work were available.

If documentary and field evidence for the existence of roads is patchy a few medieval maps survive which show the pattern of a national network. About 1250 Matthew Paris, a monk at St Albans, drew four maps of Britain based on an itinerary from Dover to Newcastle. Its Yorkshire route passes through Doncaster, Pontefract, Boroughbridge and Northallerton to Durham. Evidence of a more accurate nature is given by Gough's map of about 1360 which identifies nearly 3,000 miles of roads covering much of England. Richard Gough was the antiquarian who described the map in 1780; who first drew it, and why, are not known. It does give distances between most towns, probably in old French miles (about 1¼ statute miles), and it is interesting to see that many of the routes follow the Roman roads which had been constructed at least 1,000 years previously. However, the appearance of a Roman road on this map does not necessarily mean it was in use, and conversely the omission of such a road does not imply that one was not being used.

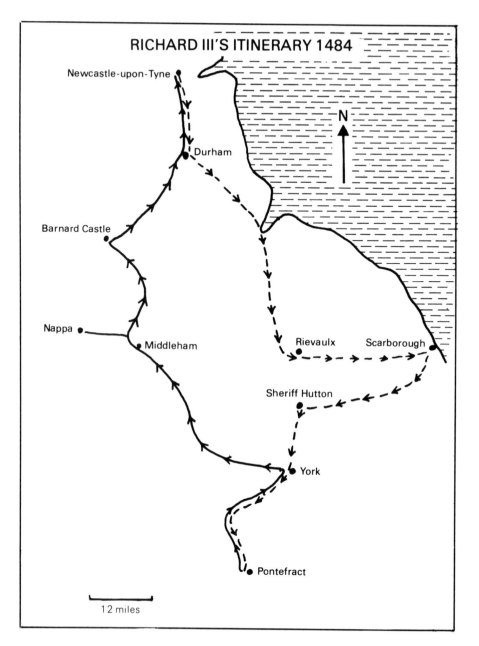

RICHARD III'S ITINERARY 1484

N

Newcastle-upon-Tyne
Durham
Barnard Castle
Nappa
Middleham
Rievaulx
Scarborough
Sheriff Hutton
York
Pontefract

12 miles

Gough's map shows a main north road through Yorkshire by way of Doncaster, Pontefract, Wetherby, Boroughbridge, Leeming, Gilling and Bowes to Brough, Appleby and Penrith (largely the A1 and A66 of today). A western branch from Doncaster led through Wakefield, Bradford, Skipton and Settle to Kirkby Lonsdale and Kendal (much of the present A65). A secondary road linked Richmond with Kirkby Lonsdale by way of Bolton (Castle), Hawes and Sedbergh. While these routes would not have the accuracy or definitive quality of those on modern maps it is reasonable to assume that where the routes followed Roman roads they were fairly accurate, while the secondary routes away from the Roman network had evolved through regular usage, and where shown on the map they were a guide to travellers. So far as the Yorkshire Dales area is concerned the relevance of Gough's map is in the apparent importance it accords to Kirkby Lonsdale (just over the Cumbria border) and Richmond.

If Gough's map offers some evidence for the course of medieval roads, relevant itineraries provide substantiation. Their value is in the fact that the person concerned must have travelled between places named, and, in the case of royalty, probably was accompanied by a large baggage train. Unfortunately, kings rarely visited the Dales area of Yorkshire, queens never. However, an early itinerary reveals that King John visited Ravensworth (142078) in February 1201, where a few fragments remain of the medieval castle of the Fitzhughs. Five years later he was at Richmond, on one of his journeys to Scotland, when it is known that he used the route of the Roman road over Stainmore between Bowes and Appleby.

Richard III, who, as Duke of Gloucester, had spent many years living at Middleham Castle, visited Wensleydale again during his brief reign of twenty-six months. Since only ten of those were spent in London, the royal administration was regularly on the move. The royal household, together with government officials, probably numbered at least 200, and travelled 20-30 miles a day, suggestive of reasonably surfaced roads having been used. Richard's northern base was York, and his 1484 itinerary includes the following places at which he stayed:

May	4	Nappa (probably)
	6-8	Middleham
	9-10	Barnard Castle
	13-14	Newcastle
	15-17	Durham

His route from York to Wensleydale is not known, but beyond Middleham he may have crossed the River Ure either by a ford below the town or by a timber bridge at Ulshaw, continuing northwards by Spennithorne and Harmby to Richmond — the route later described and mapped by Ogilby (see Chapter 4). During the twelve years when Middleham Castle was Richard's home, he frequently visited and stayed at Barnard Castle, so he journeyed regularly from Wensleydale to Teesdale, but we know no details of these journeys, so can only surmise that the Richmond-Ravensworth route could have been used, and the minor road today up Richmond Hill, continuing north-westwards to Ravensworth represents an approximation to Richard's route.

In 1487 Henry VII was in Yorkshire, and his itinerary records:

July	31	York
Aug	2-5	York
	9	Croft

11-13	Durham
14-17	Newcastle
18	Durham
20	Durham to Raby
22	Richmond
23-24	Ripon
25-26	Pontefract

Although there is no written evidence it can again be reasonably conjectured that the royal route from Raby may have crossed the Tees at Barnard Castle and continued south-eastwards to Ravensworth and Richmond. Beyond there the North Road would offer the most direct way to Ripon.

We can now consider in greater detail some of the monastic roads for which documentary evidence exists. Many of these were public highways used by all kinds of traffic — people on foot or horseback, packhorses, carts and waggons. Some lesser roads, even in medieval days known as lanes, could not be used by wheeled vehicles. Monasteries sometimes obtained rights of passage from manorial lords. The Fountains Abbey Chartulary of 1274, refers to a grant by Nigel de Plunt of free transit through his land at Grassington, except corn and meadow, for all the monks' cattle and men and carts going and returning between Fountains and Kilnsey. Further up Wharfedale grants of land were made 'for free transit for monks, their men, horses and cattle, outside corn and meadow, on the east side of the water of Wharfe' between Kettlewell and Starbotton. In monastic charters roads are mentioned frequently as boundaries but only rarely as having been built by monasteries themselves, although the system of Cistercian granges doubtless gave impetus to the evolution of a network of linking tracks. All available evidence indicates that there was very little new road-building during the Middle Ages. Roads made and maintained themselves through usage by horses and carts, by packhorses, by the movement of stock, and by people.

Mastiles Lane

Mastiles Lane was one of the most famous monastic roads in northern England. Although the name applies only to that section of it crossing Malham Moor eastwards to the site of the former Cistercian grange at Kilnsey, it continued westwards to Fountains Abbey estates in the northern Lake District. 'Mastiles' seems to be a fairly recent name, the older one being 'Strete Gate', significant in view of the probable existence of a Roman temporary marching camp which the lane bisects 300 yd east of the Gordale Beck crossing (913655).

The western continuation of Mastiles Lane in Cumbria is beyond the area of this survey, but it probably entered the Dales along the line of the modern A65 through Kirkby Lonsdale to Ingleton. It is unfortunate that so little is known of the history of Kirkby Lonsdale's magnificent Devil's Bridge (616783) spanning the River Lune on the eastern edge of the town. Its roadway is about 11 ft wide, and pontage rights for its upkeep were

MASTILES LANE

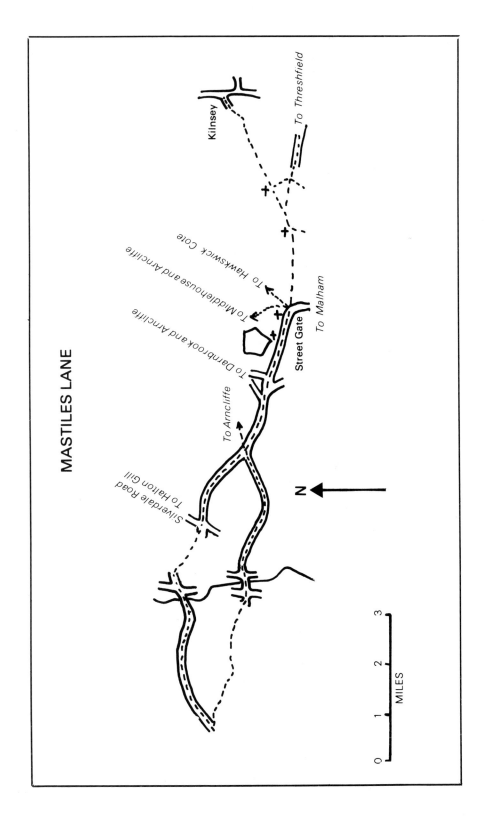

Kilnsey

To Threshfield

To Hawkswick Cote

To Middlehouse and Arncliffe

To Darnbrook and Arncliffe

Street Gate

To Malham

To Arncliffe

Silverdale Road
To Halton Gill

N

MILES
0   1   2   3

granted in 1275 and 1365 — times when monastic traffic would be considerable. However, there is no evidence to suggest that it had been built by a monastery.

From Ingleton the route eastwards probably followed the line of the 'old road' to Clapham, passing through Newby Cote (732706). The Manor of Newby belonged to Furness Abbey, and the present manor house occupies the site of the former monastic grange. Wool traffic from here, and other Furness Abbey estates, would have supplemented the similar traffic from the Fountains Abbey estates, slowly moving eastwards to the North Sea ports. Grants of passage were usually agreed between monastic owners, but it is not known if Furness Abbey used the Fountains Abbey route which continued from the northern end of Clapham village along Thwaite Lane, keeping north of Austwick to the hamlet of Wharfe (782695). From there the line is taken up by the minor road eastwards to the River Ribble at Helwith Bridge (812695).

The river here is fordable; the present bridge is a nineteenth-century structure, but there is no visible evidence of a predecessor. The monastic route climbs the hill to the east as Moorhead Lane, a steep and stony track as far as the township boundary, marked by a neatly-lettered slab of Horton slate. Beyond, the lane makes two right-angled kinks, and near the second one (830688), leaves the original track which continues as a field path to Sannet Hall, entering Goat Lane which comes up from Stainforth, by a stile. Crossing this lane, the monastic track, now adopted as a narrow motor road, goes forward into a south-easterly orientation as Henside Lane. Westside House to the north of this road, and Capon Hall farther on, were both Fountains properties, as was most of Malham Moor around and to the east of Malham Tarn.

The monastic road, now an unenclosed motor road as far as Street Gate (905657) crosses open moorland to the east of Malham Water, the outlet stream from the tarn. This is what the whole of this road, and most other roads in the Dales, would have been like before the eighteenth century when many of them became walled. To mark the bounds of the monastic tracks, as well as to provide landmarks in rather featureless country it was customary to place crosses at various prominent points. They were usually simple stumpy shafts, rather crudely squared, set in hollowed sockets cut in a stone base. Five were placed along Mastiles Lane, one near the tarn by the Pennine Way track, one near Street Gate, and the others just to the north of the lane itself. Their shafts have vanished, either for use as gateposts, or, broken up, for walling materials. Only the socket-bases remain, the best two being those about 700yd east of Gordale Beck, at 917655, and the other almost opposite the junction with Smearbottom Lane (930655).

Mastiles Lane continues eastwards as a lane across Kilnsey Moor, and, soon after Little Wood its original course is marked by a footpath (not a right-of-way) going directly across fields to Kilnsey Hall. The tarmac road to Kilnsey is a quarry road serving the vast Cool Scar quarry, behind Kilnsey Crag. A monastic grange at Kilnsey was built during the second half of the twelfth century and served all the Fountains Abbey estates of upper Wharfedale, Littondale, upper Airedale and parts of Ribblesdale, but a sub-grange was built for Malham, Malham Moor and Bordley. Kilnsey's importance accounts for the plethora of tracks which converge on it from a large area of limestone landscape to the west. After the Dissolution of 1539 Fountains Abbey estates were sold, Kilnsey Grange, with its hall and cottages, passed into the hands of the Wade family, and in 1648 Christopher Wade built the present Kilnsey Hall (974678), now used primarily as a farm store.

Kilnsey Grange was close to an old, but important road up Wharfedale which followed the eastern side of the valley, and Fountains Abbey built a bridge across the Wharfe at Conistone wide enough to take waggons. The present structure dates from the eighteenth century and is probably on or close to the original river crossing.

Other Tracks around Malham
Another important monastic road eastwards from Malham village is that now followed by the narrow, surfaced lane to Gordale House (915635), continuing as Hawthorns Lane to Lee Gate House (927644). At the top of the first hill beyond Gordale a stony track branches off south-eastwards to Weets Top, where Weets Cross, (926633) probably of monastic origin, marks the point where the townships of Malham, Bordley, Calton and Hanlith meet.

At Lee Gate House Smearbottom Lane goes forward as a green lane to join Mastiles Lane, while the monastic road continues eastwards to Bordley (942649), joining Malham Moor Lane near the prehistoric stone circle, and as Hard Gate down through Skythorns to Threshfield and Grassington. There is little doubt that the present road from Grassington over Greenhow Hill to Pateley Bridge, B6265, is the same route described in the Abbey Chartulary of the twelfth century as 'the high road which goes to Craven'. This important route divided at Pateley, one branch (now

Weets Cross, near Malham. Probably a boundary and guidepost on the edge of the Malham estates of Fountains Abbey.

a minor road past the old church) climbing Bishopside, crossing to Harper Hill (195703) and Kirkby Malzeard, the other going over Sawley Moor to Ripon.

A northwards route from Malham probably followed the present road up Malham Rakes, east of Malham Cove, crossing Mastiles Lane at Street Gate (905657). Beyond the brow of the first hill (903637) a footpath follows Trougate, another monastic track, northwards across Prior Rakes towards Malham Tarn, crossing the motor road west of Water Sinks Gate. Back at Street Gate, however, the monks' way continues northwards as a tarmac road to Middle House Farm (908677), a mid-nineteenth-century estate house. Keeping to the west of this the old track winds upwards past some small irregular fields, to the deserted Middle House, on the site of a Fountains Abbey grange (907682). Beyond, the green track divides, the westerly fork going to Darnbrook House, also an abbey grange, while the 'monks' trod', as it is called, goes north-eastwards past Dewbottoms and above the limestone cliffs of Yew Cogar, a well-defined packhorse route which descends steeply into a walled lane at Arncliffe village (932717).

To the east of this route, but also starting at Street Gate, another monastic track runs north-eastwards as a green lane, crossing Clapham High Mark (924675) and descending above the northern flanks of Cote Gill to Hawkswick Cote (947704) in Littondale. Most of this valley was

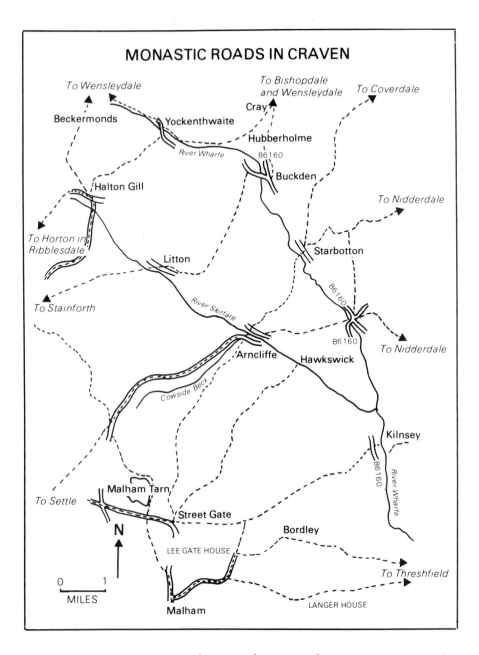

MONASTIC ROADS IN CRAVEN

To Wensleydale

To Bishopdale
and Wensleydale

To Coverdale

Cray

Beckermonds

Yockenthwaite

Hubberholme

River Wharfe

B6160

Buckden

To Nidderdale

Halton Gill

To Horton in
Ribblesdale

Litton

Starbotton

B6160

To Stainforth

River Skirfare

B6160

To Nidderdale

Arncliffe

Hawkswick

Cowside Beck

Kilnsey

B6160

River Wharfe

Malham Tarn

To Settle

Street Gate

N

Bordley

LEE GATE HOUSE

To Threshfield

0   1

MILES

Malham

LANGER HOUSE

Fountains property on or close to the original monastic way south-eastwards to Kilnsey.

West of Malham Tarn, Higher Tren House is on the site of a grange (879667). The Malham-Arncliffe road which passes it, going forward to Darnbrook and Cowside into Littondale, was another important monastic route. It picks up, near New Pasture (885691) a green track crossing Knowe Fell (part of Fountains Fell) which is a continuation of the metalled road from Settle in Ribblesdale via Langcliffe and Henside.

From Ribblesdale

Fountains Abbey also owned estates at High Greenfield (830792) in Langstrothdale, at Horton-in-Ribblesdale, and the lodge at Birkwith (800768) three miles north of this. The valley heads of upper Wharfedale (Langstrothdale) and Littondale, with their tributary becks, swing round almost in a semi-circle, stretching towards Ribblesdale, presenting convenient routes from Ribblesdale to Wharfedale. Two of these from Horton and one from Stainforth were used by monastic traffic. The northerly road from Horton, leaving the village at the Crown Hotel, formerly New Inn (807727), and following the minor road to New Houses, is now identified as a footpath to Fawber and Top Farm, and passes Jackdaw Hole to join a walled lane at 810755. This lane, now part of the Pennine Way, also leaves by the Crown Hotel, and was probably a later packhorse way to Birkwith Moor. As a clearly-defined track the monastic route continues into the extensive new forestry plantation, where, as a forest road, it becomes metalled at High Greenfield. Between High and Low Greenfield conifers now obscure the rough pastures where Arthur Young observed experiments carried out about 1774 by a farmer who had reclaimed 'black moory land by draining, burning and liming it, sowing with turnips, then laying it down to grass with a mixture of rye grass, clover, hay seed'. With walling enclosures and good grazing he managed to improve over 200 acres, and at the time of Young's visit two years later, the land was stocked with 20 horses, 40 cows, 1,200 sheep,

Lane in High Greenfield, originally part of the monastic route between Horton-in-Ribblesdale and Upper Wharfedale, used by Fountains and Jervaulx Abbeys.

with 300 young stock grazing summer pastures on the surrounding moors.

Below Low Greenfield (850802) a branch, now a footpath, initially through forest, later on rough moorland, leads to Oughtershaw, and crosses the beck by an ugly replacement for a stone packhorse bridge whose 'waisted' approach walls survive. The main monastic route continues eastwards to join the motor road down Langstrothdale beyond Beckermonds.

Another route from Horton leaves the village midway between the Crown Hotel and the church, and, as Horton Scar Lane, is adopted by the Pennine Way. On a north-east alignment it climbs as a walled lane 30ft wide as far as a derelict shooting-box (823743). Here the Pennine Way swings eastwards, but the old Foxup Road continues as a green track to Swarth Gill Gate (841758), contours round Foxup Moor and finds a narrow shelf of limestone above a spring line. At Low Bergh (870765) it descends steeply to the hamlet of Foxup and crosses a small stone bridge giving access to the surfaced road from Halton Gill at the head of Littondale.

One of the best-known monastic routes from Ribblesdale is that from Settle and Stainforth to Halton Gill. Sawley Abbey owned land above Langcliffe and Stainforth, so monastic roads would have led southwards through Settle and Long Preston to the parent monastery near Clitheroe. North-bound packhorse traffic would have left Settle at the north-east corner of the Market Place up Constitution Hill beyond which the old road, now a walled narrow lane, goes forward to Langcliffe, joining the present motor road up Ribblesdale. At the top of Constitution Hill a stony track branches off to the right, becomes a green lane, and joins the metalled road above Langcliffe (828654) which continues north-eastwards to Henside and Malham Moor. This also has a branch keeping above Langcliffe, where a footpath continues its line parallel to the railway, to Stainforth.

Goat Lane above Stainforth, now metalled, follows the monastic road up Silverdale, crossing the boundary of the ancient parish of Giggleswick near Dale Head at the head of Silverdale. By the roadside is the base socket of Ulfkil Cross (842715), a boundary mark between the estates of Sawley and Fountains Abbeys mentioned in the Fountains Chartulary. Other old tracks meet here: from Helwith Bridge to the south-west Long Lane climbs by Dub Cote Scar Pasture and eastwards by the boundary wall to Dale Head and the Silverdale Road. Opposite the junction a green track follows the edge of Rainscar south-eastwards to Henside Road. The Littondale road continues north-eastwards past Rainscar House, Penyghent House, and Upper Hesleden to Halton Gill. Just before the site of Giant's Grave a green lane branches off (856728), contours across Dawson Close and Cow Close to the village of Litton (905742). Spittle Croft, south of the river, probably marks the site of a hospice on this former monastic route.

Jervaulx Abbey had a horse-breeding farm at Horton, and monks probably used the High Greenfield route for the first part of their journey to Wensleydale. From Beckermonds, however, the route can only be conjectured, but probably went down Langstrothdale to Hubberholme (926783). Although we read in a Quarter Sessions account of 1693 that Hubberholme bridge was in 'great ruine and decay . . . the said bridge being the highe road way leading between the markett towne of Lancaster . . . the markett town of Newcastle upon Tyne and other places in the countie of Northumberland', it need not necessarily have been used in monastic times. From the minor road north of the river, leading to Cray (932792) a footpath up Cray Gill crosses a tiny packhorse bridge of primitive appearance, and joins the present road at Cray. This route over Kidstones represents an obvious, and in terms of height the easiest, way to Aysgarth and Wensleydale. The most likely alternative route to Jervaulx would have been from Starbotton, lower down Wharfedale, and this will be dealt with later.

From Nidderdale

Throughout medieval times many tracks from upper Nidderdale led north-eastwards to converge on Kirkby Malzeard, site of the castle of the Mowbrays, centre of administration of the Honour of Kirkby Malzeard of which they were the lords. They had granted extensive estates in Nidderdale to the abbeys of Fountains and Byland, and with Byland Abbey lying several miles away to the east, Kirkby Malzeard was a focal point and resting place for personnel and packhorses on the long journey from the Nidderdale granges.

From lead mines in Ashford Gill (120662) a probable monastic route climbed across the hill to Heathfield (137673) and up Nidderdale by a track now lost beneath Gouthwaite Reservoir, to Ramsgill and across

Old road from Pateley Bridge to Kirkby Malzeard, near Fellbeck. May have been part of monastic route to Fountains Abbey.

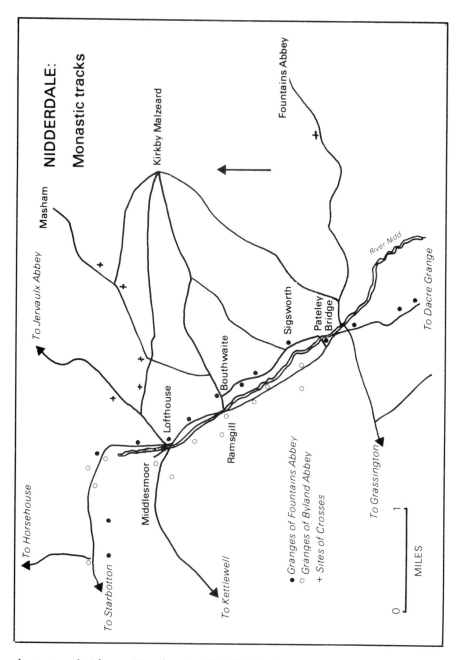

their river bridge to Bouthwaite (123713) where Fountains had a grange. From here the monks' road climbs steeply up a stony, rutted and occasionally holloway to Intake Gate (135718), crosses Covill House Moor north-eastwards, and passes close to Harry Cross Stoop. Descending as a stony lane across North Gill Beck it continues along Dallowgill Moor side near Dalton Lodge (173725), turning north-eastwards to Swetton Moor and as a modern, minor road takes a direct line to Kirkby Malzeard.

South of Dalton Lodge, in the head of Dallowgill, there are fragments of an old road, now called Potter Lane, which passes Potter Lane House, crosses the beck, and as a footpath rises over Dallowgill Moor to Kettlestang House previously referred to (163712) and is then lost on Sigsworth Moor. It is subsequently picked up as a rough moorland track at 155708 and descends to Sigsworth Grange and Wath (147677) on the opposite bank of the Nidd to Heathfield. Byland Abbey was allowed to use this route from Heathfield across Fountains estate, and the Nidderdale historian, William Grainge, writing in 1863, records that the old road on Sigsworth Moor was 4 ft wide and paved with stones. It may, therefore, have been a medieval causeway of monastic days.

From the head of Nidderdale a route of monastic origin is now largely a metalled road, leaving the north of Lofthouse village by Green Gate (102736), climbing to the Moor Gate, beyond which as Trapping Hill it continues north-eastwards over Lofthouse Level, past Benjy Guide (118755) and into the head of Agill. On Pott Moor it passes an old guide-stone pointing westwards to NewHouses, and near the crest of Pott Bank (143778) where the modern road descends towards Leighton Reservoir, the old way to Jervaulx branches off as a faint path due north to Grimes Gill, crosses a ford and climbs past High Sourmire and Towler Hill farms. Continuing to Spout House (151804) it crosses Spruce Gill Beck to Gollinglith Foot (152810).

This was the meeting place for most tracks coming down Colsterdale,

Guide stone on Pott Moor, above Nidderdale, indicating old track to New Houses and Kettlewell.

where Jervaulx monks had been granted rights for coal and iron in the fourteenth century, together with free passage for the Abbot and Convent and their men, through Mashamshire to Colsterdale. Tracks from coal pits on both sides of the valley meet at Gollinglith, from where the northwards route is now a stony lane to Low Agra and Agra, then as an indistinct footpath following the old North/West Riding boundary past the Tranmire Stone, a boundary mark, north-eastwards to Angram Cote (171836) near Ellingstring. Beyond there the route is uncertain, but may have gone through High and Low Newstead, both granges of Jervaulx, joining the main Ripon road by Abbey Hill (170854) and entering the precinct by the gatehouse farther down this road.

Corpse Roads

The sparse population of some parts of the Yorkshire Dales meant that in early medieval times parishes were large and the dead had to be carried a long way for burial in the parish churchyard. Three such 'Corpse Ways' occur in the Dales, the best-known being that in Swaledale, although it must be stated at the outset that such routes were not used exclusively for that purpose, but most probably saw the normal traffic of packhorses, driven stock, lead miners, and dalesfolk going to and from market.

The whole of Swaledale above Grinton formed one parish, with the mother-church and burial ground at Grinton (046985). Until 1580, when a new chapel and burial ground were consecrated at Muker, all

The Corpse Way — an ancient green track in Swaledale — here crossing the hill of Kisdon between Keld and Muker.

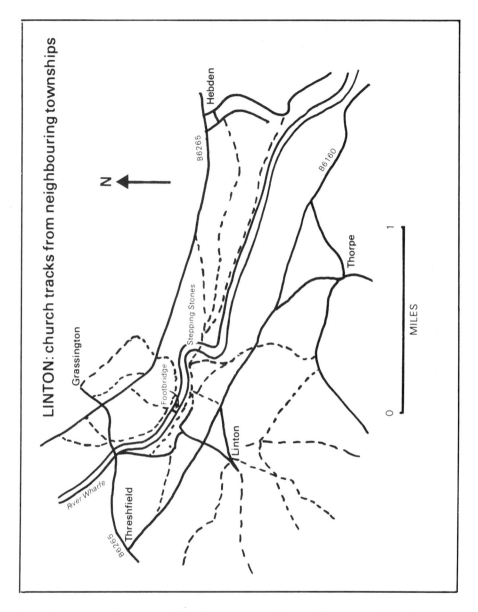

LINTON: church tracks from neighbouring townships

N

Hebden

B6265

B6160

Thorpe

Stepping Stones

Grassington

Footbridge

MILES

1

0

Linton

River Wharfe

Threshfield

B6265

burials were at Grinton; after then, corpses from the upper dale down as far as Gunnerside were buried at Muker, while those from below Gunnerside continued to be taken to Grinton. Writing about 1820 the historian Dr T.D. Whitaker describes how 'the bodies of the dead were conveyed for burial upon men's shoulders upwards of twelve miles to the parish church, not in coffins but in rude wicker baskets.' The journey from the head of the dale would take two days, depending on weather conditions, and it is said that the funeral parties stayed overnight at Feetham, possibly resting and refreshing themselves at the forerunner of what is now the Punch Bowl Inn.

There can be little doubt that the route taken was already an ancient way down Swaledale, keeping generally to the northern, or sunny side, of the valley. From Keld, the highest village in the dale, the so-called Corpse Road leaves the present motor road about 300yd south of the village (893006), descends to a ford, and climbs steeply as a stony track up the western side of Kisdon. It crosses this hill, whose commons were enclosed in 1832, as a walled lane, and descends steeply to Muker, turning back across the Carrs (hay-meadows) to ford the River Swale a few yards below the present footbridge at Rampsholme (910985). It continues eastwards along Ivelet Side, becoming a metalled lane near Calvert Houses, and passing a succession of farms to Gunnerside (950983), where it crosses Gunnerside Beck at the site of a modern road-bridge.

From the east end of the village, Lodge Green, the Corpse Way climbs as a steep, stony track deeply sunk between high banks, becoming near the deserted farm of Heights (960983) a green lane, continues diagonally up the hill as a holloway and then follows a level course over open limestone pasture high above the valley to the hamlet of Blades (981985), where the surface again becomes metalled. A possible alternative may have taken it at a lower level, below Heights, to Smarber (973977), descending to Lane End near Low Row and then by the route of the present road to Feetham, also reached by the higher route from Blades.

Beyond Blades another high-level track, walled at first, subsequently

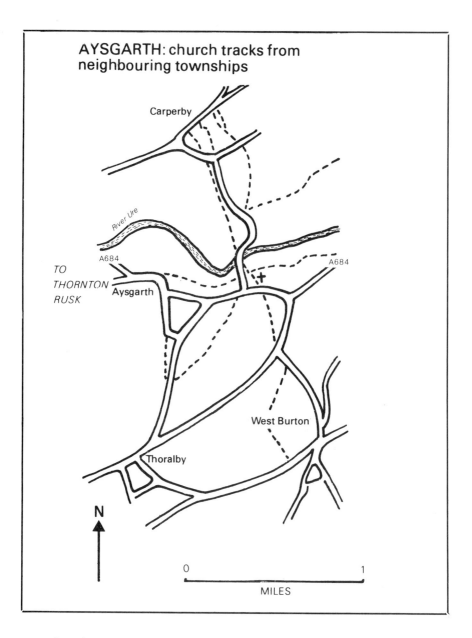

AYSGARTH: church tracks from neighbouring townships

Carperby

River Ure

A684

TO
THORNTON
RUSK
Aysgarth

A684

West Burton

Thoralby

N

0   1

MILES

unenclosed, continues to Kearton (997990), crossing three fords, and the moor road called Peat Gate which comes up from Feetham. From Kearton the Corpse Way is now represented by the metalled Morley Gate, dropping down to Barney Beck High Bridge and Healaugh, and picking up the present road into Reeth and Grinton. It seems possible that, in dry conditions with the river level low a more direct route may have been taken from Feetham, along the line of the present main road to the former ford at Scabba Wath (006984), now a road-bridge, and eastwards along Harkerside to Grinton. Jefferys's map of 1771, shows this road much more prominently than the one on the north side of the Swale. It also shows a track in the upper dale, on the east side of the river above Muker, probably a miners' track in the eighteenth century, but likely to have been the route taken by burial parties from Stonesdale, Frith and Raven Seat above Keld, in preference to the climb over Kisdon.

Aysgarth Parish in Wensleydale, 81,000 acres in extent, was formerly the largest ancient parish in England, until it was divided last century. Remotely placed at its head is the tiny church at Lunds (794945) of unknown date, although it had a curate licensed in 1713. Burials took place there, for the dead from lonely farms nearby, and also from the secluded valley-hamlet of Cotterdale (832938). Afforestation now hides the beginnings of the three mile long Corpse Way, a sketchy track over High Abbotside to High Dyke and down the fellsides by which the dead from Cotterdale were taken for burial at Lunds.

The third Corpse Way is in Wharfedale, from Buckden, over Birks Fell and Firth Fell to Litton, and down Littondale to the mother-church at Arncliffe, of which Hubberholme was only a chapel-of-ease without a burial ground. The track today is a well-defined path over the top, leaving Dubb's Lane at 936774, and climbing above Redmire Farm to cross the boundary-wall on the watershed at 1,996ft before the steep descent to Littondale, entering Litton village by the Queen's Arms (906741). From there its route to Arncliffe may follow that of the motor road, or may have forded the river to East Garth, then taking the south of the river to Arncliffe. With both the Wharfe and Skirfare liable to sudden flooding the journey from Buckden or Hubberholme to Arncliffe could be treacherous, and in the late fifteenth century one group lost its corpse in the swollen Wharfe, while another almost succumbed in snowdrifts. It seems probable that funeral processions did not continue much after that date.

Tudor and Stuart Times

That the word travel has its roots in Norman French, *travail* — meaning 'work, labour' — is significant. Until the middle of the eighteenth century travel in England away from the few main roads linking London and major cities was indeed laborious work. To do it for pleasure for most people was quite inconceivable. Almost all English travel was for business or trade. The Yorkshire Dales must have appeared very remote from the important locations of civilised life, and few accounts survive which throw much light on the state of the roads and trackways in the Dales because few literate travellers came this way.

From the sixteenth century only Leland and Camden record their observations, but even these are concerned with towns, markets, trade and important buildings. They largely ignore the countryside and say little about the ways along which they went. John Leland spent six years riding through England obtaining material for a detailed account which was never completed. Even the fragments of his *Itinerary*, written during the 1540s, were not published until 1710-12, but they do record many of the bridges he presumably crossed. Indeed, for him and travellers throughout the sixteenth and seventeenth centuries the most noted points in journeys through the Dales were the bridges and fords across rivers and streams. For foot-travellers some river crossings were by ferry — the Ure at West Tanfield and Middleham for example.

> There is no very notable bridge on Ure above Wencelaw Bridge [Wensley]. The bridge over Ure by Midleham is but of tymbar. About a mile benethe Gervaux Abbay is a great old bridge of stone on Ure, called Kilgram Bridge. There is a fair bridge on Swal at Gronton . . . the Richemount bridge.
> Nid river risethe much by West 5 miles above Pateley Bridge of wood . . . from Pateley Bridge and Village to Newbridge of Tymber 3 miles. Then to Killinghall Bridge of one great Arche of Stone 3 miles and 3 miles to Guaresbrughe, where first is the West Bridge of 3 Arches of Stone, and then a little lower Marche Bridge of 3 Arches. Both these Bridges serve the town of Knaresborow

Kilgram Bridge, Wensleydale, posibly fifteenth century and, according to Warburton, on the line of a Roman road from Catterick to Ripon.

Identifying the locations of some of these presents problems. Leland's miles are longer than present-day ones, equivalent to 1¼ statute miles. Killinghall Bridge over the River Nidd about one mile south of Ripley now has two arches, the original ribbing still visible suggesting that this method of construction was still being used in the sixteenth century, after Leland's visit. The Newbridge referred to was the predecessor of the present New Bridge west of Birstwith (236603). It is known that in 1594 the existing wooden bridge was so far decayed that it attracted a bequest for repair — and it is at least eight miles below Pateley. Leland makes no mention of the bridge at Hampsthwaite, although there must have been one in Leland's day for the village had then an important market. When, about 1638, estimates were invited for its replacement, they showed that the cost of a stone one would be £400; apparently there was not enough local timber available to build one in wood, so the existing structure was repaired for £25. All of which indicates that the existing bridge was of wood. The present two-part structure, showing an obvious widening, probably dates from late in that century (261592).

Leland makes an unusual reference to a bridge over the Swale at the Bargate foot of the town below the castle: 'Bargate Suburbe cummith down to the Bridge Ende of Swale, the wich Bridge is sumtime chaynid [chained].' This was a four-arched structure of stone depicted on Speed's map of 1610, graphically shown on R. Harman's plan of 1724, and clearly indentified on Jackson's plan meticulously drawn in 1773. Harman's plan shows the bridge to have a watch-tower over the central pier on the upstream side. The boundary between the Borough of Richmond and the North Riding of Yorkshire was along the middle of the river, and

Richmond claimed the right to levy tolls on goods crossing the bridge, whether entering or leaving the town. The watch tower was a shelter for the toll collector. When the bridge was rebuilt in 1788-9 the tower was not included.

A new bridge had become necessary by then, following repeated damage by floods. Repairs and maintenance was a joint responsibility, but the Borough of Richmond and the North Riding regularly failed to co-ordinate this work. When a new bridge was proposed, and John Carr's design agreed upon, the authorities advertised separately for tenders for their respective halves, and subsequently employed two different contractors. The differences in structure can be identified — the parapet on the county side has two courses of masonry blocks, that on the borough half has three. Between them the text of the milestone has been reconstructed: to Askrigg 18 to Lancaster 56 miles. The important road from Richmond to Lancaster was turnpiked in 1751, and travellers doubtless appreciated the new Green Bridge across the Swale. Since it was built no major repairs have been carried out on it, although it now carries far more traffic than it was ever designed for, testimony to its good design and construction. Bargate and Bargate Green were extra-mural suburbs of Richmond, and the hillside to the north-west on Harman's plan shows tenter banks indicative of cloth manufacture.

William Camden was Queen Elizabeth's historian, and his monumental *Britannia* is an account of his travels through England in 1582, written in Latin but translated in 1610. He obviously had problems in Wharfedale, describing the Wharfe as 'a troublesome River and dangerous even in Summer time also . . . for, it hath such slippery stones in it that an horse can have no sure footing on them, or else the violence of the water carryeth them away from under his feete.' He records that at Burnsall 'Sir William Craven Knight and Alderman of London there borne, is now building a Stone bridge'. That was in 1590.

When Celia Fiennes journeyed through England in the 1690s she touched only the eastern edge of the Dales, at Richmond, and was impressed by 'those high and large stone bridges I pass'd, which lay across the rivers.' Indeed, she frequently comments on the stone bridges in

Grinton Bridge, Swaledale. Widenedin ashlar stone by John Carr in 1797.

Hubberholme Bridge, Wharfedale, said to have been in great ruin in 1693. It lay on the high road between Lancaster and Newcastle.

northern England, and it must be remembered that, in her native south and especially on the Thames, most bridges were then still of wood.

Presumably the state of the roads was so awful that it defied comment, or else the few literate travellers who rode the Dales' trackways did not know, or had not experienced, anything very much better. The basic principles of road construction had virtually been ignored or forgotten since Roman times. An Act of Parliament of 1555 recognised the need for improvements by making each parish responsible for the repair and maintenance of highways within its own boundaries. Specifically, the Act stipulated that each person having land with an annual value of £50 and each person 'keeping a draught of horses or plough in the parish do provide one wain or cart . . . with oxen, horses or other cattle . . . and also two able men.' Additionally, each household had to work four days a year on the parish highways — increased in 1563 to six days for each adult male. The Act also authorised that each parish appointed two unpaid highway surveyors who had to inspect all roads, bridges, water-courses and pavements, to look after the highway, and three times a year to inspect ditches and drains by the side of it. The surveyors additionally had to watch the traffic using the parish roads, and the numbers of horses used to haul waggons — if many horses were drawing a waggon it was likely that the load was so heavy it damaged the surface of the highway. Supervising all this Statute Labour were local Justices, who could impose fines if the work was evaded. In July 1611 the parishioners of Askrigg were criticised for 'not repairing a Hie Waie lying at the west end of Askrigg Holmes' (a marshy area between the village and Paddock Beck) and were warned that 'if it be not sufficiently repaired by Lammas next, a forfeit of 10s be imposed upon them.'

Similarly, at Skipton Quarter Sessions in July 1639 we read that, 'The King's Highway within the parish of Clapham in a place called Austwick leasings, and between the market towns of Settle and Lancaster is in great decay for lack of repair . . . . A penalty of £20 is laid upon the said Michael [Howson, of Austwick] and the other inhabitants that they sufficiently repair the same before the feast of Martinmas next . . . .' The parishioners duly obliged for we read in the Wetherby Sessions the following January that a local gentleman gave evidence that the way was repaired, so the penalty was remitted. Those same Sessions also heard that 'Hubbram Bridge [Hubberholme, Wharfedale] was in 'great ruyne and decay . . . the said bridge being the high roade way leadinge between the markett towne of Lancaster and the markett towne of Newcastle upon Tyne.'

Generally, it seems, the 1555 Act was honoured more in the breach than the observance. Undoubtedly many parishes failed to carry out the work or simply could not cope with the repairs needed. Nevertheless, some improvements in travelling were made. Certainly, in the Dales area, there would scarcely have been any shortage of stone with which to fill the potholes in Tudor highways. In 1568 when Mary, Queen of Scots, was escorted into Wensleydale for her short imprisonment in Bolton Castle (with her retinue of forty servants), it is probable that her coach was the first to have been seen in the Dales.

One outcome of the increase in travel was the production of more detailed maps, the first one of Yorkshire being made appropriately by a Yorkshireman, Christopher Saxton, born in a village near Wakefield in 1542 or 1544. In 1570 he was engaged in making surveys in many areas of England, receiving grants and expenses in lieu of a salary, probably paid by Thomas Seckford, Master of Requests at Queen Elizabeth's court. Saxton visited viewpoints (including church towers), collected local information, made copious records of countless compass bearings, and travelled extensively.

Saxton's engraved and printed maps first appeared in 1575, mainly of southern and south-western counties. The four northern counties were printed in 1576, followed by a map of Yorkshire in 1577. It depicts hills, rivers, towns, villages, the important bridges — but no highways. John Speed's map of Yorkshire issued in 1610, contains similar detail to Saxton's but although at a larger scale it also does not depict highways. 'Road books' for travellers, and gentlemen's libraries, also appeared during the last quarter of the sixteenth century but it was not until Stuart times and the remarkable expertise of John Ogilby that the modern-style road-book with strip-maps introduced a new significance to travel in England and Wales.

Born in Edinburgh in 1600, it was late in life that Ogilby conceived his idea of a new road-book showing roads in a pictorial manner. Employing surveyors to travel the roads, carefully measuring all distances, noting branch roads, road junctions and features of interest near the road, his scheme was approved by Charles II, and initially seventy-three roads were thus surveyed. Small illustrations decorating the titles of the plates of the complete book show some of Ogilby's surveyors at work, using the road-wheel.

This was the first use of such a 'perambulator', a wheel of known circumference in a simple forked frame, geared to a counting device with a dial, trundled by a surveyor in front of him. Thus, every road described had been walked and all information about it was based on accurate observation. For measurements of distance Ogilby used the Statute mile, introduced by Act of Parliament in 1593 but not generally adopted until considerably later. In 1596 the word 'road' in its modern definition was first used. Hitherto a traveller followed a 'highway' or just a 'way'.

Ogilby's *Britannia Depicta* was published in 1675, made of one hundred folio plates each set out in vertical strips, and drawn to resemble a flattened spiral scroll. Towns, villages and bridges are named, distances recorded and destinations of side roads given. Villages, country seats and larger houses within about a mile of the road are also named, as are some of the more prominent natural features. So far as our area is concerned Ogilby's map gives only two roads: the London-Richmond one, spread over three plates, of which the Barnsley-Richmond section is relevant, and that from York to Lancaster. Surprisingly, no reference is made to the

Causeway near Ripley, part of the old York to Lancaster road described by Ogilby.

main trans-Pennine route on Stainmore.

An interesting aspect of Ogilby's maps is that he distinguishes between the main rivers and their insignificant feeder streams. The latter are shown as 'a Rill' or 'a Brook', while rivers merit the Latin abbreviation 'Fluv'. Thus they show 'Wharfe Fluv' and 'Your Fluv' (the Ure). Where bridges are of stone this fact is given. This point will subsequently be elaborated in a detailed consideration of the routes of his roads in the Dales area.

Neither Ogilby's road-book nor the annotated maps which followed during the early years of the next century necessarily meant big improvements in roads, for the skills of making good surfaced roads had not been rediscovered. At Rheims, Nicholas Bergier, after studying Roman road construction, published in 1622 his *Grands Chemins de l'Empire Roman*. Little notice seems to have been taken of it, and in Britain better road maintenance was sought through extra labour. In 1662 a new Act for Enlarging and Repairing of the Common Highways allowed parish surveyors to introduce a special highways levy of up to sixpence.

By then, stage waggons had been in use on the roads for about a century, having been introduced according to the historian Stowe, in the 1560s. They were very ponderous and heavy, required six to eight horses to pull them, and had broad wheels to spread the load. It was probably in the second half of the sixteenth century that an inventive craftsman evolved the idea of 'dishing' a wheel, making it run on axles each canted slightly downwards. One advantage of this was that it allowed waggon sides to slope outwards and thus increased the load carried. To compensate for the corresponding disadvantage that dished wheels would 'run on their toes', the outer circumference of their felloes, or fellies — the curved sections of the wooden rim which bore upon the road surface — needed to be bevelled.

The first regular stage-waggon service for carrying goods and passengers originated between London and towns and cities in southern England and East Anglia. Stage-coaches without windows and carrying four to eight passengers in acute misery, came on the scene at the time of the Civil War. An Act of 1662 introduced weight restriction, with a maximum load of 20cwt during the winter, 30cwt in the summer with not more than seven horses in draft. Felloes of the wheels were to be not wider than 4½in. Presumably these restrictions were either not vigorously applied, or they proved impracticable, for the Act was repealed the following year. Subsequent Acts of 1719 and 1741 reduced the width of felloes first to 2½in, and later to an unrestricted width, but only during the summer months, with weight limits raised to 60cwt. By then, however, a network of turnpike roads was becoming established, which, because it involved private financing and a system of tolls, did focus more attention on the need for better road surfaces. It had become evident that roads might even be made to pay for themselves, instead of being a liability on parishes through which they passed. The turnpikes will be considered in detail in a later chapter.

In Tudor and Stuart times there was no focus for communications within the area of the Dales. The facts of geography and the nature of the terrain mitigated against it. Since Roman times York had been the focal point for communications and trade not only in Yorkshire but for the whole of northern England east of the Pennines, and ranked first or second in the list of provincial towns between 1334 and 1662, apart from a period in the early sixteenth century. However, about that same time, Henry VIII made York the centre for his Council of the North, giving it an administrative importance it previously did not possess.

It was during Henry VIII's reign that letters were first carried by a system of post-horses, and in 1548 the postage rate was fixed at 1d per mile. The office of Postmaster-General was established during the reign of Elizabeth I, but for many years all letters were routed through London. About 1650 a York attorney organised a relay system of horses operating between there and London to carry letters and parcels for the public, and in 1667, 'A List of Postmasters, Stage Towns and Branch Posts compiled by James Hickes, Clerk of the Chester Road', shows that it was the 'North Road' with a detour to York, which related to Yorkshire. Letters to or from the Dales would have been taken to, or collected from, a selected point, probably Boroughbridge or Northallerton. Ten years later a survey shows that Wetherby was on a by-post route, with 'Ferribriggs' its post town.

By the end of the century a system of cross posts had evolved. While country letters between two post towns continued to go through London, 'Cross Post Letters' went through two country post towns situated on two different post roads, and did not go through the capital. In 1711 the postage rates for letters were:

80 miles or under	3d
Over 80 miles	4d
London to Edinburgh or Dublin	6d

The thrice-weekly service from London to Edinburgh took five days, and followed the route of the North Road already referred to, but including York.

Ogilby's survey features York on four roads. The Great North Road follows the route London-Stilton-Tuxford-Boroughbridge-Chester-le-Street-Berwick; and it is a terminus for the York-Lancaster, York-Chester, and York-Scarborough roads. Of these, only the first touches the Dales, as does the less obvious route St Albans-Oakham-Barnsley-Richmond, and it is these two which will now be looked at in detail.

York to Lancaster

From Knaresborough this road runs parallel to the Nidd, a route taken today by the B6165, joining the main road from the south which comes over Killinghall Bridge. Ogilby's road enters Ripley from the south-east, until recent years still the normal approach from this direction, but the village is now by-passed by the A61 Leeds-Ripon road.

Dr Muir has pointed out the peculiar alignment of Ripley village in

The Market Square, Ripley. The 'Ogilby' route went past the castle gatehouse (centre).

relationship to the modern roads which serve it. These are orientated north-south, but the market-place at the centre of the village has an east-west alignment between church and castle. That is far more likely to have been, not only the medieval alignment, but the Roman one mentioned in Chapter 2. Ogilby's road makes a distinct right-angled turn by the market-place to a south-west direction, passing a 'Dark hall' (Ripley Castle) on its right. By the castle entrance the cobbled market-place ends abruptly, and the way beyond is a rough-surfaced lane.

This continues as a well-defined track, between hedges and climbing slightly into Hollybank Wood (276600) where traces of laid metalling are visible. At the western end of the wood it descends and, at 269599, makes a sharp left turn from a modern surfaced road. Heading first south, then south-west, it is now a narrow footpath between hedges, and in places its surface soil and turf have been removed to reveal a good stone causeway. The track continues to a corner of a modern road (264594), which Ogilby's road follows southwards to Hampsthwaite bridge (261592) and into the village. Passing straight along the axis of Hampsthwaite the old road, now a modern one, heads south-west, then south, for Grayston Plain (252570), on Ogilby's map 'Gracies Plain Moor'. It joins the important and busy A59 — formerly a probable Dark Ages salt road — to head westwards across 'Keskie Moor', now Kettlesing Heads. It would be interesting to know the significance of Ogilby's 'two long posts' illustrated at a point about four miles from Hampsthwaite. They would be about the place where the B6451 crosses A59. A half-mile to the south-east is Long

Stoop Farm, with 'Long Stoop' in the corner of a plantation (209553). The name suggests a tall stone guide-post, but its present position is not on or very near any road or track. One wonders if it has been moved, and whether in that case, it was one of Ogilby's 'long posts'.

The way westwards crossed the River Washburn at 'Blewberrow Houses' by a pronounced zigzag, which even the present A59 fails completely to have eliminated at Blubberhouses, and then took a slightly northwards loop over Limekiln Hill and Kex Gill Moor. This is now partly a rough track becoming at 144557 the metalled Kex Gill Road. Ogilby's map names 'Keskin Moor' to the north, and the old road joins the line of the modern one again where this makes a sharp turn at 125550.

Large-scale widening and straightening of the modern trunk road has obscured not only the line of Ogilby's road but of the Skipton-Harrogate turnpike which succeeded it in 1777. However his map suggests that the route of the old road took it through 'Hassel', now Hazlewood (089538), and either by what is now a field path or by Storiths Lane to rejoin the present road at Beamsley Hospital, identified by Ogilby simply as Almshouses. This remarkable circular building, 30ft in diameter, with a raised centre, was founded in 1593 and 'finished more profusely' by the redoubtable Lady Anne Clifford, Countess of Pembroke, between 1650 and 1660. It would thus have been a distinctive, recent structure obviously worth noting by Ogilby's surveyors.

The York-Lancaster road crossed the Wharfe by Bolton Bridge, (072529) presumably the new replacement for that which had been washed away by a flood on 17th September 1673. It is known that a bridge existed here in 1318, and Saxton's map shows one, evidence of the importance of this east-west route across the Pennines. From 'Boulton' Ogilby's route seems to have been adopted by the 1777 turnpike and the modern road. The side road to 'Estby' is shown, presumably the present Eastby, and Skybeden (023530) was apparently much larger in Ogilby's time than it is now. Before entering Skipton the old road passed on the north 'Haugh Park, the Countess of Pembrokes', where Haw Park quarries have now eaten considerably into the landscape.

Entering Skipton along the line of the modern Knaresborough road by the north-east corner of the castle the old route swung right in front of the Parish Church, crossed Eller Beck by Mill Bridge, and climbed out of the town by what is now Raikes Road to White Hill, Stirton and Thorlby, joining the present route west of the village where there is a boundary stone in the angle between the two roads (963528). Almost immediately to the west the line of the old road can be identified as a green track over the shoulder of a hill at 'Stoney Bitts'. The track soon peters out but its course is followed by field boundaries for 500yd, rejoining the turnpike route below Sulber Hill (937534), and continuing along this to Gargrave.

Eshton Beck was crossed by a stone bridge, predecessor of the present Holme Bridge which has the date 1814. Most bridges on this section of the York-Lancaster road are marked as 'stone bridges' by both Ogilby and the later Warburton. Indeed, Defoe commented that the bridges of Yorkshire

Hampsthwaite Bridge, Nidderdale, probably rebuilt in 1640, but not widened since.

and Durham were of stone, and that he did not remember having seen one of timber from the Trent to the Tweed. When Gargrave bridge was rebuilt in 1638 it was recorded that 'it must of necessitie be so because there is no tymber in that part of the countrye fitt for that worke'.

Warburton's map of 1720 shows at Gargrave a side road to Otterburn running behind Gargrave House, and continuing north-westwards to the hamlet of Bell Busk. Now initially a walled lane passing through wooded parkland and the side of Mark Plantation, it becomes Mark House Lane, but a field path taking a more direct course to the south leads it directly into Bell Busk, showing in one section as a pronounced holloway. In Bell Busk (905564) it passes a low roadside stone with a clearly incised cross on it, indicative of a monastic boundary, and crosses the Aire by a three-arched packhorse bridge, widened, according to its date, in 1837.

Beyond Bell Busk this continues as a modern road, narrow and winding to Otterburn, then as the walled, rough-surfaced Dacre Lane climbs on to Hellifield Moor Top (864587), and becomes Langber Lane. Fording Bookil Gill Beck near a boundary stone (845614) it is then known as High Hill Lane and soon joins the Settle-Kirkby Malham road above Scaleber Bridge. In his *Airedale* Speight describes this moorland route as an earlier road to the north, but there is no other substantiation of this.

Ogilby's road is shown west of Gargrave as crossing some high hills to Coniston, crossing the Aire by a stone bridge east of the village. The present route takes the same line, but half a mile west of Coniston there is a divergence, near the farm now called Fogger (895553). There, the old road is identified on the north as a green track following a line of field boundaries over Coniston Moor, descending by a steep gradient to Switcher's Farm (875559) by the modern road. At Quarter Sessions in 1689 a Benjamin Rycroft was fined £10 'if he will not repair the way through his close at ffogga'. Switcher's Farm probably acquired its name through its being the place where coach-horses used to be changed. From it to Hellifield and Long Preston the old road was on or very close to the

'Switchers', near Coniston Cold, on the Keighley to Kendal old road and turnpike.

line of today's road.

Ogilby's map notes 'Hellifield P', presumably Hellifield peeltower, now ruinous, though this is a good half-mile away from the road. Three centuries ago it would not have been obscured by plantations on Tenley Hill. Near Long Preston he also notes 'Almshouses and a Chappel, a brook and a Stone Bridge'.

Beyond Long Preston there is a marked difference between the course of the old road and the turnpike which succeeded it, Ogilby's map shows the road following a direct course northwards: 'enter a Moor; a Moor; leave the Moor', all of which suggests what he felt about the wild upland crossing of Hunter Bark, at 1,025 ft. Edge Lane, as it is now called, leaves Long Preston as a metalled lane, climbs steadily to open moorland where the surface becomes rough and stony, continuing thus for nearly two miles, easing the gradient on Hunter Bark by taking a curving course (830612). As it descends northwards towards new plantations its width increases and a rutted surface shows a variety of tracks to have been taken. Reaching Mitchell Lane it becomes metalled again, the gradient is steeper, and the road enters Settle by Settle Green on the south of the town, then by Albert Street and Victoria Street to the Market Place. At Settle Green there used to be an inn, The Rising Sun, but this has now vanished.

The only existing route then was down Kirkgate, so called because it was the way leading to the church at Giggleswick, mother-church of the ancient parish. This route is aligned directly on an old river-crossing near King's Mill known as Kendalman's Ford (814637), its approach today a narrow right-of-way between the high wire fences of paper-mills. On the west side of the Ribble its route can be picked up as a narrow stretch of walled lane leading to a small modern housing estate with the street name, Kendalmans.

Crossing Bankwell into the Fellins, now a playing-field, the old packhorse way followed a causeway, paved traces of which were discovered during drainage operations, to the tall building called Armitstead

Guide stone, moved from Long Preston Moor, and re-erected about 1970 at Long Preston.

Hall, crossed Tems Beck by a small stone bridge of clapper-style construction and followed its west bank to Giggleswick church. Because of its directness this route continued to be preferred by packhorse trains long after the Ogilby road had taken its course further to the north.

There was probably a bridge over the Ribble at Settle in monastic times and the date of the present one is not known. However, it was repaired in 1662, when it was about ten feet wide and carried Ogilby's road across the river, widened when the turnpike route chose that course in 1753, and widened again in recent times. Four chamfered ribs can be seen beneath its two upstream arches.

The old road climbed Bell Hill, dropped steeply into Giggleswick, ascended westwards from the village over High Rigg to Lawkland (775664), passing 'Lakeland Hall' on the south. A narrow, winding lane follows this line today to Cross Streets where it picks up the course of the A65 at Cross Streets Inn (773676). Ogilby notes a stone bridge over Austwick Beck, but the village is named off the road to the north.

The road goes forward to Clapham, bends towards the west and follows a line probably taken by the present road to Bentham, passing through 'Greenlis, a village', (Green Close? 721693). Beyond that is a long stretch simply known as 'a Moor', now Newby Moor, still unenclosed land. The

Old Keighley to Kendal road, descending from Hunters Bark towards Settle.

Old Keighley to Kendal road at Giggleswick, with Armitstead Hall beyond.

71

next named place on Ogilby's road is 'Wellington', doubtless the Wennington of today, and the old road passed Tatham church, through part of Hornby Park into Hornby village, finally along the route of the present main road through Claughton and Caton to Lancaster.

Skipton to Richmond

The only other Yorkshire road of sufficient importance to be shown on Ogilby's map is the northern part of a route from London to Richmond. This is divided into two major sections: London to Oakham, followed by 'The Extended Road from Oakham to Richmond', which in turn is sub-divided, first to Barnsley, then to Richmond. It seems appropriate here to pick up the route at Skipton, reached by way of Halifax, Keighley and the Aire valley, crossing the river by Kildwick Bridge.

At Skipton this north-bound road would have shared the line of the York-Lancaster road for about half a mile, from the parish church to the top of Raikes Road, where it would then have taken a northerly course probably followed closely by the present Skipton-Grassington road for about two miles. Where the small, semi-derelict tollhouse at Sandy Beck now stands by the roadside (975557) the course of the old road took a slightly higher route than the modern one, its line now followed by field paths as far as Bark Brow (794578). This would have taken it just below Norton Tower, built originally by Richard Norton early in the sixteenth century, but by Ogilby's day it had become a ruin. Above Scale House, its route in a field has become a slight holloway. Descending to Rylston the old road seems to have turned right in the village centre on to a north easterly alignment, past the church and site of the old hall, and headed towards Cracoe by Chapel Lane parallel to, and a few yards east of, the modern road.

Ogilby's road entered Linton by what is now Lauradale Lane, a modern road, crossing Linton Beck in the middle of the village by a predecessor of the recent county road bridge, and continued north out of Linton, across the Burnsall road where there is a fine eighteenth-century guide-post (998632). Crossing 'a brook and a Stone Bridge' the old road then crossed the River Wharfe by 'Linton Bridg of Stone over Wharfe fluv'. Although the southern end of this is in Threshfield and the northern end in Grassington, the bridge is correctly named, being in the ancient parish of Linton, although today it is usually called Grassington Bridge.

In 1600 it was described in Quarter Sessions accounts as 'very ruinous and oak trees are needed'. Oak of sufficient size was then not locally available, so in 1603 it was rebuilt in stone, and although most other Wharfe bridges have been broken or damaged by floods, Linton bridge has survived. Its downstream part shows original ribbed arches; it was widened in 1780, its hump back lowered in 1825 and in 1984 it was further widened, again on the upstream side.

Before the various improvements the old road continued up the valley by turning left immediately beyond the bridge. Its line is now indicated by a short stretch of walled lane, leading to field paths which join Grass

Wood Lane near a barn called Rilston Hill Laithe, known apparently in 1603 as Resting Hill. The minor road up the east side of Wharfedale, past the foot of Grass Wood, to Conistone, follows the Ogilby route direct to Kettlewell.

Turning to a more north-easterly alignment from Kettlewell the road climbs out of Wharfedale, along the present line, up the steep hill of Park Rash past West Scale Park (978746). Ogilby records it as entering 'a Park', beyond which it 'enters a Moor', almost certainly the same type of wild moorland above the 1,600ft contour which exists today on this watershed between Wharfedale and Coverdale. Three centuries ago it must have been a daunting, probably frightening journey to make.

Ogilby marks Cover Head (014787), beyond which the road crosses the River Cover by a stone bridge, and kept to the north-west side of Coverdale down the valley, as does the present road down Coverdale. Immediately beyond Cover Head it is shown as passing through wooded parkland for almost five miles, through Woodall, Bradley, Horsehouse and Gammergill, to Carlton. Near Horsehouse the present map names 'Deerclose' in Horsehouse woods, and though only fragments of woodland survive this part of Coverdale did retain extensive areas of the fifteenth-century royal hunting park of the lords of Middleham.

Ogilby's map shows the road passing through Melmerby and Agglethorpe. There is an old guidepost in Melmerby, a stone whose lettering is now

Packhorse bridge with a ford alongside at Linton, Wharfedale. Probably built in the sixteenth century it was repaired in the late seventeenth century by Elizabeth Redmayne.

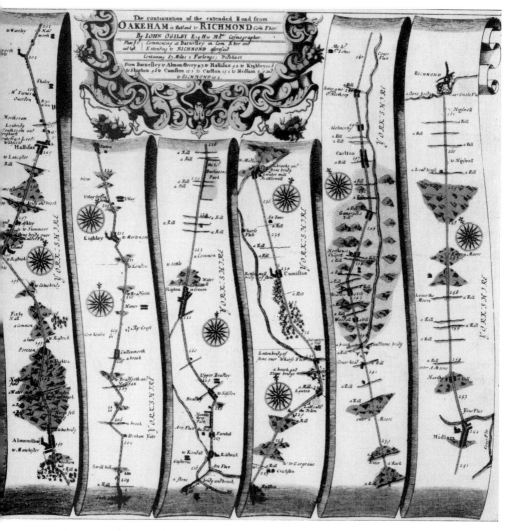

Facsimile from Ogliby's Britannia published in 1675. The right-hand strip shows the section from 'Midlam' to Richmond.

Guidestone near Burnsall, Wharfedale.

indecipherable, at the corner where the moor road to West Witton leaves the village (076853). Ogilby does not have this lane on his map, nor does he show any lane to Coverham Abbey. The most direct route today from Carlton to Middleham keeps south of Melmerby and Agglethorpe, and enters Middleham by the south-eastern corner of Low Moor. This may be the Ogilby line, but if the old road did include Melmerby and Agglethorpe in its course, which would incidentally have aligned it on Wensley where there was an important bridge over the River Ure, it would have needed to make a pronounced bend to the east to align on Middleham. Old tracks cross Middleham Low Moor from west to east and the Ogilby road may be one of these, leaving the present road north of Agglethorpe at 088870.

Middleham's significance as a place on this route from London to Richmond is probably the result of its former medieval importance. One of the great northern fortresses, home of the powerful Nevilles, it became later in the fifteenth century a royal castle, and, when Richard, Duke of Gloucester lived there during the Wars of the Roses, a northern seat of government. With the castles at Richmond, Lancaster and Skipton it formed a quartet of strongholds between which and York there would have been constant comings and goings. Each castle would have been the focal point for many tracks, and well-established crossroads would have developed between them. Ogilby's London-Richmond route would have taken one of these and developed it into a coaching road, picking up the routes from Lancaster and Skipton on the way.

The way of the old road immediately beyond Middleham can only be conjectured. Ogilby shows it leaving the northern edge of the village to cross the River Ure on a direct alignment with Harmby village, a mile north of the river. But he does not record a bridge. The present road bridge between Middleham and Leyburn dates only from 1829, before which there was a ford or a ferry. 1½ miles east of Middleham is Ulshaw bridge, of stone, dated 1674, but between this and Wensley bridge no river crossing is marked on any of the old maps. Ulshaw bridge was originally of timber, and is said to have been on an important medieval route from York to Kendal, although this claim seems unsubstantiated. Nevertheless, the fact that it was rebuilt in stone in 1674 signifies some importance of its use. There was a mill close to it, known to have been working in the mid-sixteenth century, when it formed part of the Lordship of Middleham, and thus belonged to the Crown. In 1628 the Middleham properties were sold to the Lord Mayor and Corporation of London, subsequently leased to private individuals, one of whom bought the mill outright in 1653.

Leland states that in his journey from Richmond to Middleham he crossed the Ure by a ford, but elsewhere in his *Itinerary* he writes that the

Hunter's Stone, at the head of Coverdale, possibly a guide-post on the monastic route from Coverham Abbey to Kettlewell. The road became a coach road on the route from London to Richmond, via Halifax, Skipton and Kettlewell, and is shown on Ogilby's map of 1675.

Middleham Castle. An important northern stronghold from about 1170 to the early seventeenth century.

Ulshaw Bridge, near Middleham. Rebuilt about 1670.

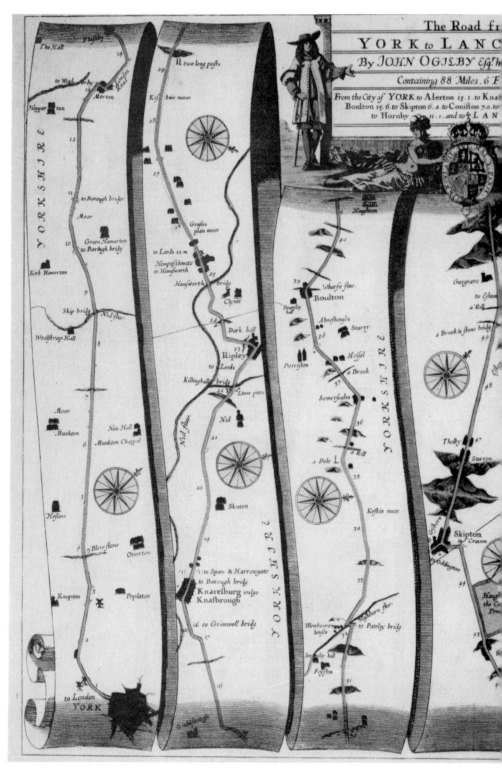

Part of the York to Lancaster road as shown on Ogilby's map, 1675.

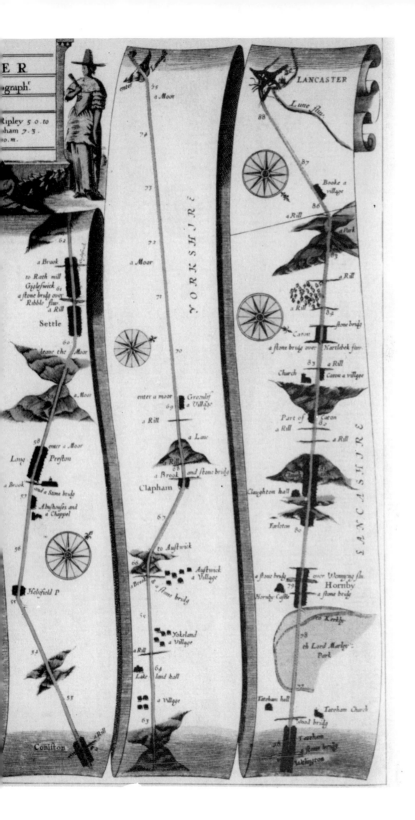

LANCASTER

Lune flu.

88

87

Booke a village

86

a Rill

a Park

85

a Rill

a Rill

84 stone bridg

Caton

a stone bridg over Hartlebek flu

83 a Rill

Church   Caton a village

Part of Caton

82 a Rill

a Rill

Claughton hall

Farleton

80

a stone bridg   over Wenning flu.

79 Hornby

Hornby Castle   a stone bridg

to Kerkby

78 th Lord Marley Park

Tatham hall

Tatham Church

flood bridg

Tatham

a ftone bridg

Wakington

YORKSHIRE

LANCASHIRE

75 enter
a Moor

74

73

72

a Moor

71

70

enter a moor 69 Greenlit a Village

a Rill

a Lane

68 a Rill

a Brook and stone bridg

Clapham

67

to Auftwick

66 Auftwick a Village

a Brook

a stone bridg

59

Yokeland a Village

a Rill

64 Lake land hall

63 a Village

62

a Brook
to Rath mill Giglefwick
61
a stone bridg over Ribble flu
a Rill

Settle

60
leave the Moor

a Moor

58 enter a Moor
Long Preston

a Brook and a Stone bridg
57
A bushouses and a Chappel

56

Helifield P

54

51

53

Coniston   a Rill

79

bridge 'over Ure by Middleham is but of Tymbar'. This was probably the 'Ulsey or Owsey bridge' reported in 1621 as being in 'decay', although 200 marks was spent in 1588 and £20 in 1607 on repairs. In 1623 £350 was allocated for the building of a new bridge, but the old one was repaired instead, for £40, in 1625, followed by £120 two years later. In April 1673 the Sessions allowed £800 for it, and £200 the next year for finishing it. Presumably these last two amounts represented the cost of the new stone bridge, whose sundial has the inscription 'RW'. All these sums for repair and rebuilding signify constant usage of an important bridge without necessarily answering the question: where did Ogilby's road cross the river?

There are two clues. A lane leaving Middleham from North Road heads northwards and vanishes in fields. At Harmby, there is a Middleham Lane heading southwards from the village, ending in fields a few hundred yards from the river, which, incidentally, floods very easily around here. Could these two lanes be the opposite approaches of the vanished river crossing of three centuries ago —perhaps by a timber bridge long since washed away? Middleham Lane at Harmby, with unusual north-south alignment of the village itself across steep contours, suggests the possibility of a very old north-south route.

Ogilby's road continued, roughly north-eastward from Harmby, adopted now by a lane through fields, becoming a footpath leading to Intake House (142918). A minor road takes its course on to Hauxwell Moor, with a fork to Hipswell, through the western part of Catterick Garrison, still as a public road, to approach Richmond by Holly Hill, at

Cornforth Hill, Richmond — the old road leading into the Market Place.

the turnpike cottage (173003) on the Richmond-Lancaster road, and crossing the Swale by the four-arched stone bridge below the towering walls of the castle. Climbing Bridge Street and Cornforth Hill, and passing through Cornforth Bar in the medieval walls, the road entered the cobbled Market Place at its south-west corner.

Lady Anne Clifford's Journeys

Few who travelled in the Yorkshire Dales during the seventeenth century left records of their journeys. One who did, however, was Lady Anne Clifford, born at Skipton Castle in 1590, and descended from three centuries of noble Clifford stock. Related to many of England's greatest families she married twice, first to Richard Sackville, Earl of Dorset, with whom she lived at Knole in Kent, and by whom she had two daughters. Her second husband was Philip Herbert, Earl of Pembroke and Montgomery. After the Civil War, and twice widowed, she succeeded after a long struggle to the vast Clifford estates which extended almost continuously from Skipton to Brougham, outside Penrith. In addition to these two castles she also inherited Barden Tower, the Bolton Abbey properties, and castles at Appleby, Brough and Pendragon in Mallerstang.

Defying Cromwell she set about a vast rebuilding programme of her slighted castles, and travelled frequently through her estates. She left a diary of her journeys and work, and this throws some light on the nature

81

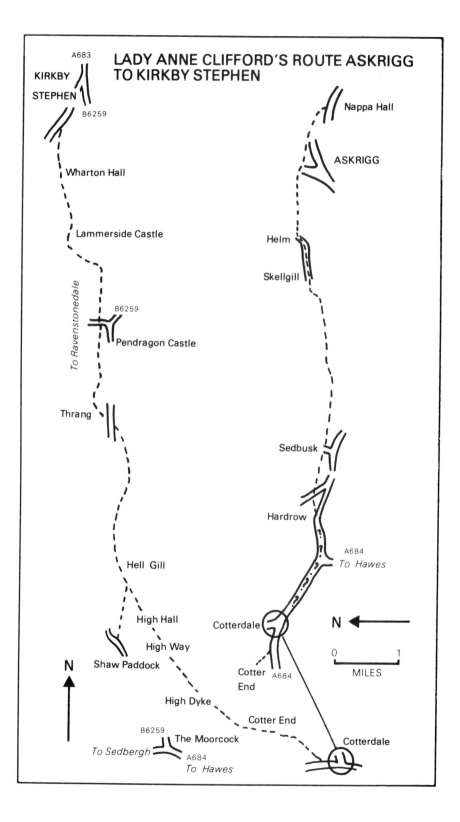

LADY ANNE CLIFFORD'S ROUTE ASKRIGG TO KIRKBY STEPHEN

A683

KIRKBY STEPHEN

B6259

Wharton Hall

Lammerside Castle

To Ravenstonedale

B6259

Pendragon Castle

Thrang

Hell Gill

High Hall

High Way

Shaw Paddock

N

High Dyke

B6259

The Moorcock

To Sedbergh

A684
To Hawes

Nappa Hall

ASKRIGG

Helm

Skellgill

Sedbusk

Hardrow

A684
To Hawes

Cotterdale

Cotter
End

A684

Cotter End

Cotterdale

N

0   1
MILES

of the roads and tracks she used during the third quarter of the seventeenth century. She travelled in a style appropriate to the leading person in the county of Westmorland, of which she was the High Sheriff, and the journeys between her castles were conducted as though she were royalty. She herself went in a horse-litter; her ladies-in-waiting and gentlewomen were in her coach drawn by six horses; her estate officials and manservants were on horseback, her women servants in another coach, while all the goods and equipment needed by such a retinue were with the large crowd that followed. This of course included the bedding carried from place to place, as well as the chairs, tapestries, curtains and carpets which were also moved from one castle to another to await her arrival. The total travelling train must, on some occasions, have numbered at least 300.

Anxious to see as much as possible of her property on these journeys she did not always take the same route. Whenever necessary she stayed a night or two at the houses of her friends in the area, as she generally mentions this fact. Twice she writes of journeys from Skipton to Pendragon. On one of these in October 1663, after leaving Skipton she spent the first night at Mr Cuthbert Wade's house, Kilnsey Hall, which had been built only a few years earlier, in 1648, on the site of Fountains Abbey grange. We are not told, unfortunately, her route from Skipton, but subsequently 'we went through Kettlewell Dale, upp Buckden Rakes, and over the Staks into Wensleydale'. Presumably she followed the road later described by Ogilby, crossing the Wharfe at Conistone, and

Kilnsey Old Hall, Wharfedale, where Lady Anne Clifford occasionally stayed overnight on her journeys.

Gatehouse to Skipton Castle, restored by Lady Anne Clifford.

continuing up the north-east side of the valley, to Kettlewell and then by the line of the present road to Buckden. Additional evidence that this road was used comes from a letter written in February 1698 by the steward of the Earl of Burlington's Bolton Abbey estate, to a Wensleydale landowner, proposing a meeting on Kidstones Pass 30 miles away. He suggested that they waited 'until the days are longer, the seasons warmer, and the Moors more passable'. He went on to detail the route, which 'crossed the new bridge at Barden for Appletreewick and Burnsall, and over Linton Bridge for Conistone... and continued to Kettlewell... through Starbotton and Buckden and up the Rakes reached Kidstones Causey on the boundary between Wharfedale and Wensleydale'.

Lady Anne would have found the track up through the Rakes (943778) very rough and stony, following the Roman route, which she kept to over the wilderness landscape of the Stake, described in Chapter 2. Descending towards Semerwater, thence either to Bainbridge or Worton, where she forded the Ure, she continued through Askrigg to Nappa Hall, where she stayed with her cousin Mr Thomas Metcalfe for two nights. Westwards beyond Nappa she kept to the north side of the valley, climbing from Nappa Hall and contouring above Newbiggin and Askrigg and crossing the fast-flowing waters of Whitfield Gill at Slape Wath, which means 'slippery ford'. Near this, today, a slight holloway leads up a grassy bank into a field, where, until recently, a narrow walled lane swung down to the former hamlet of Helm (934916), continuing in front of a former

Barden Bridge, Wharfedale, repaired 1676.

farmhouse. When I bought this property in 1967, I was told that local people still called this lane 'Lady Anne's road'. A few years ago I removed a short stretch of covering turf to reveal a nice stretch of cobbled track. Folk-memory is often a useful pointer, and I have little doubt that this was the way by which Lady Anne and her train travelled, probably more than once, over 300 years ago. Events such as one of her regal progresses would have indelibly etched themselves on the minds of local folk. When she travelled in Wensleydale, there would have been few enclosed fields, and when the Askrigg Enclosures were made in 1817 this old road would have been accepted as an ancient right-of-way, and the Enclosure walls built still to allow the passage of people and horses along it.

Beyond Helm the road continues westwards, dropping a little initially, then becoming a metalled road past Spen to Skellgill, where it is a walled lane. Where this reaches Sargill Beck it makes a sharp turn to the south (922915), soon entering open rough pasture where its course, swinging to the west again, can be picked out as a green track between more rushy ground on each side. Presumably the stone metalling of the old track produced better drainage, with no rushes growing on its course.

For the next two miles it continues westwards, always with a wall to its south, and rough pasture rising to the north. It passes Shaw Cote, a farm, and on approaching Litherskew, becomes a metalled farm road to the hamlet of Sedbusk, continuing as a narrow walled lane to the Hawes-Swaledale road at Simonstone, after which its course seems uncertain. It is likely that Lady Anne's road descended to Hardraw along what is now a field path, and at Hardraw it probably took the course adopted by the 1761 Askrigg-Sedbergh turnpike as far as the present Cotterdale lane end (842923).

There is little doubt that the old road ascended Cotter Riggs to Cotter End, a prominent hilltop spur to the north-west. Its route is now a steeply-climbing bridleway through rough pasture, following a wall, and at the top making sharp bends near a limekiln. Why this very difficult route was used we do not know. In a later journey in 1666, taken in the opposite

85

direction, Lady Anne described it as being over 'Cotter and those dangerous ways'.

We have earlier mentioned this track as a very ancient one, so it must be assumed that, bad as it was, especially for a wheeled coach, it was better than anything else available. Today this mountain bridleway contours Thwaite Bridge Common at about 1,500ft on a limestone terrace for three miles with moorland commons above and enclosed rough pasture below.

High Dike (803943) is now in ruins and, with its extensive outbuildings and former stables, stands at right angles to the track. Fronted on the south by a paved courtyard with many small, walled garths nearby, it was known to have been occupied as an inn for drovers and leaders of packhorse trains as recently as 1877, and the building appears to be of late seventeenth-century date, with mullioned windows of gritstone. Beyond it the old road is easily identified over close-cropped grass, above Shaw and High Way to the ruins of High Hall, deserted farms. Near High Way the track passes a limekiln above which is an irregular walled enclosure of about four acres, with a small, ruined building inside. Known as Horse Paddock, it was probably a resting place for packhorse trains where ponies could safely graze, the packs stored under cover in the building which would also provide shelter for the men.

The High Way, as this old road is called, gradually loses height beyond High Hall, its course less distinct on marshy ground, but finds more limestone at Hell Gill, a dramatic gorge at the bottom of which is the infant River Eden, although Camden mistakenly believed it to be the Ure. He recognised the awesome wildness of the place: 'Where this country bordereth upon Lancashire, among the mountains, it is in most places, so waste, solitary, unpleasant and unsightly, so mute and so still... about the head of the river Ure, which having a bridge over it of one entire stone, falleth down such a depth that it striketh a certain horror to as many as look down.' This last comment suggest the route was in use at the end of the sixteenth century, seventy-five years before Lady Anne experienced its hazards.

Hell Gill bridge (787968) is a single arch of stone 30ft above the beck, and carries the 10ft wide track across the ravine. The present bridge dates from 1825, replacing an earlier structure on which £3 10s was spent in 1676. A small stone at the base of its western parapet, in the middle of the bridge, is probably an old county boundary stone, between Yorkshire and Cumbria, formerly Westmorland.

North of Hell Gill the road follows a good course, and after a mile gradually descends. In one section the lower side of the track has been embanked with limestone boulders, so as to maintain a level surface, which supports the idea that wheeled vehicles did use it. Culverts take it over moorland becks on marshy ground lower down the hillside, and it joins the modern road at The Thrang (785006), where a bridge probably replaces an older ford. An overgrown path on the west of the river probably represents the old track to Shoregill, where Lady Anne's road continues as a walled lane becoming a series of field paths to Pendragon

Castle, reached by a stone bridge reputed to have been built by Lady Anne. This now carries the minor road over Wharton Fell. At 780030 the old road leaves this as a stony track contouring round the eastern side of Birkett Common towards Croop House and the meagre ruins of Lammerside Castle (773048). Indistinct across pastures it eventually picks up a good farm track leading to the historic, fortified house of Wharton Hall, continuing northwards as a road to Halfpenny House, and entering Kirkby Stephen along the line of the main Sedbergh road. The Whartons were relatives of Lady Anne and she occasionally stayed with them, usually when she was making the shorter, easier journeys between Pendragon, Brough, Appleby and Brougham.

If travel was difficult for people of the calibre and determination of Lady Anne, it must have been dauntingly formidable for others. Unfortunately, few accounts of such travel exist to throw light on road conditions in the seventeenth century. Lady Anne's accounts are significant. Although most of her journeys were between her favourite houses, Brougham and Appleby, these were relatively easily accessible, being on a direct route far different from that between Pendragon, Barden and Skipton.

The Skipton-Barden route took the Ogilby road eastwards from Skipton, through Haw Park and Skibden to Halton (042539), from where it seems probable that it turned northwards across open moorland, now enclosed, descending Hare Head Side to Wharfedale and Barden Tower. Another account describes a journey from Barden to Appleby through a different part of the area, involving spending three nights on the way, the first at Pateley Bridge, the second at 'Street House not farre from Bedell', and the third 'at a poor inne' at Bowes, a very circuitous route.

Near Barden Tower the Wharfe is crossed by Barden bridge, three segmental arches of stone spanning 55 yd, but less then 10 ft wide between parapets, with pedestrian refuges over the huge cutwaters. It was in existence at Lady Anne's time, for Quarter Sessions' accounts of 1659 noted that the 'greate summe of £300' to be spent on the bridge as it was 'not knowne who ought to repaire itt'. The Otley parish registers of 1673 record that the bridge 'was overturned by a wonderful inundation of waters'. A stone in the northern parapet records further repairs 'at the charge of the whole West Riding 1676'.

The route from Barden to Pateley can be conjectured, probably branching off the minor road on the east side of the river near Howgill (060588). 100 yd beyond Howgill Lodge there is an old milestone set in the east wall bordering the lane, bearing the legible inscription 'To Pateley Bridge M6'. Howgill Lane continues to High Skyreholme from where a moorland track with good stone metalling, heads north-eastwards over Pinder Hawes Hill to join the Grassington-Pateley Bridge motor road at Dry Gill (081634). This takes a direct route to Pateley Bridge, following closely the old line, and crosses the Nidd by a stone bridge, though in Lady Anne's day this would have been timber. This route by Craven Moor and Greenhow Hill was regularly used by 'badgers', or corn-dealers, in the

1630s, for they complained about the poor state of the causeway between Dibbles Bridge and Craven Keld (Greenhow Hill: 105639), as a result of which the township of Appletreewick hired a local stonemason to repair it.

From Pateley the road climbed steeply up from the old church to Pateley Moor, today a minor metalled road, but up to early last century according to a local historian 'nothing but a trackway across the moors indicated to travellers in misty weather and in winter by tall upright pillars of stone, some of which yet remain.' Two of these survive, one south of Harper Hill (195704), the other a few hundred yards to the north-east near the Grantley lane end. Whether these existed in the late seventeenth century is not known. Certainly this was a very old route from Pateley to the important market at Kirkby Malzeard, and Lady Anne records that for the only time in her life she went 'hard by Snape [Castle] a house of the Earl of Exeter's'. This is outside our area, so sufficient to suggest that she crossed the Ure at West Tanfield, went north to Snape and Bedale, stayed at Street House 3½ miles north, picking up the Bowes road at what is now Scotch Corner.

Right at the end of the seventeenth century another lady's travels brought her to the north of England. Indeed, Celia Fiennes, daughter of one of Cromwell's officers, who had lived through the social and political

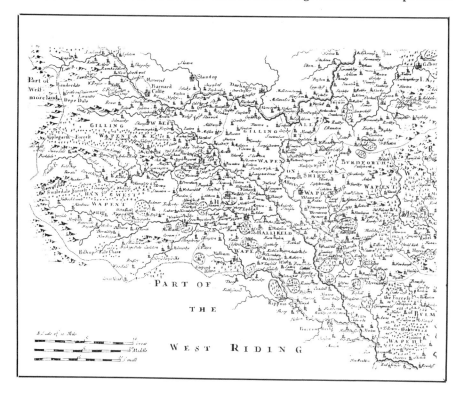

Robert Morden's 1722 map of the North Riding of Yorkshire.

The 'High Way' in Mallerstang, showing its 'engineering' on a slope.

revolution of the age, could be described as the first of the 'curious travellers'. Born in 1662, in Wiltshire, she acquired or inherited by the time she was in her mid-thirties a great urge to travel on horseback and to record scrupulously her observations. Although she journeyed extensively throughout England, she only touched the Yorkshire Dales at their eastern margins, visiting York, Harrogate, Boroughbridge and Ripon in 1697, and Darlington, Richmond and Boroughbridge the following year. On neither visit did she penetrate into the valleys and hills, but she did comment on some of the more mundane details of accommodation, food and the state of the roads.

From Darlington she rode south and crossed the River Tees by Crofton (Croft Spa) bridge, and 'went through Lanes and woods an Enclosed country'. Almost certainly her route lay through Middleton Tyas and Skeeby, so that she entered Richmond from the north-east, 'Richmond town one cannot see till just upon it, being Encompass'd with great high hills: I descended a very steep hill' (probably Frenchgate, the only way in from the north and east). 'Its buildings are all stone, ye streetes are like rocks themselves, there is a very Large space for the Markets w'ch are Divided for the ffish market, the fflesh market, and Corn. . . .'

From Richmond she rode south, by Hornby Castle along a route 'much on lanes which were narrow but exceeding long, some 3 or 4 mile before you came to any open place and there I came to a Common which was as tedious to me at least 5 or 6 mile before I came to an end of it, then I passed through a few little villages and so I came the 19 mile to Burrowbridge in Yorkshire; here I was most sensible of the long Yorkshire mile, this North Rideing of that County is much longer miles than the other parts, which I had beein in before.' Celia Fiennes frequently notes that the roads she travelled were measured in 'Long Miles', in the north the 'old British mile' of 2,428 yd was still the normal measure, even though the statute mile had been defined since 1593, and first put on the map by John Ogilby's Britannia of 1675. Present-day walkers on some Yorkshire trackways often feel that the 'Long Mile' is still operative.

Celia Fiennes seems not to have attempted to follow either of the Yorkshire roads detailed on Ogilby's Atlas, presumably because it was not small enough to be conveniently carried on her journeys. However, there had been produced in 1676 something new in the realm of county maps. Robert Morden, a map and globe maker in the Cornhill, London, produced a unique pack of playing cards: 'The 52 counties of England and Wales, described in a pack of cards. . . .'These measure only 2⅛in × 2in, each bearing at the top a county's name, with the suit and number taking about a quarter of a card's area. Apart from some particulars about the county most of the card displays a small map, and in Yorkshire's case two of Ogilby's roads are shown, the main 'Great North Road' via Doncaster, Wetherby, York and Yarm, and the Rotherham-Wakefield-Otley-Richmond route already described in detail. This was, therefore, the first Yorkshire map to indicate roads.

In 1695 Camden's *Britannia* was published with an English translation by Edmund Gibson. Its maps, though based on those by Saxton 120 years earlier, were engraved by Morden, with separate maps for each of the three ridings. Although they claimed to be 'the fairest and most correct of any that have yet appeared', that for the North Riding was brought up to date by the inclusion of Ogilby's roads, the East and West Ridings are depicted at a scale of 10 (small) miles to 2 ⅜in and measured 16 × 13½in. They were reprinted, unchanged, in 1715, 1722, 1753, and 1772.

At the end of the century Paterson's *Traveller's Guide* was introduced, a road-book which supplemented Ogilby's road maps. Paterson's 'Roads', as it became called, went through several editions, revisions and reprintings over almost 150 years. In the early nineteenth century it was extensively enlarged and re-published by Mogg and by 1826 had reached its eighteenth edition, supplied with an appendix of new maps.

1720 saw Warburton's new survey of Yorkshire, designed at a scale of

Guide-post by Pateley Bridge to Kirkby Malzeard road at Harper Hill.

five miles to two inches, the county being covered on four sheets 24½ ×
18¾in. Although many roads were added to those of Ogilby, the map
throws very little additional light on the area of the Yorkshire Dales,
although Warburton's Journal records some interesting observations:

> 1718 Oct 15: Patrick Brompton — Finghall— Wensley, on the north bank of
> the River Ure over which there is a good stone bridge, built as Mr. Leland saith,
> by a parson of the town.

From Wensley he travelled to Bolton Hall, Leyburn and Bellerby, stayed
at Walburn Hall, and continued the next day to Richmond, 'about two
miles of moorish ground and bad way'. This description probably sums
up accurately the state of most roads and tracks in the Dales in the early
eighteenth century.

Packhorse Ways and Trade Routes

Packhorses, ponies and packmules were the main form of transport in the Yorkshire Dales for over six centuries. From early monastic times until the days of the turnpikes packhorse routes gradually became integrated into the economic life of the area. As recently as the middle decades of last century packhorse trains could still be seen, particularly in those parts of the dales where lead mining and smelting still flourished and lead had to be carried to Richmond or Pateley Bridge. In hilly districts packhorses could travel across upland country much more easily than could waggons or small wheeled carts even though these may have had several horses to pull them. In the dales packhorses were usually called Galloways from their place of origin in south-west Scotland. Although a distinct breed, related to Fell and Dales ponies, they were usually brown with black legs, stood about fourteen hands, and though small were strong, sturdy and used to working in rough country. Some Scottish Galloways were bred in Swaledale and Arkengarthdale, but other breeds were also used, chiefly the German Jaeger-galloway, from which the north-country 'Jagger' derives, the name commonly given to the man in charge of a packhorse train. The word also survives in place names like Jagger Lane and Jagger Hill.

A packhorse's load, weighing up to 2 ¼cwt (just over 100kg) was carried in two panniers or baskets whose sizes varied according to the bulk of the goods. Small panniers sufficed for coal and metal, costing between 2s and 2s 6d a dozen, the larger ones for salt, corn, charcoal or peat about three times as much. Packhorses usually travelled in trains of between twenty and forty at a time, in the charge of a driver with one or two attendants. The leading pony had a bell, or a harness of bells, whose sound marked the leader, helped to keep others together, and gave a warning to travellers and the leaders of other trains so that a passing-place could be found. This was necessary in areas where packhorse tracks were too narrow for two horses and their loads to pass. Writing in 1897 Speight notes that, 'When the packhorse traffic ceased, hundreds of these sonorous bells were sold for old metal, and the brokers' shops were for a time full of them'.

In the later days of packhorse traffic packmen and carriers formed part of the large-scale dual economy system of work, combining the transport of goods with owning a little land. Such dual occupation probably explains the fact that few local records refer specifically to 'carriers'. However, an advertisement in the *Leeds Mercury*, June 1728, announces for sale, 'A Gang of Good Packhorses, containing eighteen in number, with their accoutrements and Business belonging to the same, being one of the ancient gangs which has gone with Goods from York, Leeds and Wakefield to London, being the Horses of Thomas Varley....' This team was from Kendal, a famous centre of packhorse traffic. A corollary of this comes from Wharfedale where, according to Dr Raistrick, in Bastow Wood near Grassington, many small, walled and turfed fields were made by lead miners during the seventeenth and early eighteenth centuries — enclosed crofts they were allowed to cultivate in return for looking after pack ponies which were so widely used in that industry.

Bad weather caused problems. Snow or severe frost made packhorse tracks impassable, while heavy rain channelled them down into quagmires. In summer, when roads were probably driest, carriers often subordinated their packhorse carriage trade to the more important demands of the hay harvest. Costs of packhorse transport around 1800 were about a shilling per ton per mile, perhaps a little less for long distances. In a relatively steady trade it was usual to enter into term-contracts for six months or a year, but even then shortcomings arose which seemed to foreshadow problems not unknown today. In 1801, Peter Denys owner of some Swaledale lead mines, who had negotiated a contract with local carriers for carriage of lead from Richmond to Stockton (about 20 miles) at 13 guineas for 400 pigs (about 20 tons) heard from his agent Matthew Wadeson that £14 was the normal rate, while some carriers were asking £20 or £25. Wadeson wryly added, 'The carriers are all our Masters'.

In T.S. Willan's study *An Eighteenth Century Shopkeeper: Abraham Dent of Kirkby Stephen*, the carrier emerges as the main figure in the transport system during the third quarter of the century, the period he surveyed. Carriers operated a regular service between Kirkby Stephen and other northern towns — Newcastle, Stockton, Kendal and Lancaster, Sedbergh and Kirkby Lonsdale, Barnard Castle and Richmond. Carriage costs in 1770 averaged 11d per ton-mile, which accounted for about 2 per cent of the final price of goods sold; it took two weeks to carry goods from Kirkby Stephen to London, and what is a surprising factor to emerge is the regularity of a carrier's service, even during the worst months of the winter. In spite of Arthur Young's frequent criticisms of roads, including some of the new turnpikes, the cost of carriage was the main problem of late eighteenth-century transport, which, for goods of bulk and weight but little value, was prohibitive. But a pack of knitted stockings — a common load from Kirkby Stephen to London —could stand carriage costs, as two

Tan Hill Inn, upper Swaledale, on packhorse and drove roads, later on the Reeth to Brough Turnpike, and near important coal-pits. Photographed in the mid-1960s before its appearance was altered.

sets of figures show: in 1784, it cost £2 11s 0d to carry 938 pairs of special Guards hose, subsequently sold for just over £100. During the 1780s, about 1,000 dozen pairs of stockings were carried to London, usually in packs of 50 dozen pairs weighing 22-3 stones, with a value of £30-£60.

Charges varied from winter to summer, as a result of the difference in travelling conditions and length of daylight hours. On long journeys overnight halts were needed at places where the ponies could feed; mining concerns occasionally provided pasturage, otherwise wayside inns and farmhouses offered stabling for horses, refreshment and entertainment for the men. On the old road from Kirkby Stephen to Hawes, used until the turnpike was made in 1825, the Horse Paddock on the High Way has already been referred to (796953) but most stage-houses have vanished. However, Tan Hill Inn, beyond the head of Arkengarthdale, continues its old function of providing hospitality and refreshment to passing travellers, satisfied to say they have been to the highest inn in Britain, 1,732ft.

In seeking and exploring these old packhorse tracks it needs always to be remembered that until the middle of the eighteenth century, the landscape was very largely unenclosed. There may have been a few small, stone-walled sheep enclosures on some of the monastic estates, especially in Craven, and a number of villages may have had walled crofts close to the houses, but on the hills and to a large extent in the valleys, packhorse roads and tracks passed through open country. Where they encountered boggy or marshy ground they would spread wide to get round it; occasionally, though much less in the northern dales than in the gritstone country south of the Wharfe, large flags of stone were laid across soft ground to provide a firmer trod for the ponies. Such paved stretches are called 'causeways' or 'causeys', from the Old French *caucie*, itself derived from a Latin source meaning 'trodden'. One advantage of such causeways was that they needed to be only a few feet wide and were thus cheaper to make and maintain than a full-width road; in later medieval times parishes were more prepared to accept responsibility for their upkeep.

A twelfth-century Fountains Abbey charter refers to the grant of a right-of-way for monastic carts from Hampsthwaite across 'Ulecotes' on the west of Ripley, to the causeway of 'Dalbec'. This latter may well be the present 'Dole Bank' (275642), at the head of Cayton Hill north of Ripley, and the causeway probably followed what is now Red Gate Lane from the abbey's grange at High Cayton past Dole Bank and Haddockstones (272658), another grange, to Fountains Abbey. Another Nidderdale causeway recorded in medieval times was at Rowden, south of Hampsthwaite, while in the seventeenth century there is mention of a causeway between Hampsthwaite Bridge and Ripley Park. Part of this has recently been exposed in the narrow lane west of Hollybank Wood (268598), which follows the line of the old York-Lancaster road shown on Ogilby's map, itself probably aligned on the Roman road referred to earlier. Whether the causeway is Roman, medieval, or sixteenth-century is not known. Tuke's map of 1787 names a stretch of road above Cray as Kidstones Causeway (944805).

Where packhorse tracks descended to rivers and streams these would be crossed usually by means of a ford, but where the sides were too steep or rocky, a single-arch bridge would be built. These were usually steeply humped to allow floodwater to pass beneath, and had either no parapets or very low ones to allow unobstructed passage of side-slung panniers on the ponies. Many packhorse bridges have since had their parapets raised

Packhorse bridge near Thornthwaite, Nidderdale, on an old track from Ilkley to Ripon.

for the safety of modern travellers, and have also been widened. Not every narrow, single-span bridge is a packhorse one, but many such bridges do exist on known packhorse routes. Main rivers in the dales are too wide in their mature reaches for single-span structures, and had shallow stretches which could be forded, so that it is over tributary becks that packhorse bridges are more common. Little or nothing is known about most of these, but it is likely that the earliest stone bridges in the Dales were of monastic origin. Bow Bridge (935910), spanning Grange Gill west of Askrigg, well-hidden a few yards from the present road, is probably an early thirteenth-century structure on the upper Wensleydale estates of Jervaulx Abbey. South of our area Bolton Priory is known to have spent £21 12s 9d in 1305 for building 'the bridge at Kyldwyk' across the Aire, some of the original work still being visible in the western side. Mention has been made of Byland Abbey's bridge over the Nidd at Ramsgill.

Monastic or secular overlords were responsible for providing and repairing bridges, but just before the suppression of the monasteries the state of many bridges had become so serious that in 1530 a Statute was enacted requesting local Justices of the Peace to enquire 'of all manner of annoyances of bridges broken in the highways to the damage of the King's liege people', and to find out the cost of repairing or replacing the damaged bridges, levying the cost on the local districts. Surveyors were appointed to carry out these duties but northern progress was very slow, and it was not until the following century that in both the North and West Ridings most of the important bridges had been repaired or replaced in stone, including the packhorse bridges seen today. Indeed, the period of packhorse bridge-building seems to have been between 1660 and 1760.

Public levy met the costs of rebuilding Linton Bridge across the Wharfe at Grassington soon after 1602; Sir William Craven paid for Burnsall bridge in 1609, but in 1612 the £60 needed to rebuild Ingleton Bridge was levied on 'the whole of the West Riding', as was the £30 needed for Conistone bridge in Wharfedale, which was 'never to be charged more'.

Burnsall Bridge, rebuilt 1884 on the site of Sir William Craven's bridge of 1602.

The West Riding ratepayers had to dip into their pockets twice for the important bridge at Barden (052574), in 1659 and 1676, and for the small bridge at Cowgill, near the head of Dentdale, in 1702, as recorded on a stone plaque.

Ling Gill bridge (803789) in upper Ribblesdale, is on the old packhorse route Settle-Horton-High Birkwith-Cam End-Hawes, and now carries the Pennine Way. An indistinct inscription on one wall records that it was rebuilt in 1765 'at the charge of the whole West Riding'. Nearer Ribble Head is one of the most charming of Dales' packhorse bridges across Thorns Gill (776795), while lower down the valley, between Horton and Settle, Stainforth Bridge (816673) dates from the seventeenth century and enjoys the protection of the National Trust. It is probable that Samuel Watson, who built the gauntly impressive Knight Stainforth Hall to the west of the Ribble about 1670 was also responsible for the bridge as this would improve access to the road up Ribblesdale. Contemporary with it is Swaledale's best-known packhorse bridge at Ivelet (933978), a single graceful arch built about 1690 to link parts of manorial estate on opposite sides of the river, though not necessarily on a packhorse route. Posing a similar problem is New Bridge (236603) west of Birstwith in Nidderdale. Although the present bridge appears to date from 1822, and is locally known as Packhorse Bridge, records prove a bridge here in 1594, and that may have been a replacement for an older monastic one, for it lies close to the former boundary wall of Fountains Abbey lands, with the ancient Forest of Knaresborough land across the river. Today, narrow winding packhorse tracks approach the bridge on each side, but where they came from or led to is not known.

Other evidence of former packhorse routes can sometimes be seen

Inscription on Bridge,
Cowgill, Dentdale.

Stainforth Bridge, Ribblesdale; dating from about 1675.

Ivelet Bridge, Swaledale, a packhorse bridge of about 1695.

'New Bridge' at Birstwith, in Nidderdale. An 1822 rebuilding of a bridge known to exist in 1594, possibly earlier.

where these descended steep hills and horses had to zigzag to ease the gradient. Centuries of use, allied to erosion by rainwater, has created holloways. Sometimes, where the original track had become impassable the leader of a packhorse train would start a new one alongside, and this in turn would be gradually worn away, so that some hillsides show a number of nearly parallel tracks close together. In Swaledale, above Grinton, the hillside to the west of the modern road to Redmire and Leyburn shows this (046977).

In seeking these old trading routes one is occasionally helped by guidestones or posts erected in the early eighteenth century by direction of Parliament. Meeting at Rotherham on 6 August 1700 the West Riding Justices ordered 'Stoops to be sett up in crosse highways... it is ordered by this Court [Quarter Sessions] that for the better convenience of travelling in such Partes of this Ryding, which are remote from Towns and where severall highways meet, the surveyors of the highways of every parish or place... do forthwith cause to be erected... a stone or post, with an inscription thereon... containing the name of the next Market Town...' A similar order was made by the North Riding Justices meeting at Northallerton on 2 October 1711.

Parochial response was variable, sometimes non-existent, for the orders were repeated over the next thirty years. However, the survival of some guideposts or stoops of pre-turnpike days indicates that a few parishes were conscientious. It must be conceded that many Dales farmers gained their own 'mileage' from them at the time of the Enclosure (see Chapter

7), finding that they made useful gateposts, or, broken up, incorporated them into walls. Indeed, this seems the likely explanation of so few early eighteenth-century stoops having survived. One thing does seem certain. Wheeled traffic across the hills would have been very unlikely in those days, so the guide stones were erected for the convenience of packhorse traffic using the main trading routes. Where names of market towns can still be deciphered on these stones, assuming them still in their original positions, town names face the direction in which that town lies. We can now try to trace some known packhorse tracks, concentrating on those which have not become modern roads. It must be pointed out that many routes were multi-purpose tracks, so that to describe any particular one as being a packhorse track does not mean that it was not used by drovers too. At the end of this chapter, however, some routes are picked out and described as having been used primarily for the transport of specific goods such as lead and coal.

Barnard Castle and Swaledale

Barnard Castle, in Teesdale, was an important market in medieval times, with many tracks leading south and south-west from it. One of the oldest, now a modern road for most of its length, crosses the Stang to Langthwaite in Arkengarthdale. For a short distance south of Barnard Castle its line is represented by field paths, between Thorsgill Farm (047153) and North Bitts (045138). Crossing the A66 it continues to Timpton Hill as a minor road, which deviates to the west, crosses the River Greta by Rutherford bridge, picks up the old road at Thwaite Beck (035114) and goes forward to Hill Top (027095). The old road continues ahead and will be dealt with subsequently as a drovers' route.

At Hill Top an old packhorse track, now surfaced, heads eastwards to East Hope, Haythwaite and Barningham. Between Peak Hole and East Hope a branch leaves this as a bridleway within Stang Forest, but on the forest edge at Black Hill Gate (044084) emerges on to the open moor, making an indeterminate line eastwards as little more than a sheep-trod. In 1½ miles it meets a prominent boundary wall orientated north-east to south-west, at a gate. This track across Barningham Moor is known as the Badger Way, significant of ancient trade usage, and 200yd south-westwards from the gate, is a standing stone adjoining the wall on its north side, and bearing the decipherable inscription 'Badger Way Stoop', on two faces (064076). Presumably, the packhorse track passed close to it before the wall was built about the middle of last century; if the track has not changed, the stoop would nevertheless have been a prominent mark-point, visible on a skyline from some distance to the west.

Beyond the wall the Badger Way continues eastwards to cross the Newsham-Kexwith road. Then turning more southwards it enters army firing ranges on Gayles Moor, and becomes Cordilleras Lane to the village of Marske. These last three miles follow now an almost straight alignment between walls dating from the Marske Moor enclosure of 1809.

Back at Black Gate another track, almost impossible to define, climbs

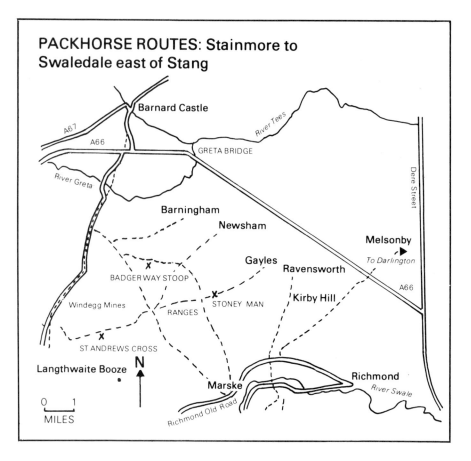

PACKHORSE ROUTES: Stainmore to Swaledale east of Stang

close to How Tallon, continuing south-eastwards over rough moorland pasture, along the western edge of Holgate Moor to Holgate itself (068038), where it descends behind the farm as a distinctive holloway. It goes forward as a path to Helwith (075028), crosses Arndale Beck, and as a rough farm track climbs and contours Skelton Moor, and enters Marske as a surfaced road. From there the old road to Richmond above the north side of the valley, now a minor road, would be taken.

Dentdale — Craven Old Way

Named thus on the 1:25,000 OS map this is a very old packhorse way from Dent to Ingleton. Leaving Dent at the southern end of the village it follows the motor road along the southern side of the valley to Deepdale Foot, branching off beyond Mill Bridge at the Methodist Chapel (723858), as a narrow, metalled lane. In 250yd a walled lane swings up to the east, and soon emerges on to rough pasture, climbing by a wall up to the north-western shoulder of Whernside. At 1,400ft OD (737850) it becomes a walled green lane, 30ft wide, with a marshy hollow to the north, marked on the map as 'Horse Well', probably a watering-place for packhorses. In another ½ mile the lane passes a well-preserved limekiln

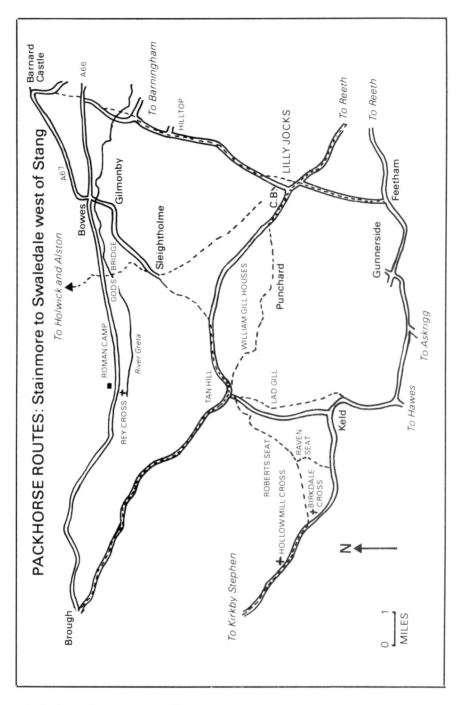

PACKHORSE ROUTES: Stainmore to Swaledale west of Stang

(745847) adjoining a small quarry.

Known here as Great Wold, the green track unerringly follows a limestone shelf across open rough moorland, past the ruins of Duncan Sike Foot, over a peaty section, before resuming on limestone at Craven

Holloway on old packhorse route at Holgate.

Great Wold, packhorse and drovers road, crossing Whernside, above Dentdale.

Wold (753833). It then loses height rapidly, descending by a fence to the aqueduct carrying Force Gill over the Settle-Carlisle railway (761816). The Craven Old Way crosses the line by a stone bridge, and follows it southwards before going under a bridge to take a south-westerly alignment to Winterscales. As a walled lane it continues to Ivescar, and through a series of hay-meadows as a bridleway to Bruntscar (738789) and Ellerbeck. After fording Ellerbeck Gill it becomes a sketchy way across rough pasture, climbing slowly as Kirkby Gate (probably signifying an old route to Kirkby Lonsdale) crosses Scales Moor at 1,300ft OD, aiming for the drier limestone land at Ewes Top, where a nick in the skyline ahead marks the only breach in Twisleton Scar (704758). Here the track follows a naturally causewayed passage through the limestone, descends a rocky stairway, and finally cuts down the escarpment as a well-graded green lane joining the Roman road above Ingleton, while in the other direction Twisleton Lane leads to the Kingsdale road and Thornton-in-Lonsdale.

Another old road from Dent to Ingleton and Kirkby Lonsdale follows the modern narrow road up Deepdale, crosses the watershed south of White Shaw Moss (723820) and makes a long descent into Kingsdale. The way for Ingleton continues the modern line, but near Yordas Cave a track leaves this road on the west, climbs above Shout Scar, and becomes a good green lane along Thorney Rigg (693773) and North End Scar,

Kirkby Gate — a continuation of the Craven Old Way, here crossing limestone on Scales Moor, near Ingleton.

eventually becoming a walled track down to Masongill (674755) and the main Kendal road. The part of this track between Yordas and Masongill is known as the Turbary Road, a reference to its use by Thornton-in-Lonsdale as the way to the parish common-land where peat was dug.

Thornton Fell was enclosed about 1820, and the Turbary Road was walled. At the same time, in the valley itself Kingsdale Beck was ordered to be straightened, presumably to give a quicker flow of water and thus reduce liability to flooding of the valley fields. The Kingsdale road was also straightened then, resulting in an almost straight alignment between the end of Twisleton Lane (693760) and Kingsdale Head (710796).

Another packhorse route out of Dent leaves the village south of the school and soon becomes a very steep and stony track up Flintergill (703867). On South Lord's Land (699859) it turns sharply westwards to join the 'Occupation road' of 1859, contouring and gradually descending to the Barbondale road (680862) which leads south-westwards and then contours round the western flanks of Barbon Low Fell as an unenclosed road to Whelprigg (635813), winds past Bellgate and descends through Casterton to Kirkby Lonsdale.

The present motor road eastwards from Dent, leading up Dentdale to Dent Head, and joining the turnpike near Newby Head was not constructed until 1802. Before then, one packhorse route out of the valley, climbing up from Stone House (772858) is described in Chapter 6. The maps of both Jefferys (1771) and Smith (1801) show a route continuing southwards from Stone House along the line of the present road. Almost directly beneath an arch of Dent Head viaduct there is a particularly attractive packhorse bridge without parapets (777844). The construction of the railway and the viaduct has completely obscured any traces of old tracks nearby, but the old packhorse route can be picked up again just beyond the twelfth milestone from Sedbergh (786836). A vague track through moorland grasses leads across Stoops Moss southwards to High Gayle Farm (786815) and Windshaw, joining the turnpike near a milestone above Far Gearstones (784803). The old packhorse track is lost in enclosed fields, but probably forded Gayle Beck south of Gearstones, or crossed by Thorns Gill bridge 200yd downstream, continuing south-easterly to Nether Lodge and High Birkwith along the route described under Drove Roads. This would lead down Ribblesdale to Horton and Settle.

Settle and Ribblesdale
Unusual among the major Dales' valleys in having a north-south orientation, Ribblesdale rarely provided a main communication corridor until the Settle-Carlisle railway thrust its impressive engineering grandeur through it in the 1870s. The present motor road, B6479, follows the valley northwards from Settle, on a slightly lower course than the old route which left the north-east corner of Settle Market Place by Constitution Hill, continuing northwards along Banks' Lane to Langcliffe, beyond which its course to Stainforth is not certain, and some of which

may have been lost in quarrying and railway construction. Beyond Stainforth the packhorse route is probably represented by field paths as far as Sherwood Brow, but from there to Horton its route can only be conjectured.

Jefferys's map shows this road along the eastern side of Ribblesdale as far as Horton, with milestones alongside it. These have all vanished. Beyond Horton, no road is shown on the western side of the valley, but a track probably existed in 1805, when Edward Dayes in *A Picturesque Tour in Yorkshire and Derbyshire*, wrote 'Horton is about six miles from Settle, and the last village on the upper road to Askrigg. From Horton I immediately entered on the moors, where all is dreary, wild and solitary'. This was the old packhorse route from Horton to Askrigg, and is today surfaced as far as High Birkwith (800768). It leaves Horton by the New Inn (807727) and goes forward past New Houses as a walled lane with a grass verge. High Birkwith, now a farm, was an inn on this important packhorse way, and the track beyond, now a farm road, climbs to Old Ing (804773) and winds northwards as a green lane, walled mainly on one side, occasionally on both sides, past Dry Lathe Cave to Ling Gill bridge already referred to. It then climbs over unenclosed rough moorland to join the Cam High Road on Cam End. *Paterson's Roads*, fifteenth edition of 1811, describes this section precisely, as part of the recommended route from London to Askrigg, via Halifax, Skipton and Settle:

'Old Inge. Three miles farther you encounter the road from Lancaster, through Hornby and Ingleton, to Askrigg (the Richmond-Lancaster turnpike) and then

Constitution Hill, the old road out of Settle northwards into Ribblesdale, used by Scottish drovers.

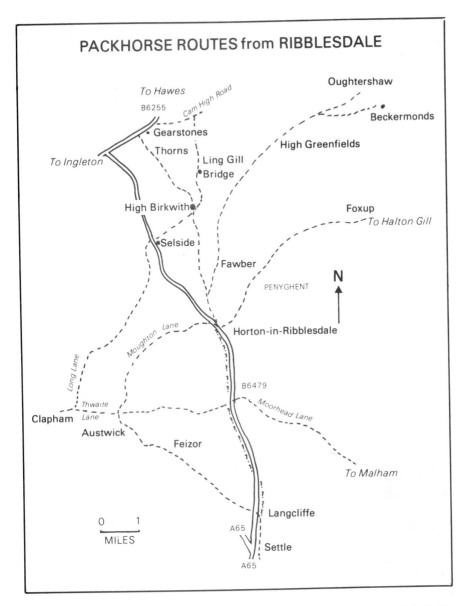

PACKHORSE ROUTES from RIBBLESDALE

To Hawes
B6255
Cam High Road

Oughtershaw

Beckermonds

Gearstones

Thorns

High Greenfields

To Ingleton

Ling Gill
Bridge

High Birkwith

Foxup
To Halton Gill

Selside

Fawber

PENYGHENT

N

Horton-in-Ribblesdale

Moughton Lane

Long Lane

B6479

Moorhead Lane

Thwaite
Lane

Clapham

Austwick

Feizor

To Malham

0   1
MILES

Langcliffe
A65

Settle
A65

turn on the right at the 12th milestone from Settle, and just beyond the 26th from Lancaster. Beyond the 28th milestone on Cam Hill you may turn on the left, through Hawes to Bainbridge, a circuitous route'.

Jeffery's map shows all these milestones, so presumably Paterson merely extracted the information from there. His alternative route branches off the Cam Road at Kidhow Gate (830834), continuing north-eastwards as a high-level green lane to the western flanks of Ten End (843869) where it descends northwards above forest plantations, over Backsides, and as a walled lane 32ft wide, joins the turnpike road (860895) west of Hawes. From Old Ing to Ten End the Pennine Way follows the packhorse route, diverging eastwards from it on Ten End.

Another important packhorse route from Settle went eastwards to Malham, leaving the Market Place at the south-east corner by High Street, Victoria Street and Albert Street to Upper Settle. Climbing steeply up the present Malham road the old road diverged northwards about a mile from Settle (836630), its course now signposted as a bridleway to Malham. As a walled lane it continues along Stockdale, keeping north of Stockdale Farm (855638). Maintaining a regular width of about six feet and with an increasingly rough surface it climbs out of the valley head, passes over slate, steep sections of bare limestone, and emerges on to open grassy moorland at 1,700ft OD.

As a well-defined green lane it crosses three boundary walls, at one of which a huge upright slab of Horton slate serves as a gate-post, but whose skyline situation suggests an earlier guide-post use (873638). Beyond the third wall the packhorse track starts its long descent to Malham. 200yd to the north-east the re-sited Nappa Cross, probably of monastic origin, occupies a prominent wall-top position (875643). The track passes Pikedaw Caverns, former calamine workings, beyond which one branch heads south-eastwards by Hoober Edge and enters Malham village on the west, while the other keeps to an easterly alignment through Far Sleets Gate, joins the moor road west of Malham Cove, and descends the hill to enter the village at Town Head.

When John Housman travelled from Malham to Settle in 1800 he described this route: 'The road (when it can be called such) leads us over a wild, hilly country and extensive tracks of moors'. He refers to 'several

Old Road from Settle to Malham in Stockdale.

This packhorse track may be part of the western continuation of Mastiles Lane as it enters Feizor.

calamine pits close to the road', and notes 'stone walls dividing the fields'. (They had been enclosed twenty to thirty years previously). He adds, 'the road is nowhere good, and some of it almost impassable, notwithstanding the abundance of excellent materials everywhere at hand: but its being not much frequented is probably the reason why so little labour and care are bestowed upon it. . . . This road between Settle and Malham is by no means to be recommended to strangers except in clear weather . . . that by way of Long Preston, though tolerably good, is a circuitous route of about fifteen miles.'

Although Settle was the focal point for many packhorse routes it is worth mentioning three others to the west which do not enter the town, but do enter and cross Ribblesdale higher up the valley. The hamlet of Feizor (790676), about a mile north of the main A65, lay on the monastic route which was a westwards continuation of Mastiles Lane, and both Fountains and Sawley abbeys had estates there. A walled lane runs from Stainforth bridge (817672) into Little Stainforth, then climbs westwards as an unenclosed track below Smearsett Scar and Feizor Scar to enter Feizor as a holloway between tumbled walls. Its course beyond Feizor is probably represented by the field path to Austwick, or by Hale Lane, coming into Austwick by the bridge to the east of the village (769683). West of Austwick the route can only be conjectured — it may have picked up Thwaite Lane to the north or be represented by field paths to Clapham, from where its further course was probably along the 'Ogilby' road to Newby Cote and Ingleton already described.

Some tracks from Lancaster and the Forest of Bowland approached the Dales area via Ingleton or Bentham; if the latter they then headed for

Clapham or Austwick. A well-attested packhorse track runs north-eastwards from Clapham leaving the village at the church, passes through the tunnels which re-routed its course beneath the grounds of Ingleborough Hall about 1833, and, as the western part of Thwaite Lane, climbs out of the village to Summit Clump (752695). There, as Long Lane, the track runs northwards beneath the limestone walls to the head of a valley, turns eastwards over the unenclosed Long Scar, and as Clapham Lane — a fine green track through open limestone country — goes through Sulber Gate (776733) above Thieves Moss, eventually descending gradually to the enclosed fields of the very old farm settlement of Borrins (784747), and becoming a walled lane again near Selside (783757).

Jefferys's map shows this road from Clapham to Selside continuing northwards to Lodge (Ingman Lodge) and Caber (Gauber), ending short of the turnpike at Ribble Head. Smith's map of thirty years later shows it completed to Ribble Head, along the line of the present motor road. The old packhorse track continued north-eastwards from Selside as a walled lane beneath the railway, fording the Ribble probably near the site of the present footbridge (793762), its course beyond represented by the footpath to Low and High Birkwith (800768). From there it takes the line of the Horton-Askrigg track already described.

The route from Austwick to Horton is not shown on Jefferys's map. This leaves the village at Town Head (770869), follows the walled Crummack Lane northwards to the corner of White Stone Lane

Long Lane, near Clapham, the packhorse route from Clapham to Selside and Askrigg.

110

Moughton Lane in Crummackdale.

(773706), where one branch goes forward to Crummack to join Clapham Lane south of Sulber Gate. Another branch, now a field-path, heads north-eastwards, crosses Austwick Beck by a clapper bridge (778715) and joins Moughton Lane coming up from the hamlet of Wharfe (784696). This then climbs as a narrow, walled lane past an old shooting-box on to the limestone scars and pavement of Moughton. Its eastwards line to Beecroft Hall and Horton has been wrecked through quarrying and an alternative footpath has been created to the north. From the Crown Hotel, Horton, the route northwards went to New Houses, then probably through Fawber and Top Farm, the course now represented by field paths, joining a walled lane at (810755), forward to High Birkwith and the old Settle-Askrigg road.

To work out long-distance routes for packhorses is rarely more than an exercise in conjecture. Documentary evidence is sparse; field-work often reveals evidence of packhorse use over a long period, but to an increasing degree the use of old tracks by farm tractors and four-wheel drive vehicles has completely obscured the original nature of old tracks. Common sense suggests that a network of packhorse routes served local and market needs for centuries, but it is probably wisest to consider examples of some relatively short-distance ones, particularly those which 'cross the grain' of the area.

Littondale and Upper Wharfedale
No motor road crosses the high ridge separating these valleys, but at least five packhorse tracks can be identified — Halton Gill to Beckermonds,

Halton Gill to Yockenthwaite, Litton to Buckden, Arncliffe to Starbotton and Arncliffe to Kettlewell. They are so similar that space justifies mentioning only two, but all are still public footpaths or bridleways.

Halton Gill to Yockenthwaite   This is a continuation of routes from Horton and Stainforth. The track leaves the Foxup road west of Halton Gill (879766) and zigzags steeply up the hillside on to Horse Head Moor, sometimes as a stony track, sometimes a green one. It crosses a boundary wall at Horse Head Gate (889776) at about 1,950ft OD and soon descends steeply by Hagg Beck with a final series of zigzags to Raisgill (906786) opposite Yockenthwaite. Packhorse trains bound for Wensleydale's markets at Askrigg or Hawes then had a choice of routes, either by Deepdale, Oughtershaw and Fleet Moss, the line of the modern road, or from Deepdale and directly northwards by Deepdale Gill (899816) either to Marsett (903862) or Cragdale (919837), above the head of Semerwater, and so down to Bainbridge and Askrigg. Jeffery's map shows the Marsett road, but all traces of this have now vanished. So far as the Cragdale one is concerned a local tradition asserts that an inn once existed in this remote valley. There is certainly a short stretch of cobbled causeway south of Bank Wood near the ruins of an old building (918837). The Horse Head track between Littondale and Wharfedale was used regularly between 1807 and 1833 by the incumbent of Halton Gill to take Sunday services at Hubberholme (925783), which was a chapel of ease to the mother church at Arncliffe.

The packhorse route from Arncliffe to Kettlewell would have forded the River Skirfare near the site of the present bridge (933720); it then probably followed the line of the footpath immediately beyond, and crossed the motor road to continue as a field path slanting up the hillside through Byre Bank Wood, becoming a steep, rocky track where it crosses limestone scars. On Old Cote Little Moor it is a clear track through heather, crosses the boundary wall (953723) and continues in an easterly direction to descend very steeply through the Slit, a nick in the limestone scars, to the bridge at Kettlewell. The County Bridge Book of 1752 describes this as 'paved', which suggests packhorse use, and the present 'New' bridge probably dates from the eighteenth century. It partially collapsed in February 1985, and extensive repairs are needed. In 1457 the Fountains Abbey Bursars's Book records an item of 2s 8d 'for labour on the bridge of Ketylwell'. The track described, though considered in a local context, could form a section of a long-distance packhorse route from Settle to Kirkby Malzeard.

Wharfedale to Wensleydale and Nidderdale
A number of packhorse tracks cross the watershed between Wharfedale and lower Wensleydale, and between Wharfedale and upper Nidderdale. The only metalled road is that from Kettlewell, via Park Rash and Coverdale, to Middleham and Jervaulx, already described. Kettlewell was formerly the market town for upper Wharfedale, much more important

than Grassington. Fountains Abbey, Bolton Priory and Coverham Abbey had land there, and in medieval times its manor was shared between Coverham Abbey and the Nevilles of Middleham Castle. In the eighteenth and early nineteenth centuries lead mining brought additional importance, as well as packhorse traffic.

One of the most distinctive packhorse tracks leaves Kettlewell where the Coverdale road makes a sharp bend (973725), and Top Mere Road arrows up the hillside ahead, a walled green track which continues over open fell pastures to Cam Head (971753) where it joins a similar track that has come up from Starbotton. Nineteenth-century enclosures of Top Mere and Starbotton Cam Pasture have caused a deviation of tracks here, but the Top Mere road continues to the township peat grounds at Tor Mere Top (972764). By turning westwards down the Starbotton Road (another green lane) for a few hundred yards, a northwards branch of this is picked up contouring along the Out Moor, and this in turn joins the Walden Road from Starbotton at 962772.

This Walden Road leaves Starbotton at the north end of the village (953748), climbs as a stony track steeply northwards to reach open fell on Knuckle Bone Pasture, gradually swinging north-eastwards, carefully avoiding marshy ground, and, in places, showing clearly as a holloway. At the head of Cam the track forks, one branch being the Out Moor track just mentioned, leaving the Walden Road climbing steeply to a ruin on the crest of the hill (965775). Far too high for a farm building this was

Kettlewell across the River Wharfe. Top Mere Road can be seen slanting up the hill behind the village.

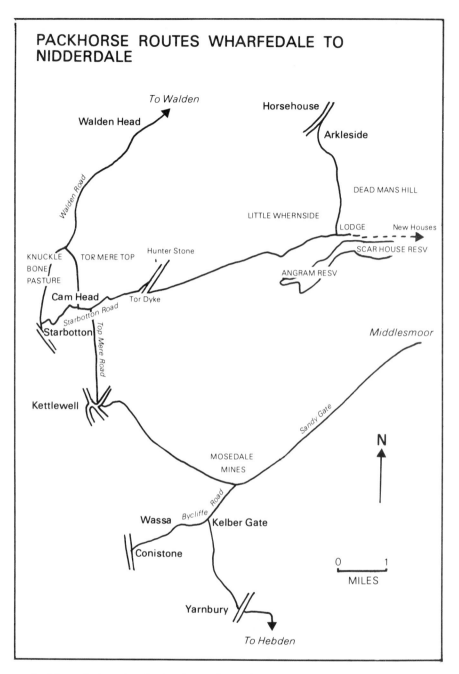

PACKHORSE ROUTES WHARFEDALE TO NIDDERDALE

To Walden

Walden Head

Horsehouse

Arkleside

Walden Road

DEAD MANS HILL

LITTLE WHERNSIDE

LODGE

New Houses

KNUCKLE
BONE
PASTURE

TOR MERE TOP

Hunter Stone

SCAR HOUSE RESV

ANGRAM RESV

Cam Head

Starbotton Road

Tor Dyke

Middlesmoor

Top Mere Road

Starbotton

Kettlewell

Sandy Gate

N

MOSEDALE
MINES

Bycliffe Road

Wassa

Kelber Gate

Conistone

0   1
MILES

Yarnbury

To Hebden

probably a shelter for the leaders of packhorse trains. There is some rough grazing nearby. Near the second gate beyond this, just past a wall, there is a prominent low boundary stone (966778) with the letters 'B' and 'O', though the latter may have been a 'C', for the boundary wall separates the parishes of Buckden and Carlton Highdale. The track continues northward through heather, past a small cairn identifying the long-disused Hard Rake quarries, and gradually descends Walden Moor to Walden Head (987807) where it becomes a surfaced road subsequently following the west side of Walden to West Burton and Wensleydale.

Returning to the Starbotton Road, which may well be a 'short-cut' continuation of a packhorse track from Arncliffe, from Cam Head this swings round eastwards below Top Mere, becomes mixed up for a while with the prehistoric earthwork Tor Dyke, but then takes a north-easterly course to join the Coverdale road on Great Hunters Sleets. A few hundred yards north along the motor road Hunters Stone (994767) is probably an old guide post.

Where Tor Dyke crosses the motor road, a packhorse track slants north-eastwards by Hem Gill Shaw, continuing as a slightly sunken way to a small skyline nick near a cairn (008765) at about 1,950ft OD, descending along the southern flanks of Little Whernside to the ruins at Lodge (048774) above Scar House Reservoir in upper Nidderdale, where it meets another packhorse track which has come from Horsehouse in Coverdale (047813). This starts as a surfaced road, crosses Arkleside Bridge and keeps to the south side of the River Cover to Arkleside,

Boundary stone on Starbotton Fell, on the old Walden Road.

becoming a green lane climbing the hill to a shooting box before descending to Lodge near Dead Man's Hill. This track is known to have been used by pedlars, packhorse trains and Scottish drovers.

Lodge is probably named from its having been a lodge in the ancient forest of Nidderdale. In packhorse days it was an inn regularly used by Scottish pedlars, and in the township books of Middlesmoor an entry dated 30 May 1728 states that 'three murder'd Bodies were found burr'd on Lodge End without heads'. Various stories grew up round the event, but it seems most likely that the corpses were of Scottish pedlars murdered for their money, the killers taking them to this remote spot on the boundary between the old West Riding and North Riding in the hope of confusing any possible enquiry. The name Dead Man's Hill commemorates the discovery. From Lodge the old packhorse track continues eastwards but becomes confused among the works involved in the construction of the reservoirs at the head of Nidderdale in 1913 and 1936. Indeed, Jefferys's map shows this road from near Hunters Stone crossing the col between Great and Little Whernsides and coming down to West House, now lost in Angram Reservoir, and continuing to Middlesmoor, where In Moor Lane, of Enclosure date, may represent part of the route. Jefferys also shows a road from High Woodale, through Low Woodale and New Houses (095767), following the north and east banks of the Nidd to Lofthouse, but the course of this has also become confused in the reservoir construction.

Packhorse tracks which are now footpaths climbing across the limestone scars of Langcliffe east of the village mainly led to old mines and peat moors. A more definitive route, however, can be traced from Conistone, farther down Wharfedale. This turns off the Kettlewell road north of the church (981675), and for the first half-mile it is a surfaced road. Initially, and significantly, called Scot Gate Lane it is walled as far as Wassa Hill. Where it winds past Hill Castles Scar (992683) it shows a well-preserved cobbled surface, and beyond the moor gate on to Conistone Moor it becomes the Bycliffe Road. At Cappleside Gate it divides, one branch going northwards, as Conistone Turf Road, to Capplestone Gate and the old Silver Rake workings, the other branch swinging eastwards and north-eastwards past Kelber Gate (003685), where three distinct holloways, almost parallel, can be identified.

Beyond Kelber Gate the Bycliffe Road continues north-eastwards as a well-defined, rough-surfaced track past Mossdale Caverns (017697) into Mossdale and climbing to cross the watershed and old Riding boundary on Conistone Moor. Its yellow colour across Friar Head Moor merits its name, Sandy Gate, and it gradually descends along the northern flanks of How Stean Beck, past High and Low Riggs (077744) and then as field paths to Middlesmoor and Nidderdale.

Back near Kelber Gate a green track leaves the Bycliffe Road, cutting southwards across heather moor to join a walled lane on Green Hill (007677), then turning south-eastwards, where it becomes Limekiln Lane leading directly to Yarnbury above Grassington. This was not a cross-

Bycliffe Road, above Conistone.

valley route but merely gave access from Grassington to the lead mines and peat moors, and was doubtless a busy track from the mid-eighteenth century onwards. Limekiln Lane can be continued opposite Yarnbury House (015658), keeping right at the first fork, then as a well-defined track southwards down Hebden Gill into Hebden village (025632). The north branch of the fork leads to more mine workings on the moor, and is known as the Duke's New Road, after its construction about 1820 by the mining agent of the Duke of Devonshire to eliminate difficult gradients on an old road to the mines whose output was then expanding.

One old road not yet mentioned in detail is wholly in Wensleydale and was formerly an important highway between Middleham and the hunting forests of its medieval lords in Bishopdale Chase. It subsequently became a packhorse track and was probably also used by drovers. From Middleham its course is now lost in the training gallops on Low Moor which is still common land, but is probably represented by a footpath leaving the motor road west of Middleham Castle (123875) on a westward alignment for two miles to Agglethorpe Gate (093874) where it joins a surfaced road continuing the line as Common Lane across the lower edge of Middleham High Moor as far as Penhill Farm. For much of its length Common Lane is a wide lane, with broad verges, between early nineteenth-century enclosure walls.

At Penhill Farm the road divides, one branch turning south as a modern road over Melmerby Moor, the other descending Witton Steeps towards West Witton. At the first hairpin, where the motor road twists back on itself, the old road continues ahead as a green lane; at this junction an early

An early eighteenth-century guide stoop above West Witton, on an old road up Wensleydale. The near face reads Middleham the right one Askrigg.

eighteenth-century guide stoop shows directions and distances to Middleham and Askrigg. Never less than 30ft wide between walls, the packhorse track maintains a constant height for almost two miles, and this stretch is known as High Lane. At one point it is 60ft wide between walls, suggesting possible use as a cattle stance during droving days, or as grazing for packhorses. Beyond here the track swings south-eastwards, and on the 1854 OS map is known as Morphet Gate, changed on modern maps to Morpeth Gate (030878), and descends steeply as a stony lane, eventually becoming a surfaced one, and crosses Walden Beck by an attractive packhorse bridge into West Burton village at the foot of Bishopdale.

Jefferys shows this route clearly, with a continuation up Bishopdale along the line adopted by the present road, B6160, over Kidstones into Wharfedale. This road, incidentally, was never turnpiked, being a good example of one that evolved through the linking of existing tracks. Near the crossroads to Thoralby and Newbiggin, Street Head Inn dates from about 1730, probably about the time when the local road network acquired its present form. A century later it had become an important coaching inn.

Returning to the Wharfedale area, among a number of probable tracks one in particular merits further attention. Significantly named Badger Gate, this is a very old way from Beamsley across the southern edge of Denton Moor to Harrogate. At Beamsley its course is not certain, but it

Packhorse and drove road, known as Morphet Gate, above West Burton —probably also a medieval route from Middleham Castle.

probably followed the line of the present minor road round Bowers Hill south-eastwards to Beacon Hill (095517), then leaving the motor road on to an easterly alignment past Wards End (105517), keeping to the edge of enclosed land to the south and an open moor to the north. It meets another track on Long Ridge, follows it along Foldshaw Ridge to the Hunger Hill Road (117516). It is then lost for nearly a mile on the moors north of March Gill Reservoir, continuing eastwards near Cross Bank and across Denton Moor to Ellercar Pike (159523), and named in this section Low Badger Gate, with High Badger Gate to the north. Following a line of boundary stones and a wall north-eastwards to Sourby Farm (167530) it crosses the surfaced road called Psalter Gate, and as a metalled road follows Trimble Ridge to Fewston, diverted by reservoir construction. East of Fewston, Penny Pot Lane continues its course to Harrogate, the straight alignment representing the surveyors' re-drawing of its route when the ancient Forest of Knaresborough was enclosed in the 1770s.

Lead-Mine Tracks and Roads

Many of the Yorkshire Dales have experienced some form of mining. Ores of lead, copper, zinc and to a small extent, iron, have been exploited, some workings having continued into the present century. Enormous quantities of limestone have been quarried, for burning in hundreds of limekilns, the resultant lime being used as a sweetener for sour moorland soils or as the basis for a lime mortar used in building, especially during the seventeenth and eighteenth centuries. Stone itself for building farms, barns, houses, mills and field boundary walls, has also been quarried, usually on a very local scale. On the high gritstone fells thin seams of coal have yielded their own mineral wealth from medieval times until as recently as the 1930s. All these activities have resulted in many miles of roads and tracks, mostly very localised, but some, traceable today over quite long distances, concerned with the transport of products from within the Dales area to places far outside the scope of this book.

Within the Dales the lead mining fields cover two large areas where mining was for at least two centuries the dominant occupation. The northerly one embraces practically the whole of Swaledale and Arkengarthdale above Marske, together with parts of the north side of Wensleydale. The other main area of mining extends in a narrow band from near Pateley Bridge in Nidderdale, westwards across the moors of Greenhow Hill and Appletreewick, keeps to the north flank of Wharfedale and over the moors of Hebden, Grassington and Kettlewell, reaching across the watershed to the south side of Wensleydale near West Burton.

Lead mines were far more numerous than the smelt mills to which the dressed ore was taken and smelted in order to obtain the pure metal. Jefferys's map of 1771 identifies only four smelt mills: at Marrick, in Swaledale (078995); Braithwaite, also known as Burton Mill (018855) in Wensleydale; Heathfield near Pateley (144665); and Grassington Low Mill almost opposite Linton Church, in Wharfedale (007633). There were certainly many others, some in places far removed from known roads. From the mills smelted lead was carried, mainly by packhorses, to the lead markets. Lead from the northern area went to Richmond, Stockton or Yarm, and, when horse drawn carts were used from the late eighteenth century, to Richmond and Darlington, where a street is still called the Lead Yard. From there shipping agents arranged its transport from the ports of Stockton or Yarm, along the coast or across to the continent. Nidderdale lead, as well as that from Grassington and Wharfedale up to about 1800, went to Boroughbridge, but afterwards the Grassington product was carried to Gargrave for shipment on the Leeds-Liverpool Canal.

Not only was there this long-distance carriage of the finished product, together with the shorter-distance movement from mines to mills, but miners themselves evolved paths from their homes in villages to the mines and mills, which may have been two or three miles away. Many paths in the lead mining areas originated in this way, undocumented and unrecorded on early maps, although the 6in Ordnance Survey of the middle of the last century shows a number of such tracks. However, information can be gleaned occasionally which helps to throw a little light, with map and fieldwork to supplement it. A mine agent for Grassington Moor arranged in 1756 for a Newcastle engineer to produce some iron machinery for the whims (horse-operated winding engines), but pointed out in a letter that: 'the roads are so excessive Rotten that it will be difficult to get Timber and other Materials Led till they be better. . . . I say it will be better to defer Erecting the Engine till April or May when one may hope the Weather and Roads will be much better.' The carriers were advised to come through Richmond as the most direct road to Grassington, presumably by the old Ogilby route via Middleham, Coverdale and Kettlewell, or, since there was no bridge at Middleham they may have crossed the Ure at Wensley bridge.

In the seventeenth and eighteenth centuries successive Lords Wharton owned many lead mines in Swaledale, as well as others in the manor of Ravensworth to the north. A large-scale map of Healaugh by Richard Robinson, engraved by Jefferys in 1770, shows four smelt mills in the course of Mill Beck, later called Old Gang Beck, between Swaledale and Arkengarthdale. These were on the Wharton estates, and were listed by the mine agent, Philp Swale, in 1682, together with mills at Ellerton (068976), Waitwith (now lost beneath Catterick Camp) and Hartforth (159057) by Smelt Mill Beck three miles north of Richmond. In 1680 Hartforth Mill was a collecting and forwarding centre for lead from the other Wharton Mills, whence it was weighed and sent to merchants in Stockton either for sale or shipping. Thus, three centuries ago there was a network of lead roads converging from the Swaledale mills on Hartforth.

Road to the lead mining ground on Grassington Moor, probably mid-eighteenth century walled at the enclosure of the moor.

As other smelt mills were introduced at various places throughout Swaledale and Arkengarthdale mining field the number of miners' and packhorse ways increased to produce a complex tangle of tracks over many square miles.

The Moresdale Road   This road is regarded as a ridgeway, although its moorland course from Arkengarthdale to Arndale Beck follows more of a slightly domed plateau than a ridge. Nevertheless it may be of prehistoric origin, but from medieval times to the nineteenth century was part of a saltway by which salt from sources on the Durham coast was carried by packhorse to the northern dales of the Yorkshire Pennines. It was also used in the opposite direction to carry lead eastwards to the coast. From Langthwaite a steep walled lane (metalled) leads to Booze (015025), above Slei Gill, site of an eighteenth-century smelt mill, and lanes from Booze climb northwards on to Low Moor. Their courses converge as a well-defined green track by a wall, heading northwards round the ravaged head of North Rake Hush, then more north-easterly to the broken ground which marks the location of the famous Windegg Vein. To the east of this a footpath continues due eastwards through bracken and heather, contouring the hillside to 'Stony Man or St Andrew's Cross' (032040), a four-foot stone pillar, carrying a bench-mark and the date 1867, together with the letters 'FM'. Another stone, 200yd to the north-west is similarly inscribed, and though both stones mark a boundary, the 'Stony Man' is

Moresdale Road — a medieval saltway and a lead mining road of the eighteenth and nineteenth centuries, above Arkengarthdale.

Moresdale Road, on Gayles Moor. 'Stone Man' — a guide-cairn now within Army Ranges, hence the metalwork.

almost certainly the older, although the explanation of its saintly name is not known. It is shown on a map of Marrick parish of 1592, the earliest map depicting mines in Swaledale. The Moresdale Road continues east-north-east into the valley of Moresdale Beck at the farm of Kexwith (053051).

Beyond Kexwith it is a metalled road climbing Holgate Moor where one branch leads northwards to Long Green Gate, where it becomes a walled road 30ft wide. Its north-eastern course, as Moor Lane, for Newsham three miles away is a straight alignment resulting from the early nineteenth-century enclosures on Newsham Moor. The name Holgate, or Hall Gate, formerly Hollow Gate, almost certainly indicates packhorse use when moorland tracks would have been worn deep through continued use in muddy weather.

The direct continuation of Moresdale Road from Kexwith to the east is lost in moorland for short stretches on Gayles Moor — now used by the Army as firing ranges, with limited access — but crosses Rake Beck near the hairpin bend in the present road from Marske to Newsham, picking up the route at the tumulus called 'Stone Man' (098062), from which Stony Man Lane leads to Gayles. A stone cairn on the tumulus which lies about 60yd north of the road, occupies a prominent skyline situation for packhorse leaders to see from either direction of approach. Stony Man Lane is over 40ft wide between enclosure walls, with the stony surface 8ft wide, and at Pace's House (ruin 116067) it bends north-eastwards and decends as a narrow motor-road to Gayles. Traffic for the Hartforth Mill would then have turned south-eastwards along what is now a motor road through Kirby Hill to Whashton, continuing as a bridleway to Smelt Mill Beck, then as Lead Lane joining Jagger Lane at 165055 for Hartforth, across the Scotch Corner-Bowes turnpike, now the A66, to Melsonby and subsequently Stockton.

Undoubtedly much Swaledale lead was carried along the old Reeth-Richmond road, following the modern road to Fremington and keeping to the north of the valley, a route now taken by a minor road running eastwards from Fremington (046987) and soon climbing steeply past a limekiln along the southern edge of Copperthwaite Allotment and Marrick Moor. The well-preserved ruins of Marrick Smelt Mills (077995) lie a quarter of a mile south of this road, linked to it by a broad green lane through Smelting Mill Plantation. Lead was smelted at Marrick Mills for three centuries, ceasing about 1890.

The Richmond road goes eastwards to Marske, descending into the village and climbing north-eastwards to Richmond Out Moor. It then continues into Richmond, passing the former racecourse at the top of the hill above the town. Lead may have been carried into Richmond for marketing or, on the Out Moor, taken along Jagger Lane (134025). This is now a footpath across rough intakes, swinging north-westwards past Jockey Cap Clump, and along the edge of Black Plantation. At the north-eastern corner of this (155046) where it crosses the Richmond-Kirby Hill road, the boundaries of Easby, Gilling and Kirby Ravensworth parishes meet. Dr Raistrick makes the interesting observation that the place-name 'Black' is often associated with boundaries.

Jagger Lane crosses the road into Gilling Wood, emerging into open country and making a direct, well-defined course for Hartforth, part a stony track, part a green lane. This becomes a distinct holloway between trees as it approaches Leadmill Gill Beck, where the abutments of a former packhorse bridge can be identified (168060). This is now a wooden footbridge. Beyond, Hartforth Beck was probably forded but is now spanned by a rustic, early nineteenth-century park bridge. The track goes through the hamlet, crosses Hartforth Lane, and becomes a very overgrown, hedged bridleway to the main A66, and as a metalled lane beyond to Melsonby.

An alternative northwards route across Richmond Out Moor is the modern road, Sturdy House Lane, from 127025 to Ravensworth four miles away. The long, straight stretches of this, between early nineteenth-century enclosure walling, obscure the line of the original track. At Sturdy House (135051) the metalled road keeps north-east, then swinging north, down Stonygate Bank to Ravensworth. Another track, now over Army ranges, takes a more north-easterly alignment towards Gayles, and is subsequently lost near old quarry workings, from where a lane does turn northwards towards Ravensworth, as a metalled road down Flats Bank. Between the two is Kirby Hill, with no visible evidence of a direct link to Sturdy Hill. However, north of the church at Kirby Hill (140066) a field path makes a carefully-graded, partially causewayed descent of the

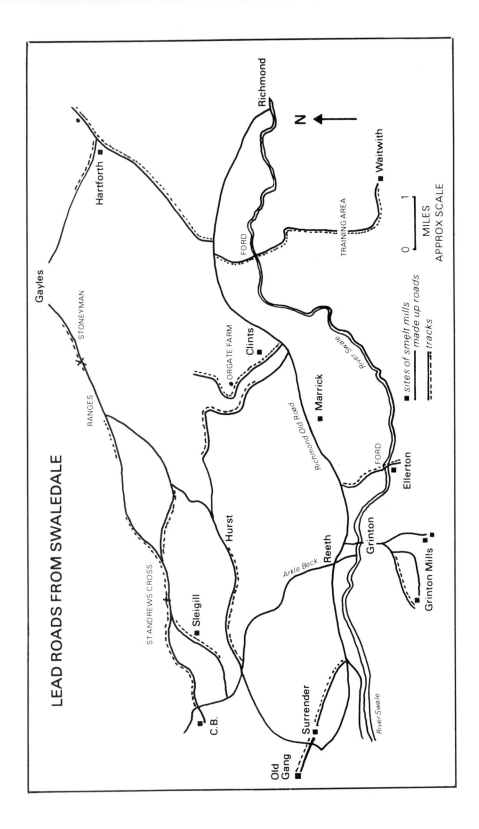

LEAD ROADS FROM SWALEDALE

sites of smelt mills
made up roads
tracks

MILES
APPROX SCALE
0 1

Access track to Marrick Smelt Mill, from Richmond Old Road.

escarpment, and follows field boundaries across 'The Park', entering Ravensworth by the earthworks of its castle. Waitlands Lane and New Lane link Ravensworth with the turnpike road (A66).

At a more local level Gunnerside Gill, on the north side of Swaledale between Reeth and Muker, is a typical example of a concentrated area within a mining field, with a multitude of tracks associated with activity during the eighteenth and nineteenth centuries. Miners' paths running northwards from the village follow both sides of the beck, the better ones being on the east. West of the village a bridleway now firmed by the passage of four-wheel drive vehicles to shooting-places on the moors, follows the contours below Jingle Pot Edge. At least four tracks, including the two mentioned, follow almost parallel courses at different levels northwards up the sides of Gunnerside Gill.

On the west side Lownathwaite Mill (936006), very ruinous, was working from about 1760 to the late 1820s, dealing with lead from mines on Lownathwaite Moor. An 1822 plan marks a track from the mines to the mill as 'Smelt Mill Road', with a northward continuation to Blakethwaite Mines over a mile away at the head of the valley (935030). A mill was built at Blakethwaite and seems to have operated from about 1820 to 1880. Near it are the ruins of the peat-house and a limekiln, and a small stone-slab bridge carries a track across the beck. Smelt Mill Road shows distinctly in the view of the complex, from near the limekiln, and other prominent tracks can be identified on the north-east side of the valley. On this eastern side, near the Bunton Level (940013) tracks climb steeply up the hillside, meeting on Melbecks Moor (947014), their old

Lead mine track (right) in Gunnerside Gill, Swaledale. Ruined building left of the beck was the peat store. The smelt mill was below the lime kiln, whose mouth is in the foreground.

nature lost in the maze of recent tracks made during the reworking of old spoil. In a mile they reach workings in the Hard Level Gill, where the many ruined buildings of Old Gang comprise the most extensive of Swaledale's surviving lead mine complexes. Among the structures is a small neat stone bridge (973006). Back in Gunnerside Gill a good green track climbs from near Bunton Level towards Winterings Edge, serving a limekiln at 945997, and continuing south-eastwards at a high level to the farms at Winterings (947993), eventually descending steeply as a good track to Lodge Green at the eastern end of Gunnerside village.

Coal Roads

Coal mining in the Yorkshire Dales can be documented as far back as the end of the thirteenth century, in the 'New Forest' of Arkengarthdale, belonging to the Lords of Richmond Castle. It was then used domestically, and by blacksmiths and armourers, but in later times — until early in the present century — apart from domestic use it went to fuel the smelting mills of the lead industry. Collieries at Tan Hill were supplying coal to Richmond Castle in 1384, and from the seventeenth century to Appleby, Brough, Kirkby Stephen, Penrith, Hawes and most of upper Wensleydale, and Swaledale. Workable seams of coal occur at the base of the Millstone Grit which caps the higher fells, with lesser seams among the strata of the Yoredale Series of rocks. The best coal went for domestic use, the poorer quality — usually in the Yoredale Series — had a ready sale to the limeburners about 1760-1850, and the smelt-mills. Indeed, many collieries were little more than purely local pits supplying farms and limekilns nearby. The more commercial ones were associated with tracks along which the coal was transported greater distances.

Initially, packhorses were used, but small carts were slowly being introduced about 1790. Adam Sedgwick, the eminent geologist, born at Dent in 1785, remembered as a boy:

> Some roads in Dent so narrow that there was barely room for one of the little country carts to pass along them....I remember too when the carts and the carriages were of the rudest character; moving on wheels which did not revolve about their axle; but the wheels and their axle were so joined as to revolve together. Four strong pegs of wood, fixed in a cross-beam under the cart, embraced the axle-tree, which revolved between the pegs, as the cart was dragged on, with a horrible amount of friction that produced a creaking noise...called 'Jyking'. The friction was partially relieved by frequent doses of tar, administered to the pegs from a ram's horn which hung behind the cart. Horrible were the creakings and Jykings, which set all teeth on edge while the turf-carts or coal-carts were dragged from the mountains to the houses of the Dalesmen in the Hamlets below.

Sedgwick wrote this in 1868, adding that he thought no young person then alive in Dentdale would have seen such carts. He also thought that, 'our power of transport, to be perfect, only wants a better line of road', and admitted to regretting that 'Dent has lost the picturesque effect of its trains of packhorses'.

Dent's coal came from the Garsdale collieries which extended over an area of about one square mile around Cowgill Head. Many old shafts are scattered over the moorland on both sides of the Galloway Gate, linked to it by short stretches of green track. To the south-west, Fountains Fell, between Malham and the head of Littondale, has extensive coal seams a short way beneath its Millstone Grit cap. These were worked at the end of the eighteenth century, and by 1810, after many shafts had been sunk, a road was constructed to replace the various packhorse tracks down from the summit plateau. A colliery account for that year shows the payment

To Edward Watson, to Banking and Making the road to the new pit 114 days at 3/- per [day]   £17.2s.0.

Fountains Fell colliery was worked for a number of years, producing 900-1,000 tons of coal a year, that is 8,000-11,000 packhorse loads annually, carried down the road, now used as part of the Pennine Way, between 'Old Pits' on Fountains Fell (8867720) and the Malham-Arncliffe road on New Pasture (885692). From there the coal road runs south-

Coke oven, about 1810, on the summit plateau of Fountains Fell, near Malham.

westwards across Knowe Fell, identified now as a footpath, for one mile, when it turns off towards the south as another, poorly-defined path, crosses a minor road north of Higher Tren House (879666), and follows the Malham road south-eastwards, past the restored chimney of the Malham Smelt Mill. This was smelting lead-ore from a number of small, local mines from 1815, finally ceasing in 1910, and in its early years used much coal from Fountains Fell.

Calamine, an ore of zinc which, when calcined and subsequently combined with granular copper produced brass, was mined at Pikedaw Caverns (875639) in the late eighteenth and early nineteenth centuries. Calcining — a roasting process —needed coke, brought from Fountains Fell, for which the coal road, already bringing fuel to the lead smelting-mill, was then routed from Langscar Gate(887648) westwards and south-westwards to the 'Calamine House', the calcining building near the mine. Later, a larger Calamine House was built at the northern end of Malham village, now a private house, and the raw materials brought there, down the old Settle-Malham road. The coal road itself continued down the line of the present motor road to the west of Malham Cove into the village. The calamine was sent on to Cheadle, Staffordshire, for making into brass, and after the westwards extensions over the Pennines of the Leeds and Liverpool Canal in the 1790s, Malham calamine was carried in wooden casks by packhorses through Airton to the canal wharf at Gargrave.

Around Tan Hill

The Tan Hill coal seam was worked over a large area astride the North Yorkshire-Cumbria-Durham border, centred roughly on Tan Hill (897067), and almost wholly above 1,600ftOD. Tan Hill Inn probably owes its presence to the long tradition of coal-mining in that very remote area, and the roads which converge nearby would all have been used by packhorse traffic carrying coal away, across Stainmore to the north, to Arkengarthdale and Swaledale, and westwards over the watershed to the Vale of Eden. The track from Sleightholme in the Greta valley has already been described. At least six other routes converge on Tan Hill, three of them now modern roads, the other three moorland tracks.

One of these, leading south-westwards to Raven Seat and Birkdale has become indistinct through lack of use, but it is still marked as a footpath on the OS maps. Its start can be identified 250yd down the Keld road from Tan Hill, where a sketchy track leads off to the south-west near the second stone post by the roadside. It is then lost in peat hags, but can later be picked up climbing the south side of Thomas Gill (880055) from where it gradually descends past a new plantation to the hamlet of Raven Seat (863034).

Only two houses are now occupied at Raven Seat, but before the middle of the eighteenth century at least seven families lived there, sufficient to justify a public house and a small chapel. These have gone but a good

Coal roads near Tan Hill ('Pitt Houses') surveyed by Anthony Clarkson, 1836.

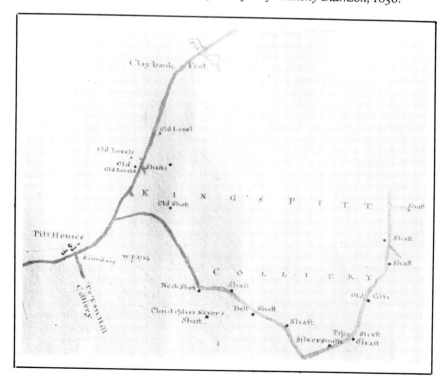

Packhorse bridge at Raven Seat, upper Swaledale.

packhorse bridge survives, used by packhorse trains with their loads of coal or other goods being taken to or from Kirkby Stephen. From Raven Seat the line of the jagger road is lost in enclosed fields, to be picked up as a good green track above Friar Side, keeping to the north side of Ney Gill, climbing steadily westwards towards a corrugated iron shed used by shooting parties. This old road from Raven Seat to Birkdale is mentioned in Quarter Sessions records of 1788 as being in a poor state of repair. It was then 8yd wide, and described as 'a certain common and ancient highway leading from the market town of Kirkby Stephen... towards the village of Raven Seat... for all the liege subjects of our lord the King... on horseback or on foot... and to drive their cattle at will.' Two years later £50 was to be spent on repairing it, and the road was then stated to be 'a Pack and Prime Way from Kirkby Stephen to Barnard Castle.' Its route then would have taken it to Tan Hill, picking up the Sleightholme track across Stainmore towards Bowes.

At 839028 a signpost marks 'Coast to Coast Path', which, from Raven Seat, the old road has now become. This unofficial long-distance path heads north-west at this point for Nine Standards Rigg, but the packhorse route continues westwards indistinctly, to join the motor road up Birkdale north of Birkdale Cross (834025). This slender pillar of rough stone is sited above the road and is easily visible from some distance along the old route; almost certainly it served as a marker. A short way down the Keld road is Crook Seat, named on old maps as Crook Seal. Now a barn, it was an inn, but ceased to be occupied about the middle of last century.

The modern road from Keld continues the line of the old track from

Raven Seat up Birkdale to the North Yorkshire/Cumbria boundary at Hollow Mill Cross (812041), but no cross exists now. In 1664 a packman, John Smith, was murdered nearby, but there was insufficient evidence to bring the felon to justice. Smith's body was apparently discovered in one of a series of limestone shake-holes north of the road, their name — Blue John Holes — probably commemorating the tragedy, and indicating that his pack contained blue knitted stockings being taken from Swaledale to Kirkby Stephen. The county boundary is marked by two roadside stones over 100yd part, one inscribed 'Township of Nateby 1856', the other 'Hamlet of Birkdale County of York'. Beyond the watershed the road descends Tailbrig into the village of Nateby two miles from Kirkby Stephen.

Returning to Tan Hill and its coal tracks. Immediately opposite the inn a 'Pennine Way' sign points southwards towards Keld. This popular long-distance footpath has adopted the old packhorse way over Tan Hill Moss, Lad Gill Hill and Low Frith, passing close to open shafts of some former pits (895055). Initially stony, it soon becomes a peaty track, crosses Lad Gill by a ford, and for a short way at Low Frith is a walled lane. Keeping well to the east of, and high above, West Stonesdale, it descends by Pry Hill as a walled lane, dropping steeply to the River Swale east of Keld. Until the great storm of 1899 which washed away many small bridges in upper Swaledale, there was a small packhorse bridge over the river, with a

Boundary stone near Hollow Mill Cross, Upper Swaledale.

low arch and low parapets, but this was replaced by a wooden footbridge (896011).

Coal for Keld would have been carried up the steep holloway (now the Pennine Way) into the village. Packhorses taking coal to the Beldi Hill smelt mill a mile east (909006) would keep north of the river, crossing East Gill Bridge, and follow the good track contouring above the Swale gorge. At Stony Hill one branch climbs to Crackpot Hall, now in ruins, and Swinnergill, with an eastward extension to the smelt mills in Gunnerside Gill, while the more important route for Beldi Hill heads south-eastwards. Domestic coal for Swaledale would then be carried down the east side of the valley, now a grassy track to Calvert Houses opposite Muker, picking up the Corpse Road from there.

150yd east of Tan Hill Inn, where the Arkengarthdale road is marked on the map as 'Long Causeway', a green road leads south-eastwards to King's Pit Colliery. It is known that coal from this pit was sent to Lord Wharton's smelt mills in lower Swaledale in the seventeenth century, and subsequently to the Old Gang smelt-mill. A road serving King's Pit is clearly shown on Clarkson's survey of 1833, for the Reeth-Tan Hill Turnpike. To the north of King's Pit a good packhorse track, clearly visible across Mirk Fell Edge, continues to the ruins of William Gill Houses (920057), site of another colliery, then heads up the east side of William Gill before following the contours eastwards as a green track. It follows firm, dry ground along the top of Annaside Edge for almost two miles to the head of Punchard Gill (946044) where coal was worked extensively. As a green track it crosses a stone bridge, follows the north side of the gill to Tongue End, passing old lead mines on the way, fords Little Punchard Beck and heads, indistinctly, directly eastwards to join the turnpike near Whaw Gill Bridge (980044), thus avoiding the toll house at Punchard three-quarters of a mile up the road.

The other roads from the Tan Hill colliery have become motor roads, that down Arkengarthdale having been turnpiked in 1770, when one of the reasons for its justification was to exploit the Tan Hill coal more easily. Tan Hill colliery's long years of productivity were responsible for many miles of coal roads radiating from there.

Seams of the Tan Hill coal were extensively worked on the southern flanks of Great Shunner Fell (848973) with access tracks up Cotterdale and Fossdale, north-west of Hawes. A metalled road up Cotterdale ends at the hamlet (833941) and a footpath beyond crosses the beck and zigzags up a hillside now afforested, to former pits a mile to the north. Cotterdale pits are also reached from Hardraw, initially by the Pennine Way route up Pen Lane by the side of the school. In less than a mile this forks, the western branch following the contours along the side of the spur to the pits, the Pennine Way itself keeping to the crest of the ridge, and another path following the desolate flanks of Hearne Beck to the West Pits in Fossdale. The 1:25,000OS map refers to this as 'Hearne Coal Road', and at the beginning of this century it was in so much use that it was as white as a modern quarry track. The various stone cairns, curracks or beacons so prominent in the landscape were probably marker points to identify the sites of the pits, for miners walking to work when mist shrouded the fells, or when they were blanketed by snow.

South of Wensleydale, on the long ridge between Walden and Coverdale, Fleensop was a well-known colliery which supplied coal to Coverdale. A lane from Gammersgill, (055830) walled at first, but rising south-westwards over unenclosed moor by Fleemis Gill, leads to Fleensop, where it is joined by a moorland track from the village of Carlton. The shafts and levels of Fleensop colliery lie south-west of the remote hamlet, astride a coal and packhorse road between Walden and Horsehouse.

Walden to Horsehouse

From above Whiterow Farm (016838) the track rises steadily as a green lane, climbing more steeply to a gate in the moor wall. Beyond this it is slightly sunken, then becomes a 6-10ft wide track across cotton-grass moor, greener than its surroundings. At a boundary wall it swings southwards with heather moor on Snod Side. Where it leaves the wall there is a good boundary-stone with the letters 'F' on its eastern face and 'W' on the western one, identifying Fleensop and Walden. For almost a mile, the track shows signs of stone metalling beneath the surface, and beyond an impressive ravine, passes extensive remains of old workings on Fleensop Moor. Coal and lead were mined here from the seventeenth to the nineteenth century, and the track from Walden would have been used by packhorses to carry lead-ore to the smelt mill at West Burton. On Fleensop Moor occasional causeway stones suggest that the track was sufficiently important to have been metalled.

The track branches about 600yd south-east of the ford at the head of Fleemis Gill, one arm going eastwards as a grassy moorland path, and dropping steeply to Horsehouse in Coverdale, entering the village by the school. The other branch takes a south-south-east line, crossing open moorland, and becoming less well-defined as it descends steeply to the hamlet of Bradley, 1¼ miles farther up the valley. In the middle of last century there was an inn at Bradley to cater for the packhorse traffic crossing from Walden, as well as that climbing over the watershed from Kettlewell in Wharfedale.

Another track across Carlton Moor used by packhorses, though not necessarily carrying coal, climbs steeply from near Cote Farm (018855) as a walled, winding lane, above the south side of Thupton Gill, to become a narrow path over the moor to Howden Lodge, then as a well-defined track becoming a walled lane into the village of Carlton.

Above Redmire

The largest area of coal workings in the Dales extends over nearly three square miles of lower-level moors between Wensleydale and Swaledale, roughly within the triangle enclosed by the Redmire-Grinton, Redmire-Bellerby, and Grinton-Bellerby roads. The area is named on Jefferys's map

as 'Coalpit Moor'. Pockmarking the landscape are hundreds of bell-pits and shafts of the Grinton Moor, Redmire Moor, Preston Moor and Bellerby Moor collieries. All except the Grinton pits were within the royalties of the Bolton estates, with records of coal-working going back to 1569. In the first half of the seventeenth century great quantities of coal were carried from these collieries to alum works at Guisborough in Cleveland, and in the late eighteenth century leases on the Bolton estates collieries were taken by principal lead mine operators at Grassington. Coal was worked over most of this area until the late nineteenth century by when the development of the north-eastern railway network brought the better.quality Durham coal to Richmond and Wensleydale. The area of old workings is a tangle of tracks and paths, but most of the main routes by which coal was taken beyond the area are now modern roads. However, one section of unchanged road leaves the Richmond-Lancaster turnpike at a crossroads above Preston (074920), goes northwards towards Broomber Rigg, initially as a walled lane, then as an open track, stony-surfaced, bearing westwards past the ruins of Cobscar smelt mill (059931) to join the Grinton road above Redmire quarries. From Broomber Rigg and from the smelt mill well-defined tracks lead northwards on to Preston Moor where there is a concentration of old pits.

A similarly unchanged road by which coal was carried eastwards to Richmond leaves the Grinton-Bellerby road on Preston Moor at a

Boundary stone on Old Road, Grinton Moor.

distinctive boundary stone (074945), and as a green track through heather follows a boundary wall eastwards and north-eastwards, down the north side of Stainton Moor Beck to Stainton, Downholme and along the crest of Downholme Moor to Hudswell and Richmond. This section is now a surfaced road. Both this and the Cobscar road are shown on Jefferys's and Tuke's maps, but unfortunately the moors east of the Grinton-Bellerby road are now Ministry of Defence land, so the track to Stainton cannot be followed. However, tracks associated with the coal and lead mines on Redmire Moor, and East Bolton and Whitaside Moors to the west, including the very distinct track through Apedale (042941-983964), can be explored.

Swaledale, from the ruins of Crackpot Hall, near Keld. Pollution from lead-mining activities in the eighteenth and nineteenth centuries has made farmland nearby untenable. An old coal road followed the left bank of the River Swale down to Muker.

Drovers' Roads

If packhorse ways were one type of trade route the droving traffic formed another. Although we do not know for certain when droving began we can be reasonably sure that in prehistoric times herds of livestock were moved from one grazing area to another. It is probable that 'British Trackways' marked on Ordnance Survey maps, sometimes called 'ox droves' or 'drift ways', were ancient drovers' routes, and, as we have seen in Chapter 1, they could be regarded as the earliest roads, preserved for us through continued usage by herds of oxen and sheep, and successive generations of drovers and traders.

Droving became important during the Middle Ages, reaching its peak early last century, in the decades before the building of railways resulted in the quicker and more convenient movement of cattle over long distances. A late twelfth-century charter refers to a road called the Galwaithegate (the Galloway Road) running southwards from Low Borrow Bridge (610014) near Tebay in the Lune valley, and continuing southwards to Kirkby Lonsdale. A letter of safe conduct, in 1359, refers to two Scottish drovers, with three horsemen and their servants, travelling through England with horses, oxen, cows and other merchandise.

By the sixteenth century, when towns and cities were becoming too large for their meat supplies to be met by the products of their immediate countryside, and the meat demands of the Navy were also increasing, droving increased in importance. Drove roads were an integral part of the road network of the country, and cattle often shared them with other trade traffic such as waggons and packhorses. In the reigns of Mary and Elizabeth I drovers had become so numerous that the authorities decided to control them through Statutes licensing 'badgers of corn and drovers of cattle', specifying that a drover must be at least 30 years old and a married householder, and that his licence was to be renewed annually. Anyone contravening this was liable to be fined five pounds. One outcome of this Statute was that it gave status to the true drover, whose profession became recognised as an honourable one to such an extent that drovers not only controlled large-scale movements of livestock but carried important messages, and, more significantly, became travelling bankers.

It was quite usual for a drover to have over £1,000worth of cattle in his charge, and it was quickly realised that this 'money on the hoof' was far less vulnerable to highway robbers than its equivalent in guineas carried in saddlebags. Hence, a merchant who may need to pay a bill in some other town or city on a drover's route would pay him, and the drover would keep the money at home and settle the account at the end of his journey from the proceeds of the sale of his beasts. Drovers and the men they dealt with often used promissory notes or bills of exchange, which constituted a system of credit. These notes often remained in circulation for some time before encashment, being used in the same way as bank-notes later. It was a Welsh drover, David Jones, having married into wealth, who established the Black Ox Bank at Llandovery, its promissory notes carrying an engraving of a black ox. These were only accepted by the bank from sound customers and were useless to thieves. London agents were appointed to cash them; the business grew, more branches were opened, and the bank was taken over by Lloyds in 1909.

At some of the more important fairs and markets temporary booths were set up by banks where bills and promissory notes could be exchanged. At Malham Moor Fair the notes were issued by the Craven Bank and bore an engraving of a large fat ox against a view of Bolton Abbey, while at Middleham Moor Fair the Wensleydale and Swaledale Banking Company circulated their own five-pound notes which had engravings of Dales beauty-spots.Middleham Bank is said to have given its customers a nip of whisky! A law passed in Queen Anne's reign forbade any drover from declaring himself bankrupt as a means of escaping financial obligations. An earlier law of Charles I's time prohibited him from Sunday droving, presumably for the good of his soul rather then out of any consideration for his beasts, which, in any event, were rarely driven more than a dozen miles a day. With herds of up to 200 cattle or 2,000 sheep, progress would inevitably be slow and laborious. Herds would be split so that one drover would have up to 50 cattle or 500 sheep, and would be helped by dogs. It is known that, if drovers had to spend a day or two conducting business at the end of their journey their dogs would often be sent home by themselves, probably stopping for food at the same inns used by their masters on the outward trip. Early last century drovers were paid three to four shillings a day —about twice as much as a farm labourer — out of which they had to pay their own lodging expenses, up to ninepence a night in winter, half this in summer; they were also allowed ten shillings for the return journey.

The profits from droving are hard to evaluate. Costs and returns varied with the time of the year and the conditions of the beasts. On an average drove of 200 cattle they could be between 2s 6d and 5s a head early last century. It was obviously in a drover's interest to do his best to ensure that his beasts were in good condition by the time they reached the big markets

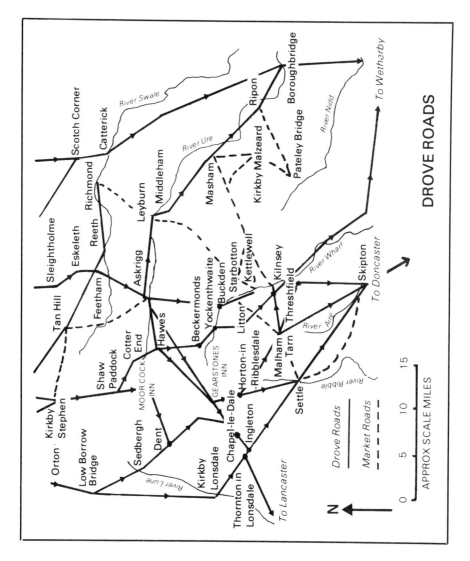

in the Midlands or Smithfield, and since several hundred miles had to be covered the animals' feet were shod. Cattle have cloven hoofs, involving eight small shoes for a complete shoeing, which, by the middle of last century, cost one shilling per beast. Sheep were not shod, and geese had to walk through a mixture of sand, sawdust and tar. Geese-driving was, of course, a shorter-distance affair, and some Dales-folk today can still recollect their being driven — in one case told to me — from Wharfedale over the Stake into Wensleydale for Hawes market. At Threshfield, in Wharfedale, the door of a barn near the road bridge over the beck displays a variety of iron horse and cow shoes, made by a blacksmith in nearby Grassington for use during droving days.

It has been estimated that, at the height of the droving trade around 1800 some 100,000 cattle a year were annually driven from Scotland into

England, and the greater proportion of these probably passed through the area of the Dales. A Malham schoolmaster, Thomas Hurtley, writing of Great Close on Malham Moor in 1786, states 'this Great Close pasture (732 acres)... was for many years rented by Mr. Birtwhistle of Skipton, the Craven Grazier, and on which you might frequently see 5,000 head of Scotch cattle at one time. As soon as these were a little freshened, notice was dispersed among the neighbouring markets and villages that a FAIR would be held in this field on a particular day.... As soon as these Lots (often several hundred) were disposed of, a fresh Drove succeeded, and besides Sheep and Horses frequently in great numbers, Mr. Birtwhistle has had Twenty Thousand head of Cattle on this field in one summer. Besides Mr. Birtwhistle... there are now several other Graziers who go to the Highlands on the same business, and vast quantities indeed are fed in every part of Craven for the Markets in the populous Towns both in Yorkshire and Lancashire.'

Contemporary with this Great Close Fair on Malham Moor was a smaller one on Boss Moor, four miles to the south-east, where large herds bought at Great Close were resold in smaller quantities to local farmers with less pasture to feed them. The former ale-house on Boss Moor, the Waste Inn, and another on Great Close, have both vanished, but radiating tracks help to pinpoint their sites.

Drovers tended to stick to familiar, well-defined routes known to have overnight stopping-places, lodgings, inns, overnight pastures and stances. The routes followed were usually wide, even though drovers preferred

Road menders on the Askrigg to Muker road, at the top of Oxnop Gill, from Walker's *Costume of Yorkshire, (1814).*

their beasts to move gently in columns rarely more than three abreast, being easier to control that way. Until Enclosure days (1770-1830) drove roads were unwalled and unsurfaced; many still survive as green lanes between walls of Enclosure date. Where subsequent surface metalling has been added the existence of a wide grass verge provides evidence of a former droving use. Sometimes Roman roads were followed; upland routes were preferred to valley ones because they kept away from farmland and enclosed fields. Routes altered through time, perhaps because of the decay or rise of markets, the enclosure of former open country, or the introduction of new turnpike roads with their attendant and disliked tolls.

Drovers' roads took the best routes available to them, twisting and turning with the lie of the land, easily distinguished from those new roads made at the time of Enclosures which tended to be much more straight. In the area of the Yorkshire Dales they tend to be orientated from north to south, unlike most packhorse and market roads whose inclination is more east-west, and along the valleys.

Evidence of the known routes followed by the drove roads comes from a variety of sources, which, with the physical evidence on the ground, enables an overall picture to be built up. Documentary evidence such as details of fairs attended by drovers is useful, as are the accounts of travellers who met with drovers on their journeys. In 1792 the Hon John Byng (later Lord Torrington) was crossing the Dales from Askrigg to Ingleton by the then recognised route of the new Richmond to Lancaster Turnpike which itself followed the Roman road from Bainbridge over Wether Fell and Cam Fell, down to the ford over Gayle beck (786804), to stop awhile at the inn at Gearstones, a predecessor of the present late nineteenth-century building. His diary records the occasion:

> I was much fatigued by the tediousness of the road whereon we met two farming men, with whom we conversed about the grouse, and their abundance. Crossing a ford, Mr. Blakey led me to a public house — called Grierstones, the seat of misery, in a desert; and tho' filled with company, yet the Scotch fair held upon the heath added to the horror of the curious scenery: the ground in front crowded by Scotch cattle and the drovers; and the house cramm'd by the buyers and sellers most of whom were in plaids, fillibegs etc. The stable did not afford hay. The only custom of this hotel or rather hovel, is derived from the grouse shooters, or from two Scotch Fairs; when at the conclusion of the days squabble the two Nations agree in mutual drunkenness; the Scotch are always wrap'd up in their plaids — as a defence against heat, cold or wet; but they are preventions of speed or activity; so whenever any cattle stray'd, they instantly threw down the plaid, that they might overtake them.

Later he records that at Ingleton 'I saw vast droves of Scottish cattle passing to the south.'

An old Arkengarthdale man has recollected that, even in the last decade of the last century there were still 'vast droves of cattle and sheep coming over the Stang and Tan Hill tracks from the border of Scotland.' Apparently they either continued down the dale to Richmond or crossed the moor southwards to the fairs at Askrigg, Leyburn or Middleham. Documentary evidence supporting the route to Askrigg comes from the accounts of Edward Broderick, a farmer at Summer Lodge (964956) on the south side of Swaledale:

> July 1848. Received of a Scotsman for 137 Galway cattle one night on Sumside pasture £2.5.0., also the same month 105 bullocks on the moors 15s. Received of Mr. Johnson for Gimmer Hoggs [young sheep] on the moor for two nights £1.16.0.

The evidence of place- and field-names, though not always reliable, sometimes gives a clue. Galloway Gate in the Lune valley has already been referred to, but the Galloway Gate above Garsdale and Dentdale is equally significant, though whether it comes from the breed of packhorse ponies using it, or the Scotch cattle driven along it is debatable. Scot Gate is the name for part of a lane above Conistone in Wharfedale, on an ancient route to the head of Nidderdale. The orientation is not typical of Dales' drove-roads, although for Scotch cattle coming down the eastern side of the area it would be on a route leading to Malham Moor by way of Mastiles Lane.

Overnight halts, usually 6-12 miles apart, offer further evidence. Ideally these would be inns with pasture available for grazing, and although inn-names may suggest a former association with the Scottish droving trade it must be remembered that inns do sometimes change their name. The only 'Drovers' Inn' names in our area are both on the south-eastern edge — at a crossroads near Bishop Thornton (268638), and south-west of Kirkby Malzeard (210720).

Galloway Gate, above Garsdale, looking south — a coal road, a packhorse road, and a drovers' road.

'Drovers' — near Bishop Thornton, Ripon.

Perhaps the strongest evidence comes from the location of cattle fairs. These, which were far more numerous than is generally thought, played not only an important part in the economic and social life of the country, but also in the droving trade. Those in the Dales area which provide evidence for routes taken by drovers were at Appletreewick, Askrigg, Malham Moor, Middleham Moor and Skipton. On the eastern edge of the area Boroughbridge and Wetherby were very important, while those at Appleby and Brough to the north were on the busy route southwards from Carlisle taken by many Scottish drovers.

Drove roads through the Yorkshire Dales fall into two groups: those forming the main routes from Scotland, the drovers' 'trunk roads', so to speak, and those more local ones within the Dales themselves which were linked to the main system. Drovers from Galloway, Dumfries and the Southern Uplands would converge on Carlisle and continue southwards to Penrith and Eamont Bridge, where one route kept forward to Low Borrow Bridge and Kirkby Lonsdale while the other branched south-eastwards, roughly along the line of the present A66 to Appleby. There it forked again, the eastern arm going to Brough and across Stainmore to Scotch Corner — a significant name — meeting other drove roads which had come down from Corbridge by way of Wolsingham. The other route from Appleby followed a line to Kirkby Stephen, and then through or

144

above Mallerstang towards Garsdale.

Another important route, crossing the Border at the Larriston Fells eventually followed the South Tyne valley to Alston, down Teesdale to an important stance and halt at Birkdale, continuing down the Tees to Holwick, then roughly southwards by what is now the Pennine Way and crossing the Greta by God's Bridge west of Bowes; and forward over the moors to Arkengarthdale, meeting with and crossing a route from Brough that had come by way of Tan Hill and was heading for Reeth and Richmond. Thus, Kirkby Stephen, Brough and Bowes were the northern approach points for the drove roads through the Dales, and we can consider more closely the subsequent spread of these likely routes and their links, travelling southwards.

Kirkby Stephen to Gearstones

From Kirkby Stephen the drovers' route probably kept to the west of the River Eden towards Wharton Hall and the ruins of Lammerside Castle (773047), then contoured round the eastern side of Birkett Common. The presence of fords (777045) near Round Hill might be an indication that there was a recognised track through Nateby along the line of the 1822 turnpike as far as here. A stretch of common land adjoining the river's north bank would certainly have been an ideal stance, and continues to be favoured today, not by drovers with beasts but drivers towing caravans. The drovers would remain west of the Eden probably as

Environs of Hawes, Wensleydale, from Jefferys's map of 1771.

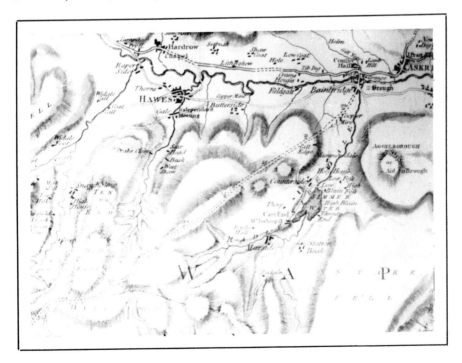

far as Shoregill (780015) or Thrang, half a mile to the south and their route then took them up the same way as that travelled by Lady Anne Clifford.

Mention has already been made of the former drovers' inn at High Dyke, used by those continuing eastwards to Hawes. An alternative route left the High Way at Hell Gill Bridge (786968) and descended the hillside by a wide grassy track to Shaw Paddock (785952). This has been a farmhouse for many years but up to the end of last century was the Shaw Paddock Inn, and in the 1820s was known as The Bull, and was a popular stopping place for drovers, probably heading for Gearstones and Ribblesdale.

A footpath from near the Lunds lane end leading directly to Garsdale Head may represent the line of the drovers' track, but what is more certain is its continuation, now as a metalled road, steeply up on to Garsdale Common, a track long known as the Galloway Gate, reaching a height of 1,760ft near Cowgill Head (796894). For much of its length this has good grass verges beside the metalled surface, and goes forward between limestone walls to the head of Monkeybeck Grains, where the motor road continues one branch, past Dent Station, to Lea Yeat in Dentdale, while the other contours southwards as a green lane round Pikes Edge. This stretch is known as the 'Driving Road', most likely a corruption of Droving Road, and goes round to the head of Arten Gill to be joined by a steep, stony lane from Stone House, in upper Dentdale.

Along most of its upland course the Galloway Gate and the Driving

An old road in Mallerstang, near Shaw Paddock, used before the 1826 turnpike to Kirkby Stephen, and possibly used by drovers.

146

The 'High Way' at High Dike, formerly a drovers' inn.

Road is joined by small, undistinguished branches linking it to the many shafts of Garsdale Colliery, identified now by their raised discs of grass-covered spoil. At the head of Arten Gill (796863) the old road from Dentdale to Hawes continues as a well-defined track down the western side of Widdale, crossing the beck at Widdale Foot by a packhorse bridge rather crudely enlarged. Drovers heading southwards would most likely have contoured the eastern side of Wold Fell, although there is no sign of a track now. However, Newby Head (795840), now a farm, is known to have been a drovers' inn, and high on the fell to its north-east is a 'Cow Pasture', from which footpaths lead to Newby Head, and to Newby Head Gate on the Dent road (791835). From nearby another track continues southwards to High Gale, Low Gale and Holme Hill and the present motor road which is at this point joined by the Roman road over Cam Fell. Gearstones is less than half-a-mile down the main road.

Upper Ribblesdale

From Gearstones, which ceased to be an inn in 1911, and which was previously the site of a busy weekly market as well as regular fairs, drovers had a choice of two routes. One followed the valley west of Ingleborough to Ingleton, heading for Lancaster and the important markets of Lancashire. The other headed down Ribblesdale to Horton where another choice presented itself. The drovers' road to Horton forded the infant River Ribble below Gearstones about 50yd above a modern footbridge (783798), and crossed rough moorland, aiming for the site of a former monastic grange at Thorns, now a ruined farm. A footpath follows its

147

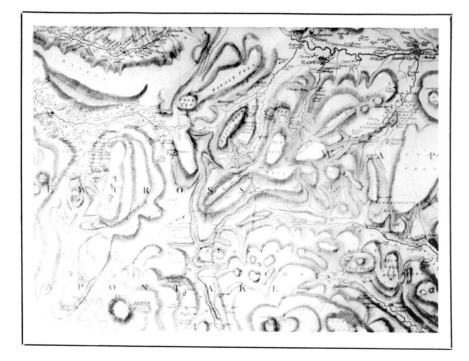

Upper Wensleydale, Garsdale and Widdale, from Jefferys's map, 1771.

course through the drumlin country east of the river to Nether Lodge, fording Ling Gill and winding over the western side of Cow Close to God's Bridge (a natural limestone arch over a small ravine) and High Birkwith (800768) once a drovers' inn. There the drove road joined the old road from Wensleydale, and followed that to Horton, entering by the Crown Hotel.

From Horton one route continued down the east side of Ribblesdale to Langcliffe and Settle, probably on or close to the line of the present motor road as far as Langcliffe, where the old route branches off near Bowerley to enter Settle by Constitution Hill at the north-east corner of the Market Place. In a letter written some years ago a Langcliffe resident recollects that, probably in the 1870s or 1880s the annual arrival of large droves of Scottish cattle was an eagerly awaited event. This old way into Settle from the north would have enabled drovers to avoid paying tolls on the new turnpike near the bridge. Similarly by continuing out of the town by Upper Settle and following the old coach road over Hunter Bark into Long Preston, another tollhouse on the Keighley-Kendal Turnpike could be avoided. Beyond Settle drovers would head for the Lancashire markets at Clitheroe, Blackburn and Preston.

Ribblesdale to Wharfedale

The drovers' route from Horton to Malham is by no means certain in its early stages. It may have climbed by Dub Cote and the limestone pastures

Gearstones, a former drovers' inn near Ribblehead.

above to cross the southern shoulder of Penyghent and drop down the eastern side to Dale Head, now a large farm with many outbuildings (840715). This was once an inn used by drovers and packmen at the crossing of two important old roads — that from Stainforth to Halton Gill and Wharfedale, and the road we are now following, which continues south-eastwards as a green lane round the western and southern sides of Fountains Fell to join the western continuation of Mastiles Lane near Westside House (848680), thence eastwards by Malham Tarn to Malham Moor and Great Close.

Beyond Great Close Mastiles Lane would be followed to High Long Ridge (937657) where a branch leads south-eastwards, crossing Malham Moor north of Bordley, and passing close to the prehistoric stone circle mentioned earlier. The lane east of this is now metalled between grass verges, and leads direct to Threshfield, picking up the line of the present motor road B6160 to Burnsall. This road up Wharfedale seems to have been created piecemeal and was not turnpiked, so drovers were not faced with the payment of any tolls. Crossing the Wharfe at Burnsall, either by a ford or by Sir William Craven's stone bridge of the early seventeenth century, recorded in 1752 as being 'a good bridge and all paved', the drovers' route headed for Appletreewick. Until the beginning of the present century the annual fair here, dating from 1310, was one of the most important in the district, held on 2 October, particularly for horses, cattle from the Highlands, and sheep from southern Scotland. During the period of the fair stock grazed land between the village and river, in a field still known as Sheep Fair Hill. A number of stone water-troughs used for

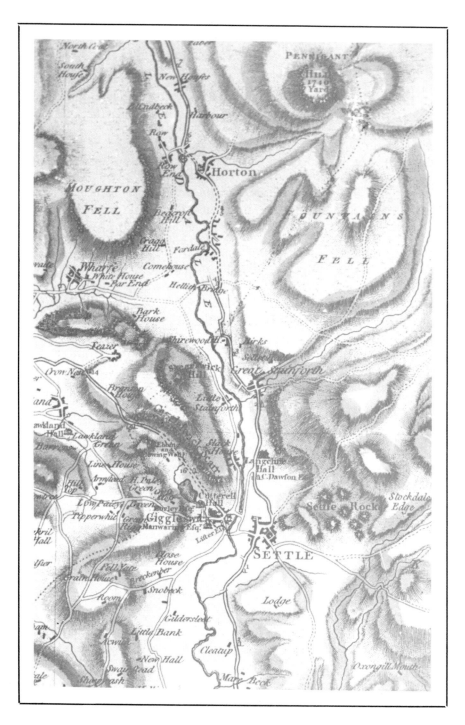

Settle and Ribblesdale, from Jefferys's map of 1771.

drinking can still be seen down a farm track called Cork Street. Beyond Appletreewick the minor road down Wharfedale's eastern side was formerly a green lane, possibly the drovers' route to the Storiths and the Bolton Bridge-Blubberhouses road at Hazlewood. An alternative would have been a higher-level way, contouring round the western slopes of Barden Fell and across Hazlewood Moor to join the Bolton Bridge-Blubberhouses roads at Pace Gate (116547), which then offered routes eastwards to Ripon or southwards to Otley, both of which would converge at Wetherby.

Other drove roads from Malham and Boss Moor almost certainly headed southwards towards Skipton, and since the Skipton-Cracoe road was not turnpiked until 1853, it is likely that the old road, one or two fields' distance to its east, may have been followed by the drovers. From Skipton, cattle not sold at the fairs or markets would be driven on to Skipton Moor by the old road, reaching the 1,000ft contour near Standard (010505), crossing High Bradley Moor and Silsden Moor to Cringles (049485), Windgate Nick and the Doubler Stones to Black Pots Farm, formerly a drovers' inn called Gaping Goose. There is a story that the lady of the inn married a Scottish drover. From Morton Moor the drovers' route descended to Bingley, well outside the area of this survey, probably heading for the important fair at Wibsey on Bradford's southern outskirts.

Bowes-Swaledale-Wensleydale

A well-attested drove road crosses Stainmore west of Bowes, crosses the River Greta by the natural limestone arch called God's Bridge (957126) and climbs Wytham Moor to Sleightholme (955102); this section from the A66 now adopted by the Pennine Way. Beyond Sleightholme its course is impossible to identify although a footpath on the map suggests it kept east of Coney Seat Hill and Mud Beck to enter Arkengarthdale at Ravens Park (973069), continuing south-eastwards to Low Faggergill where a farm track may represent its line, becoming a metalled road above Whaw, high above the Arkle Beck, crossing it at Eskeleth. In the field above the river, the first building, Plantation House, was in the late eighteenth and early nineteenth centuries a drovers' inn called Lilly Jocks, named as such on the 1836 turnpike map.

Southwards from Arkengarthdale the course of the drove road is now followed by a motor road, climbing steeply past lead mining spoil heaps to Bouldershaw House and the col between Reeth Low Moor and Reeth High Moor. It fords Bleabury Gill (993009), crosses Hard Level Gill by Surrender Bridge, and drops steeply into Swaledale at Feetham. In its course over the moors it is still an unenclosed road. However, overwhelming evidence shows that much of the valley land of Swaledale had been enclosed by the end of the sixteenth century, with the moor edge 'intaked' in early nineteenth-century days, so the drovers' way across the valley and river is not clear. Rowlith Wath (968975) between Feetham and Gunnerside is an old ford, and Isles Bridge below Low Row probably

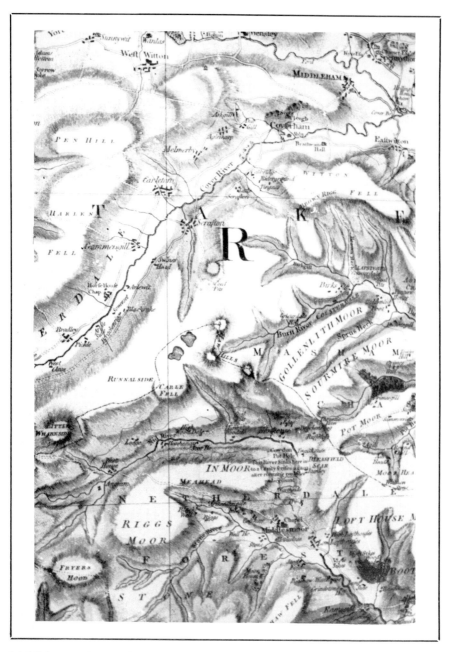

Middleham and Coverdale, from Jefferys's map of 1771.

replaces a ford.

Both crossings have lanes leading to Crackpot and Summer Lodge, so it is probable that this was the drovers' route over Summer Lodge Moor and Askrigg Common, to Askrigg and Wensleydale. This is now metalled only to Summer Lodge from where it becomes a rough moorland track for half a mile to the crest of the moor (965948) where it joins another road coming up across Whitaside from Grinton or Healaugh. The joint road, unenclosed, continues south-westwards to Askrigg.

Askrigg's Enclosure Award of 1817 shows the 'Fair Allotment' to the west of the moor road about half a mile from the village, adjoining High Straits Lane (948923). During much of the eighteenth century Askrigg's October Fair took place in the village in the small area around the Market Cross. Another fair, held in early May, subsequently in June, and eventually in mid-July, seems to have originated on Carperby Sleets, lower down the dale, about 1785. At the turn of the century it moved to Askrigg Common, was held for a short time above Gayle, near Hawes, and returned to Askrigg Common where it stayed until the coming of the railways resulted in a decline during the 1870s and 1880s.

From Askrigg drovers with their beasts crossed the River Ure either by a ford at Worton or the bridge at Bainbridge to pick up the old road over Wether Fell to Gearstones, already described, or the track via Stalling Busk and the Stake, over the moors to Buckden in Wharfedale, joining the route down this valley to Kettlewell and Kilnsey, with the option of diverting to Malham Moor or going forward to Appletreewick and Skipton.

The important fairs at Middleham Moor and Masham may have attracted some drovers to continue their journey following the Richmond-Lancaster turnpike down Wensleydale to Redmire and Leyburn, although,

'Lilly Jock's' — a drovers' inn near the foot of the Stang, Arkengarthdale.

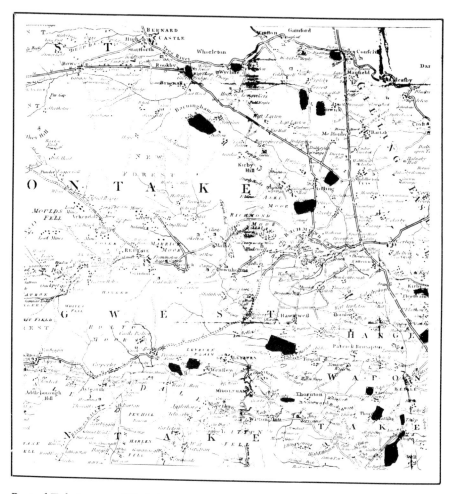

Part of Tuke's map of Yorkshire, 1787

by following a lane eastwards near Fair Hill, Askrigg, by Heugh (963917), Ox Close and Castle Bolton, three toll-gates could be avoided. Middleham's charter for a fair was granted by Ralph Neville, Earl of Westmorland, in 1389 and held in early November for three days on Middleham Low Moor, over 360 acres of common land, still unenclosed, where the public are free to wander. The November Fair continued in importance until late last century, when plaided Scottish drovers still attended with their cattle and sheep.

Masham Fair, also dating from the late fourteenth century, became in later years predominantly a sheep fair, held around the middle of September. This remained an outstanding annual event up to the days before World War I, as shown by a newspaper account in which a writer recalls how, as a child then, 'no other part of the year, except again to Christmas, did we as children look forward with such excited anticipation of delight [as 17 September]'. She remembers 'shepherds in long coats

154

Road over Oxnop, between Muker and Askrigg. The open space on the left was formerly occupied by a smithy.

and fustian trousers. . . and Irish drovers, excitable and getting drunk long before an Englishman on the same amount of liquor would have turned a hair.' Presumably the Irish had taken over the mantle of the Scottish drovers, and brought 'Cheviots and little horned Scotch sheep with fleeces almost as long as petticoats were in those days.' Presumably, too, in this area of enclosed land, they would have followed the now toll free road eastwards through lower Wensleydale.

Another well-used drove road from Brough, now a minor motor road, runs eastwards from Church Brough to Barras (846123) and climbs the south-western shoulder of Stainmore, continuing as an unenclosed road over Kaber Fell to Tan Hill (896067). This is a crossing-point of routes going back possibly to the twelfth century when castles at Brough, Bowes and Richmond, with their attendant markets, were already important centres. Such a point was an obvious site for an inn, and although the present building is not earlier than nineteenth century, there is little doubt that it had predecessors patronised by castle servants, packmen, miners, drovers, and other travellers on these wild uplands seeking shelter.

Eastwards from Tan Hill the drovers' route can only be surmised. It may have followed that taken by the Reeth-Tan Hill Turnpike in the late eighteenth century; it may have used a well-established miners' track about a mile to the south of the motor road across Arkengarthdale Moor, the two joining near Whaw (980043). This course would avoid the tollgate at Punchard. Beyond Whaw the drove road joins that coming into

Arkengarthdale via Eskeleth already described. When Arthur Young made the journey from Brough to Askrigg in 1771 it is not clear which route he followed, although his description suggests the moor road by Tan Hill, Arkengarthdale, Feetham and Askrigg Common:

> From Brough, the road, if I may give it that name, to Askrigg, lies over one continuous range of mountains, here called moors. The cultivated vallies are too inconsiderable to deserve mention. Most of these fifteen miles [it is actually nearer 25!], however dreadful the road, are tracts of very improveable land: if a good turnpike road was made from Askrigg to Brough, the first great step to cultivation would be over; for it is almost impossible to improve a country with spirit, the roads of which are impassable.

His comments did not fall on deaf ears. By the end of the century a turnpike had been created between Askrigg and Sedbergh, and that along Mallerstang to Kirkby Stephen and Brough followed about twenty-five years later.

By the eighteenth century many farms in the Yorkshire Dales were engaged in the cattle trade. It had become quite a common practice for farmers, graziers and dealers to buy young Scottish black cattle at the autumn fairs and fatten them over winter for sale the following spring. The north-south routes of the Scottish drovers have been identified and described, but there is very little evidence to define the local links by which Dales farmers' cattle approached the main routes. Place-names may occasionally provide a clue. The Norse-derived word 'wath', meaning a ford, can be suggestive, and examples of this have already been

Middleham Market Place

mentioned. When it does occur on maps it is indicative of long use, although not necessarily by drovers' beasts. However, it needs to be realised that small, quick-flowing rivers and becks could be more difficult for cattle to cross than wider, shallower ones, which could be waded or even swum without serious hazard. Walker-topographers may well like to try identifying various 'waths' as possible drovers' crossing places. Many fords so named are on local packhorse tracks, however, and would not necessarily be associated with drovers. Slape Wath (936917), Slapestone Wath (032896) east of Aysgarth and Wanless Wath (065896) north of West Witton, are examples of these in areas where Norse settlement occurred.

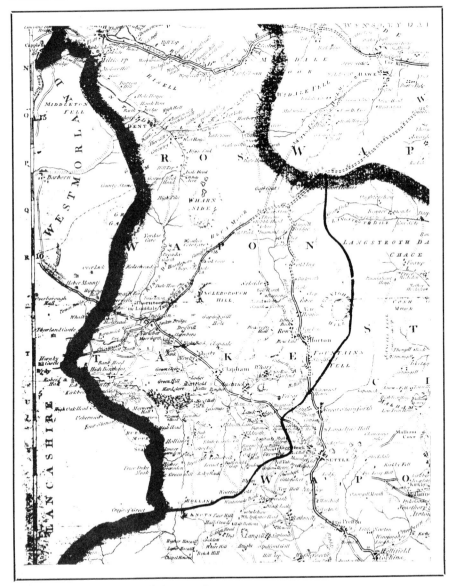

Part of Tuke's map of Yorkshire, 1787.

Turnpike Roads

It is almost impossible for us to imagine how vile were even the few roads in the Dales during the seventeenth and early eighteenth centuries. Contemporary travellers who ventured into such a remote area rarely recorded their experiences. One traveller described a road near Leeds as being 'in so great decay that travellers can hardly pass', while the historian Ralph Thoresby observed in 1680 that the waters on the roads round Leeds were very deep. In 1720 Defoe described the busy Leeds-Ripon road as 'crossing a continued waste of black, ill-looking, desolate moors, over which the travellers are guided, like racehorses, by posts set up for fear of bogs and holes, to a town called Ripley.' At the beginning of the eighteenth century fast coaches could do the 200-mile journey from York to London in four days in good weather, a week in winter months.

The decades around the turn of the century saw a period of peace and prosperity in which trade could expand and flourish. Although agricultural improvements were slow to reach the Dales, farming did thrive, encouraged by the growing markets resulting from increase in population of the peripheral towns. A woollen trade centred on Richmond, Keighley and Kendal was well established, as Defoe recognised in the early 1720s:

> . . . and as before, all was clothing and all the people clothiers, here you see all the people, great and small, a knitting, and at Richmond you have a market for woollen or yarn stockings, which they make very coarse and ordinary, and they are sold accordingly. . . . The trade extends itself also into Westmorland, or rather comes from Westmorland, extending itself hither, for at Kendal, Kirkby Stephen, and such other places in this county as border upon Yorkshire, the chief manufacture of yarn stockings is carried on. . . .

Among other manufactures, particularly in the Dales where lead ore was mined and smelted, was lead itself. In most mining areas there were recognised carriers, like Joseph Calvert of Bewerley in Nidderdale, who, at an Exchequer Deposition in 1750, stated that 'he kept a set of carriage horses [packhorses] for the carriage of lead and servants for that purpose.'

He was mainly employed to transport pigs of lead from Yarnbury, above Grassington, to Pateley Bridge. Some roads existed which did allow carts, but these were on the lower land at the eastern edge of the area.

Dr Raistrick gives a graphic account of the estimated amount of movement of horse traffic associated with the lead mines at Yarnbury. By 1760 the output of smelted lead had risen to an annual 600 tons, which naturally implied a vastly greater weight of ore and rock to be dealt with. The finished lead was carried either to Pateley Bridge or Skipton to be sold. Packhorse loads were such that a ton of lead required at least eight horses, that is, about 5,000 horse loads of lead and probably 7,000 horse loads of mined and dressed ore. It was calculated that 4,000 horse loads of coal from moor colleries above Threshfield and Thorpe were needed in the smelt mills, in addition to which stores, timber and iron rails had to be brought from various woods and foundaries. Thus, along the few miles of roads between Yarnbury, Skipton, Gargrave and Pateley Bridge, as well as in the mining field itself, at least 16,000 horse loads were carried in a normal year, over 500 for every working day. A similar situation would apply in the Swaledale-Arkengarthdale mining area, which was even more extensive, but with outlets concentrated towards Richmond, Darlington and Stockton. It is apparent that the transport problem was reaching unmanageable proportions requiring a solution. This was the construction of roads of surface quality good enough to carry waggons and carts during winter as well as in the summer, and to ensure that they were maintained.

Turnpike roads provided the answer. In 1663, the first turnpike act in England had been passed, allowing tolls to be levied to provide money to repair a section of the Great North Road in the counties of Hertford and Huntingdon. This established the important principle that those who used the roads should contribute towards the cost of their maintenance. Thirty-two years elapsed before the next turnpike act was passed. But by 1706 an Act of Parliament created a turnpike trust in which a body of private persons, mainly landowners and other prominent local people, were appointed as trustees to manage the highway between Fornhill in Bedfordshire and Stony Stratford in Buckingham. This marked the real beginning of the system of turnpike roads which over the next 140 years or so resulted in about 23,000 miles of English roads being so created and managed. Between 1700 and 1750 authorising Acts averaged about ten a year; from 1750 to 1790 this increased to forty a year, while the century's last decade saw this peak at fifty a year. Obviously this remarkable expansion made a strong contribution to the burgeoning Industrial Revolution, yet at its heart it remained an essentially local affair.

The turnpikes were not planned by government but by local landowners, traders, manufacturers, merchants, councils — anybody with an interest in improving local roads and thus promoting increased trade and travel. But, being local and generally small in scale, rarely involving more than thirty miles of road, usually much less, they suffered from lack of capital, central organisation, and sometimes from any real control. There seems to have been little co-operation between adjacent trusts, and inevitably there was opposition from farmers, drovers, carriers — especially those involved with the packhorse trade. Some traders opposed the establishment of trusts on the grounds that they believed new roads would harm their interests by changing market patterns or by raising costs through the necessary imposition of tolls.

The word 'turnpike' was used in 1477 in the Paston Letters in the context of a gate in a walled town. In its newer use it referred to the spiked tollgate at the entrance to a stretch of road controlled by a turnpike trust authorised by Parliament, where tolls could be collected from travellers and others using that road. The tolls were usually mortgaged in advance to provide the necessary capital for road improvements. Initially, turnpike trusts were intended merely to be temporary bodies to be dissolved when road improvements were concluded, after which it was hoped that the old Statute Labour system would keep them in good repair, and the original creditors repaid. Early Turnpike Acts were therefore usually limited to twenty-one years, after which time Parliament hoped that the tollgates would be removed with resultant free travel. This did not happen, and turnpike acts were almost automatically renewed. Manifestly, if a trust maintained its roads and kept out of debt it must have been well managed, thus justifying encouragement. In any case, experience showed that maintenance was as expensive as the initial improvement, so that tolls were constantly needed.

In most cases turnpike trusts did not at first make any new roads but generally took over existing ones, concentrating on improving worst sections. Most of the routes were already in existence as packhorse ways, which took little account of steep gradients, often crossing lonely, unpopulated moorlands, so that in a number of cases new roads, avoiding the steepest hills, were created. One outcome of the work of the trusts was that they reduced the multiplicity of routes into a single, usually more direct, line, consequently concentrating traffic using it, and establishing the basis of the main roads of today.

During the decades of 'turnpike trust mania' methods of road construction showed little real technical advance. Repairs were done in the old way, potholes being filled with stone from nearby quarries, ruts levelled, and drainage ditches dug. Travellers who did venture along the recently improved roads were not always impressed. In 1773, riding on the Keighley-Kendal turnpike, Thomas Pennant wrote 'I descended an exceedingly tedious and steep road' into Settle — the old Settle road over Hunter Bark. In 1793 the Hon John Byng, having stayed at Askrigg, rode south-westwards to Ingleton, climbing from Bainbridge by the Richmond-Lancaster turnpike which had exactly followed the line of the Roman road, crossing a shoulder of Wether Fell at about 1,900ft: 'The Ascent of the Mountain Cams is one of the longest, steepest and most stoney in Great Britain; for they say it is 9 miles to the summit: the first 4 are very steep.' The distances are about right, as measured from Askrigg, although the first mile is across the valley-floor of Wensleydale. Cam End is some way beyond the highest part of the road.

Turnpike roads were not popular. The ordinary countryman was content with his old road, rough though it may be, but free from tolls. Packmen, carriers and drovers resented the tolls which, increasing the costs of their journeys, reduced their profits. The new roads may have made for quicker movement but the delay at tollgates slowed it down, particularly on a drove where stock were allowed to pass only singly so that they could be counted.

Nevertheless, the creation of new roads without the use of public money is an interesting example of private enterprise directed towards the public good, and it is worth noting the method of promoting a turnpike. When a group of trustees had decided to build a new stretch of road — usually referred to as a 'diversion', they raised the capital by advertising in the newspapers and by appealing to their acquaintances, offering 4 per cent or 5 per cent interest, sometimes with ¼ per cent 'promotion money', ie commission. The security against this loan capital was the income from the tolls to be levied. Being public highways neither the road nor its diversions could be a security, nor were the trustees personally liable. Thus, a turnpike trust was like a modern joint stock company with no ordinary or preference shares, but only loans or debentures secured by the statutory right of the trustees to levy tolls during the lifetime of the Act of Parliament authorising that particular trust, which, as we have seen, may or may not be renewed.

The system of tolls, with its tollbars, tollfarmers and turnpikemen, was obviously the chief source of revenue for the trustees, but it was difficult to manage and was open to fraud. A number of trusts tried initially employing their own servants to collect the tolls, paying turnpikemen, perhaps, £10 a year for being on duty each day from 4am or 5am until late at night. It is hardly surprising that this sytem was short-lived in favour of the arrangement, gradually adopted throughout the country, of 'letting' the tolls. In this the right of toll collection was put up for auction, sold to the highest bidder who subsequently became the 'farmer' of the tolls at one or more tollgates. For such a person this was always a speculation, but often became a profitable one, for after paying the trustees and the toll collectors, any balance left over from the tolls he could keep for himself.

For the toll collectors either old buildings were converted into tollhouses or new ones were specially constructed, rarely costing more than £50 each. Erected close to the gate itself and near the edge of the road, they provided rent-free accommodation. Eventually, after their toll collecting days had ceased, they were sold, and many still survive, adapted to modern use, often inhabited. In 1835 tollhouses on the Skipton-Knaresborough road were advertised for sale by auction, that at Blubberhouses being sold for £138 and the one at Kettlesing Head for £56.

Every tollhouse was supposed to display a list of tolls charged. Those levied at the Craven Cross Bar at Greenhow, on the Grassington-Pateley Bridge turnpike, reflect the importance attached to the cheap movement

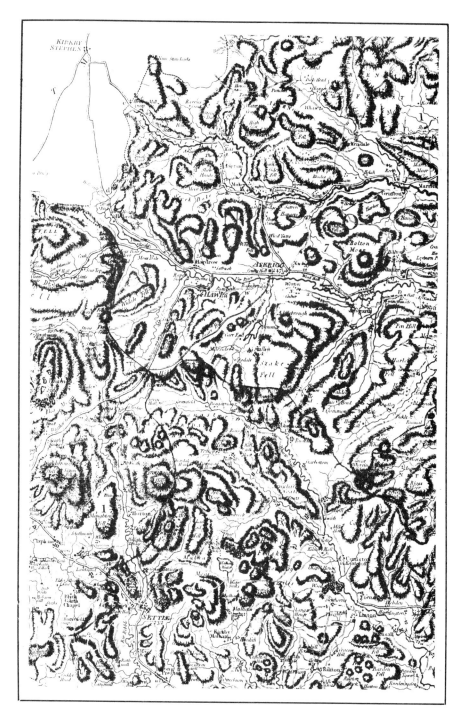

From Smith's map of Yorkshire, 1829.

of coal from local pits around 1780:

	s	d
One horse		1½
One horse cart		6
Two horse cart	1	1½
Three horse cart	1	6
Four horse waggon	1	10½
Four horse chaise	1	10½
One horse coal cart		1
Two horse coal cart		3
Four horse coal cart		6
Cattle, one score		10
Sheep and pigs		5

This makes an interesting comparison with the toll charges at Askrigg, on the Richmond-Lancaster turnpike, in 1751:

Every Coach, Chariot, Landau, Berlin, Chaise, Calash or Hearse drawn by Six or more Horses, Mares, Geldings and Mules 4s. 6d.

decreasing to

Every Drove of Calves, Hogs, Sheep or Lambs, the sum of 10d a score.

Carts carrying coals were exempt from toll, but this was so taken advantage of that by 1756 a second Act needed to be passed to impose a toll on these vehicles, while at the same time reducing toll charges on those which had earlier been so high. At this, as at most other tollgates a wicketgate provided for the free passage of pedestrians.

When the promotion of a turnpike was undertaken the inaugural meeting of trustees would be held usually at a larger inn in one of the market towns or villages on the proposed route. At a meeting of the trustees of the Richmond-Lancaster turnpike held in the Red Lion, Askrigg, in June 1751, Alexander Fothergill was unanimously appointed surveyor at an annual salary of £30, subsequently raised to £40. The first meeting of the Keighley-Kendal Trust was held 'at the dwelling-house of Robert Johnson in Settle', and although about forty gentlemen attended it was only a handful of trustees who subsequently did all the work, most of these from the Settle area.

Toll income provided money for creating and repairing roads, but parishes through which the road passed were expected to supply the labour. Justices at Highway Sessions assessed parishes for the amount they should provide, but this work could be avoided by the payment of 'composition money'. In 1768 an Askrigg Statute List assessed 115 persons liable to pay sums from 8d to 5s 4d, with twenty-four of them additionally expected to supply a horse and cart. It seems that the money was often preferred to the labour which frequently was so unskilled as to be useless, or drunk, or may even have been women and children. Far more likely it was left to the 'undertakers', partnerships of men who supplied tenders to contract at an agreed price of 5s to 7s 6d a rood (5½yd).

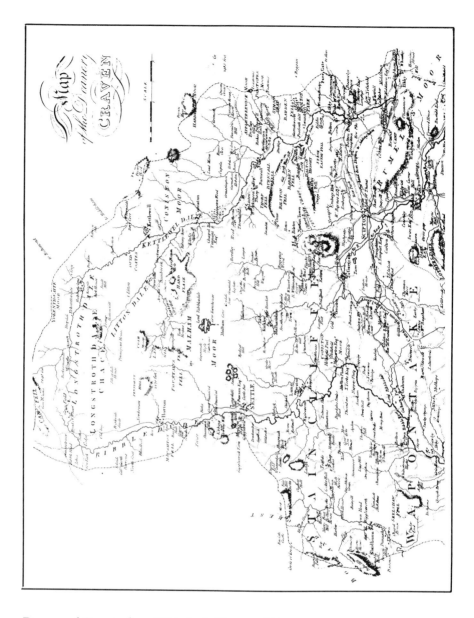

Deanery of Craven, from Whitaker's History of Craven, 1822 edition.

Strict specifications were laid down:

The road is to be casten six yards broad within the trenches, to be well formed and as near as can be Levell taking down ridges and filling up hollows. To be stoned four yards broad and ten inches thick. To be very small brocken and well covered with the best gravill and earth, conduits to be made where necessary. Three fourths of the price to be paid at the end of each sixty rood made and the residue to remain as a security for keeping the said road 12 months in repair. The said road to be completed on or before the last of September next.

Thus an agreement of June 1754 for one of the highest sections over Green Side, of the Richmond-Lancaster road.

Specifications varied from one trust to another, according to the amount of traffic expected, the type of terrain, and the money available. The Keighley-Kendal turnpike was slightly wider than the Richmond-Lancaster one, 7yd wide of which 5yd were to be maintained as a metalled track. Contracts were agreed for road repairs:

> John Birtwhistle agrees to repair the road 'from the end of his undertaking on Conistone Moor to the gate going upon Tarn Moor at 12/- per rood, to be stoned like Parson's contract, but to be first covered after stoning with the materials at the side of the road, and then with good gravel if it can be had within half a mile, if not, with a solid covering of stones to be broken'.

Although there were repeated attempts by the State to improve road construction, it was not until the late 1750s that a technical break-through was achieved, and this through a blind Yorkshireman. John Metcalf was born at Knaresborough in 1717, and, after an attack of smallpox at the age of six, he became blind. After the 1745 rebellion he set up in business as a carrier and plied the first stage-waggon between York and Knaresborough. His Scottish experiences had probably introduced him to the road-building exploits of General Wade, and he became the first engineer of the turnpike era to recognise the need for solid foundations and good drainage for the road being improved. The road between Knaresborough and Boroughbridge was particularly bad around Minskip and Ferrensby, and Metcalf repaired it so well that he was asked to advise on that between Harrogate and Knaresborough. This very boggy route had defied earlier efforts at improvement, but 'Blind Jack's' solution was both original and effective. He simply covered the bog with hundreds of bundles of heather and floated the road surface on these. The result was a firm dry highway.

Within a few years Metcalf had become the leading road engineer in northern England, and was responsible for constructing about 180 miles of roads in Yorkshire, Lancashire, Derbyshire and Cheshire. His surveying methods never varied. Using nothing but a stout staff with which to test the surface and the gradients, he walked the ground over which the route was intended, and from his observations decided on the eventual course, noting where culverts, embankments and new earthworks were needed.

'Blind Jack of Knaresborough' was responsible for only one road in the Dales, between Pateley Bridge and Grassington. Other specialist contractors were often entrusted with the responsibility of initially making up the roads. Thus, John Smith contracted in June 1758 to construct a section of the Knaresborough-Pateley Bridge road, at 8s a rood, to be 27ft wide between the ditches, with an 18ft-carriageway of stones 14in thick at the crown diminishing to 4in at the edges, all 'sufficiently covered' with gravel. Smith estimated the work to take five months. A month later he took on the Ripon-Pateley Bridge road between Pateley and Sawley Moor Top, and two years later he contracted to make up the Pateley-Greenhow road, of similar specifications, with the added proviso that 'all ascents shall be made easy and regular.' This was costed at 10s a rood. The

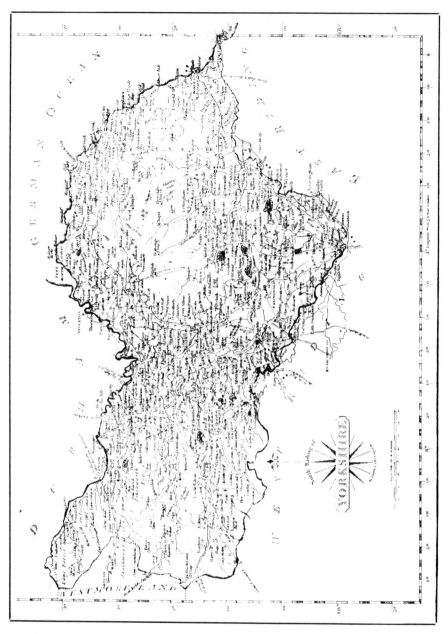

Cary's map of North Riding, 1789.

remainder of the roads between Pateley and Ripon and Knaresborough, contracted to other men, were constructed at a cost of about £3250 for the twenty-five miles, excluding bridges, tollhouses and overheads.

Compiling a list of the turnpike acts relating to the area of the Yorkshire Dales is not a straightforward matter. There is no single source concerned only with roads in Yorkshire, let alone the Dales, which were under the jurisdiction of both North and West Ridings. The national lists given in W. Albert, *The Turnpike Road System in England*, and E. Pawson, *Transport and Economy — the Turnpike Roads of Eighteenth Century Britain*, give poor indication of the detailed routes. Most turnpike acts were for only a limited number of years after which they had to be renewed. These renewals are not given in the national lists. Some turnpike acts were not actually implemented, and the roads they promulgated never came into being. The following list is therefore not the full one.

Turnpike Trusts relating to the Yorkshire Dales 1743-1853

1743	Bowes to Brough-under-Stainmore
1744	Middleton Tyas to Bowes
1751	Richmond to Lancaster
1753	Keighley to Kendal
1756	Ripon to Pateley Bridge
1758	Wetherby to Knaresborough — Pateley Bridge —Grassington
1761	Askrigg to Sedbergh
1762	Kirkby Lonsdale to Sedbergh
1765	Sedbergh to Kirkby Stephen
1770	Reeth to Tan Hill
1777	Skipton to Harrogate
1802?	Sedbergh to Dent
1836	Richmond to Reeth
1853	Skipton to Cracoe

The most important map relating to the new turnpike roads is that of Jefferys, published posthumously in 1772. The county was surveyed between 1767 and 1770, but when the initial surge of turnpike mania had just ended, so that many of the roads which were turnpiked during 1743-68 are likely to be included.

Thomas Jefferys (1732-71) became the most prolific cartographer and engraver of the eighteenth century, and was appointed Geographer to the Prince of Wales and George III. He co-operated with another engraver, Thomas Kitchin, in producing *The Small English Atlas* in 1749. Ten years later the Royal Society of Arts offered a prize of £100 for new, accurate county maps on a scale of at least one inch to one mile — much the largest scale employed to that date for maps covering a large area. Benjamin Down surveyed Devonshire and won the first £100 award, and Jefferys engraved it for him. After publishing maps of Bedfordshire, Oxfordshire and Huntingdon he surveyed the northern counties of Westmorland and Yorkshire.

Jefferys's map of Yorkshire, completed in the year he died, is on the scale of one inch to the mile, engraved on twenty plates each about 23in square, and the whole bound into an atlas. Each sheet is divided into squares five geographic miles wide, numbered 1-20 from west to east, lettered A-Q from north to south. An accompanying gazetteer lists all towns and villages on the map, giving number and letter references to the appropriate square. A key map at the front of the atlas indicates the area shown on each sheet; there are engraved plans of many towns, and views

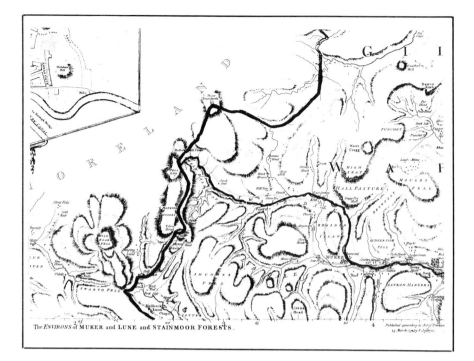

Environs of Muker and Lune and Stainmoor Forests, Jefferys 1771.

of historic buildings such as Fountains Abbey and Middleham Castle occupy large areas in corners which otherwise would have been empty.

An innovation on large-scale maps is Jefferys's attempt to represent the outline shape of hills by the use of hachuring — finely-engraved lines, thick where a hill is steep, thinning where its slope decreases. In the Dales area this strikingly shows the uplands and valleys. Turnpike roads are usually, but not always, indicated by the use of heavier lines; tollhouses and milestones are shown, although the absence of these does not necessarily mean they did not exist. The large scale allowed new features to be included — lead, iron, and coal mines, and mills. Many farms are individually named, churches and chapels are frequently shown pictorially. Inaccuracies occur, particularly with the heights of mountains — Ingleborough being given as 1,760yd, more than double its true height of 2,372ft!

It is probable that Jefferys did not penetrate to the remoter parts of the area. No road, for example, is shown beyond Whaw in Arkengarthdale although one did exist from Tan Hill — an important route serving the old coal pits there — which became turnpiked just after Jefferys completed his survey. With relatively few turnpike roads in the Dales the significant aspect of his great map is the light it throws on the pre-turnpike roads, proving that there already existed a comprehensive network of routes along the valleys, and across the hills.

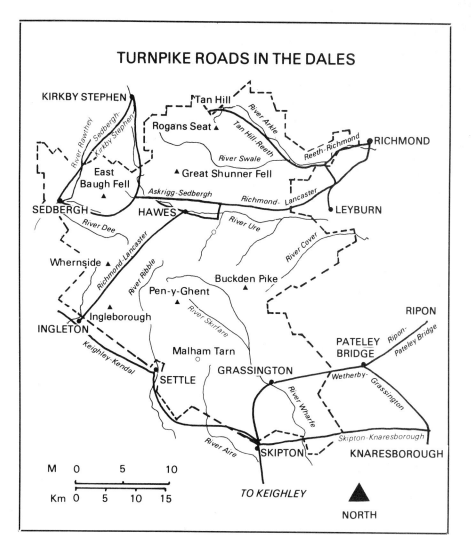

TURNPIKE ROADS IN THE DALES

KIRKBY STEPHEN

Tan Hill

Rogans Seat ▲

RICHMOND

River Rawthey

Sedbergh-Kirkby Stephen

River Arkle

Tan Hill-Reeth

River Swale

Reeth-Richmond

East Baugh Fell ▲

▲ Great Shunner Fell

SEDBERGH

HAWES

Askrigg-Sedbergh

Richmond- Lancaster

LEYBURN

River Dee

River Ure

Richmond-Lancaster

River Cover

Whernside ▲

River Ribble

Buckden Pike ▲

Pen-y-Ghent ▲

River Skirfare

RIPON

Ingleborough ▲

INGLETON

PATELEY BRIDGE

Ripon-Pateley Bridge

Keighley-Kendal

Malham Tarn

GRASSINGTON

Wetherby-Grassington

SETTLE

River Wharfe

Skipton-Knaresborough

River Aire

SKIPTON

KNARESBOROUGH

| M | 0 | 5 | 10 |
| Km | 0 | 5 | 10 | 15 |

TO KEIGHLEY

▲ NORTH

Keighley and Kendal Turnpike

The Keighley to Kendal road of 1675 followed for much of its length the Roman road described earlier. It is largely the Skipton to Clapham portion of the route with which we are now concerned, its pre-turnpike course having already been described under Ogilby's York to Lancaster road of 1675. This was confirmed in Warburton's survey of about 1718 which resulted in a new map of Yorkshire, on a scale of five miles to two inches. The state of this road may be judged from the preamble to the private Act of 1753 'for the road between Keighley in the Westriding of Yorkshire and Kirkby in Kendal in Westmorland' which was described as 'from the narrowness thereof in many places and the nature of the soil very ruinous and in great decay and, not only impassable for wheel-

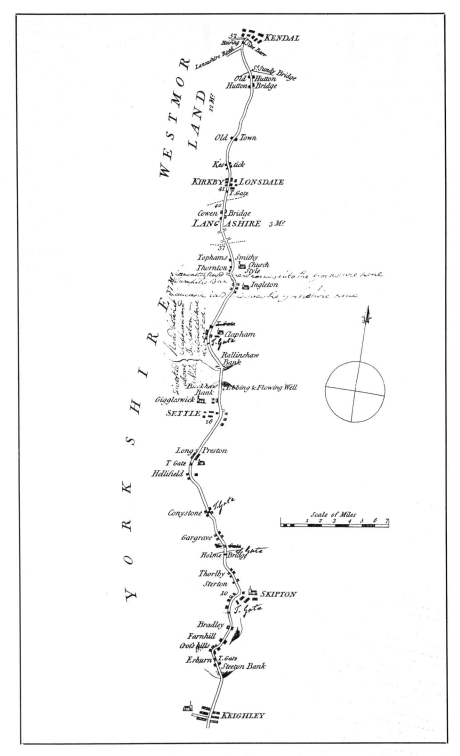

Route of the Keighley to Kendal Turnpike, from an original survey (WYCRO).

Tollhouse on the Shode Bank, Skipton, on the old Skipton to Ilkley road.

carriages, but very dangerous for travellers.'

A broadsheet, probably published in 1753, was very persuasive in its arguments addressed to all persons 'of what degree soever, having Property, Real or Personal in Craven', about the merits of the proposed Turnpike Trust:

> . . . a TURNPIKE wou'd make a better Trade and a greater Number of Passengers.
>
> The Woollen Manufacture . . . is daily increasing in Craven, for which it is better situated in every respect (save the scarcity of Coal) than any other part of the Country. Good Roads wou'd lower the Price of Coal at least one-Third, this wou'd be a prodigious advantage to all the inhabitants. . . .

In the 1753 Act the new road through Skipton followed Ogilby's route, entering from the south along the line of the present Keighley Road, continuing into High Street to the parish church, descending to Mill Bridge below the castle, and climbing north-westwards out of the town by Raikes Road. The line is now followed by a minor road over White Hills to Stirton and Thorlby, where it joins the present A65 west of the village by a boundary stone (962528). This route out of Skipton suffered from a steep gradient, but not until 1824 was the present Gargrave Road improvement introduced. This was intended to come across Water Street, making 'a beautiful entrance to the town of Skipton' over the canal (the Leeds-Gargrave section of the Leeds-Liverpool Canal was operational by 1777, including the Springs branch into Skipton), the brook and the mill-goyt, entering High Street half way down its western side. Money was raised for all but the last few hundred yards so the entry into the town took the Water Street approach, joining the old road near Mill Bridge.

West of Thorlby the 'Stoney Bitts Diversion' was made in 1828 to avoid a relatively low hill. Marked on the 6in OS map of 1846, 'the old turnpike road' is now identified as a green track crossing the shoulder of Sulber Hill, rejoining the present road at 957534.

West of Coniston Cold and across Coniston Moor the 1753 line took a more northerly course from Fogga Farm (895553), recognizable now as a field boundary and bridleway which rejoins the A65 at Switchers Farm (875559), so called because coach horses were changed there. This 1824 improvement necessitated placing the new road in a cutting, at the eastern end of which survives a milestone of that date.

The present road keeps to the 1753 line through Hellifield to Long Preston, where the house on the west side of the road beyond the bridge was the Long Preston Toll Bar. In 1823 the bar was moved and a new tollhouse built near Runley Bridge (813623) a mile south of Settle. Opposite this, at the lane corner, is a tall, square-sectioned milestone indicating 1 mile to Settle, 13 (or 15) to Skipton, and 17 to Clitheroe.

There is a similar milestone on Long Preston Green, re-erected in this position in the early 1970s, having been found some years previously buried beneath rubble in the churchyard. It records 3 miles to Settle, but that to Skipton is not clear. Almost certainly it came from the hill called Hunter Bark, to the east, which the pre-turnpike road crossed between Long Preston and Settle, following the Ogilby route described in the previous chapter. The difference between this old road and the valley route favoured by the new turnpike is most striking. Gradients were eliminated, but at the expense of spectacular and wide-ranging views.

In the 1753 Act many exceptions were introduced doubtless to placate local interests of those original Trustees who lived in or near Settle. For instance, '... no Gate or Turnpike shall be set up or erected nearer to the Town of Settle than the Town of Long Preston on the One Side and the Town of Clapham on the Other Side of Settle aforesaid. . . .' In any case, no tolls were charged on the carriage of fuel, manure, building materials, corn going to the cornmill, cloth or wool going to a fulling mill, livestock going to water, residents going to a place of worship on Sundays, to the funeral of a neighbour or to vote at an election, and carriers of the Royal Mail were also exempt.

The turnpike road, now the A65, entered Settle by a new road, called Duke Street, direct into the Market Place, then turned sharp left down Kirkgate and sharp right to Settle bridge. A bridge across the Ribble had existed here in 1498, its importance recognized by later Quarter Sessions records of the seventeenth century imposing the costs of successive repairs upon the West Riding. Following the increased use resulting from turnpike traffic it was more than doubled in width in 1783. Its old, ribbed arches are still visible on the upstream side. Unusually, Jefferys's map of 1771, still marks Kendalman's Ford as the main road, and not that over Settle bridge. In 1804 the road through Settle from the Market Place to

Tollhouse at Ingleton on the Keighley to Kendal Turnpike.

the bridge was changed to its present line along Church Street, thus eliminating two awkward corners which doubtless caused problems for coaches.

Beyond Settle the 1753 road was diverted from the old course at the top of Bell Hill, and, in effect, was constructed to by-pass Giggleswick, the line taken by the modern road. An existing lane was engineered into the most dramatic section of the whole route, to the crest of Buckhaw Brow (797658) beneath the limestone crags of Giggleswick Scar. When the poet Gray travelled eastwards along this road in 1769 he appears to have been singularly unimpressed by the scene: 'In approaching Settle the crags on the left draw nearer to our way — till we descended Brunton Brow into a cheerful valley to Giggleswick, a village with a small piece of water by its side.'

Just beyond the second milestone from Settle (794659) the original turnpike deviated from the present main road, north-westwards past Brunton House, dropped steeply to Rawlinshaw Bottom, picking up Kiln Hill Lane from Feizor, and rejoining the modern road at 780675. Brunton Lane marks this course, which was superceded by the newer road, on an easier gradient in 1792, forward to Cross Streets Inn. Unusually, the old road from Lawkland, which is rejoined here, was still favoured by travellers, according to advice offered by early nineteenth-century road books.

When Housman travelled this way about 1800 he thought that the turnpike road was 'the most eligible route for people unacquainted with

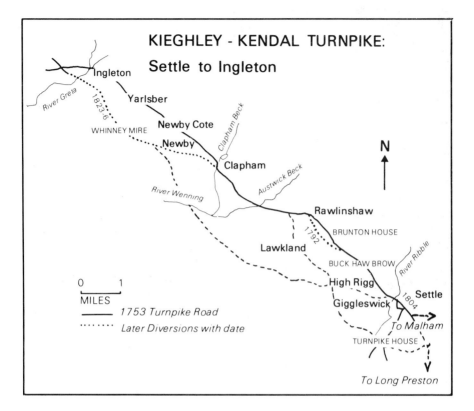

KIEGHLEY - KENDAL TURNPIKE:

Settle to Ingleton

Ingleton

River Greta

Yarlsber

1823·6

WHINNEY MIRE

Newby Cote

Clapham Beck

Newby

Clapham

N

River Wenning

Austwick Beck

Rawlinshaw

BRUNTON HOUSE

1792

Lawkland

BUCK HAW BROW

River Ribble

High Rigg

Settle

Giggleswick

1804

To Malham

TURNPIKE HOUSE

To Long Preston

0   1

MILES

——— *1753 Turnpike Road*

········· *Later Diversions with date*

the country.' Recent improvements to the A65 have straightened and widened sections of it, particularly near Austwick, where a new bridge now spans Austwick Beck. Midway between here and Clapham the Old Toll Bar still stands on the east side of the road (753685). This had been moved here in 1823 when the line of the road through Clapham was altered. The original turnpike entered the village by the New Inn, still standing, crossed Clapham Beck and turned north, keeping to the west side of the beck to the top of the village, then turned sharply left to leave Clapham by what is shown on the 1:25,000 OS map as 'Old Road', now a minor road, to Ingleton.

In 1753 two tollbars were ordered at Clapham, one at Thornber Lane end and the other at the foot of the village. Jefferys's map of 1771 shows a turnpike at the top of village by the old Ingleton road, and this is marked on the 6in OS map of 1847 as 'Old Turnpike House'. When the new deviation was planned, originally in 1792, but not implemented until 1823, it was ordered that the road to Ingleton should start 'at or near the old Lower Turnpike at the South West end of the town of Clapham.' Whereas the original road clung to the lower slopes of Ingleborough, with a number of short, steep hills and a sharp descent into Ingleton, the new road was diverted through Newby and across Newby Moor to the southern edge of Ingleton.

The 1753 road entered Ingleton from the east, joining the Richmond-

Lancaster Turnpike near the site of the present police station. Continuing down the main street to the church it then made a very steep descent to the River Greta before climbing to Thornton-in-Lonsdale and Westhouse. To avoid the steep hills of Ingleton, the 1823 deviation took the new road south of the village along the present line of the A65. This necessitated a new bridge across the Greta, near which a tollbar was set up (on the south side) in place of one on the old road in Ingleton. This tollhouse is still there (680727) contemporary with the Bridge Inn opposite built to attract the coach traffic using the new road.

The road between Ingleton and Thornton was shared with the Richmond-Lancaster Turnpike, doubtless complicating the question of tolls. The 1847 OS map shows 'Thornton Toll-gate' on this road west of the twin becks in Ingleton, and another one opposite Blue Hall, at the eastern end of the village. It must be remembered that not all tollbars were necessarily in operation at any one time. Indeed, a 1778 turnpike map shows only four working along the whole Yorkshire section of the route from Keighley, at Steeton, Holm Bridge near Gargrave, Long Preston and Clapham. A comparison of the annual tollbar lettings for 1835 — a prosperous time for the trust — shows:

Holme Bridge tolls let for £353
Hellifield tolls let for £457
Rundley Bridge tolls let for £496
Clapham tolls let for £451
Greet Bridge tolls let for £361

The Keighley and Kendal Turnpike Act expired in 1878, and the road was 'disturnpiked' and its eight tollhouses sold for a total of £520. All

175

roads disturnpiked since 1870 became 'main roads', their maintenance cost ordered to be shared equally between the district through which they ran and the county ratepayers, and in 1888 the new county councils assumed the whole cost of maintaining these 'main roads'. In 1894 the new Rural District Councils accepted responsibility for local roads other than the main roads.

In 1909 central government made the first grants to local authorities for road maintenance. The Ministry of Transport was established in 1920, and ten years later the County Councils assumed responsibility for all roads. In 1936 the former main roads, by now trunk roads, came under the ministry's responsibility, and the Keighley and Kendal Turnpike was one of these. Thus, what may have been a prehistoric route through the Aire gap, then a Roman road, then an important trade route through to the eighteenth century, then a turnpike, has become the main route from West Yorkshire to the Lake District.

Wetherby-Knaresborough-Pateley Bridge-Grassington Turnpike
There is little doubt that the successful promotion of the Keighley-Kendal turnpike encouraged traders, merchants and landowners, particularly with interests in the lead mines around Grassington and Pateley Bridge, to follow the example. By the middle of the eighteenth century it was becoming evident that roads of good enough quality to take waggons and carts in winter as well as in summer were needed.

The preamble to the 1752 Leeds-Harrogate-Ripon Turnpike Act confirms this need for all-weather roads: '. . . from the narrowness thereof and in several places the nature of the soil and many heavy carriages

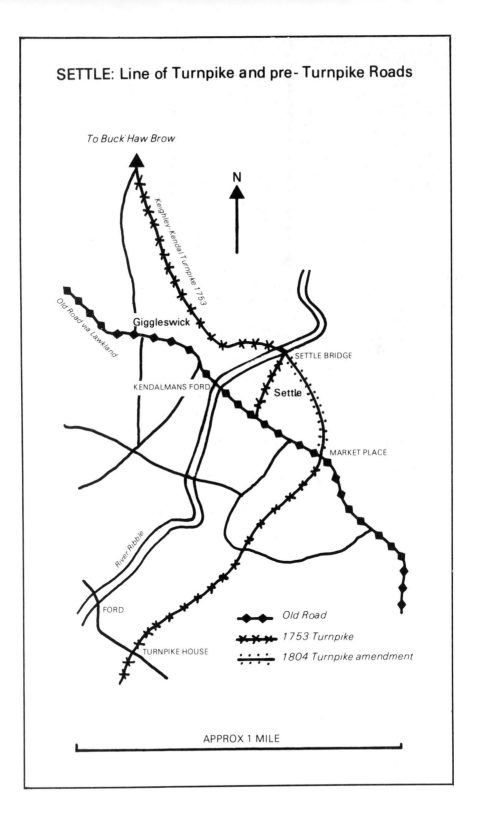

SETTLE: Line of Turnpike and pre- Turnpike Roads

To Buck Haw Brow

N

Keighley-Kendal Turnpike 1753

Old Road via Lawkland

Giggleswick

KENDALMANS FORD

SETTLE BRIDGE

Settle

MARKET PLACE

River Ribble

FORD

TURNPIKE HOUSE

◆——◆ *Old Road*

✕✕✕ *1753 Turnpike*

∙∙∙∙∙ *1804 Turnpike amendment*

APPROX 1 MILE

177

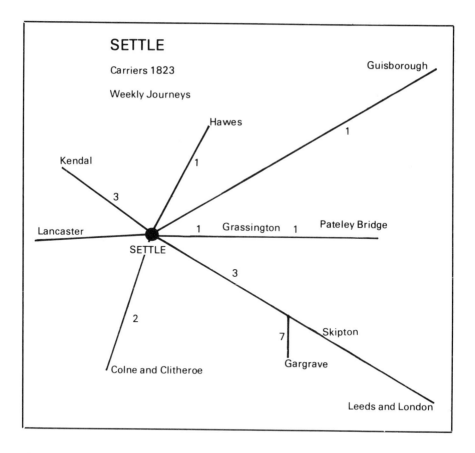

SETTLE

Carriers 1823

Weekly Journeys

Guisborough

Hawes

Kendal

1

3

Lancaster

1 Grassington 1 Pateley Bridge

SETTLE

3

2

7 Skipton

Gargrave

Colne and Clitheroe

Leeds and London

frequently passing through, the same are become very bad, especially in the winter season, so that travellers cannot pass without danger. . . .' Similar descriptions were made of the existing Ripon-Pateley and Wetherby-Pateley-Grassington roads, and in 1758 an Act was promoted '. . . for repairing and widening the road leading from Wetherby . . . through Knaresborough, Ripley . . . Pateley Bridge, Greenhaugh Hill and Hebden, to Grassington.' In a subsequent Amending and Continuing Act the Grassington-Pateley Bridge section was made separate from the rest, being almost wholly concerned with lead mining traffic between those principal markets. Because lead ore carried to smelting mills was toll-free, and the only tollgate was at Craven Cross, west of Greenhow, where the lead from the smelt mills being transported did not pass through it, this section of the turnpike was never profitable. Indeed, between 1801 and 1810 the annual income of £7-£8 a mile was insufficient to repay even the interest on the capital outlay, with road-surfacing between Pateley and Greenhow costing £160 a mile. No turnpike records of this road survive beyond 1822, and eventually its maintenance reverted to the townships through which it passed.

One outcome, if only temporary, of turnpiking the section from Pateley Bridge to Grassington was to divert Upper Wharfedale's market and trade

178

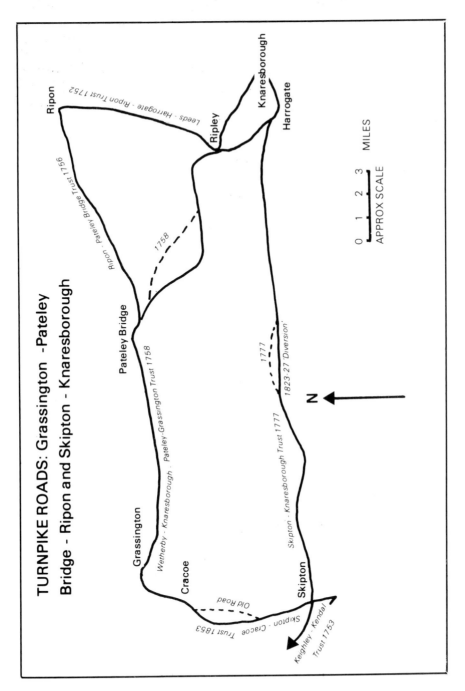

TURNPIKE ROADS: Grassington -Pateley Bridge - Ripon and Skipton - Knaresborough

Ripon

Leeds - Harrogate - Ripon Trust 1752

Knaresborough

Ripley

Harrogate

Ripon - Pateley Bridge Trust 1756

1758

Pateley Bridge

Pateley-Grassington Trust 1758

Wetherby - Knaresborough -

Grassington

1777

1823-27 'Diversion'

Skipton - Knaresborough Trust 1777

N

Cracoe

Old Road

Skipton

Skipton - Cracoe Trust 1853

Keighley - Kendal Trust 1753

APPROX SCALE

0 1 2 3

MILES

interests from Skipton to Pateley Bridge and Ripon. However, in 1777 the Leeds and Liverpool Canal was completed from Leeds to Holme Bridge, Gargrave. Wharves and warehouses at Gargrave and Skipton re-orientated trade, especially coal, there. In 1790 when the supply of local coal for the Grassington and Greenhow smelt mills was becoming irregular and

inadequate, agents of the Duke of Devonshire, who owned the Grassington mines, sought a more reliable source of supply to be brought by canal to Gargrave. The road from Grassington to Gargrave, passing through various Devonshire lands, was improved without the need for a turnpike, following a direct course through Cracoe, Hetton and Flasby. This increased mineral trade southwards from Grassington, coinciding with more cattle dealing, resulted in a revitalization of Skipton market at the expense of those of Pateley and Ripon. Wharfedale's interests once more returned to Skipton, and the importance of Gargrave eventually diminished. In 1853 part of the old road from Grassington was realigned between Cracoe and Skipton, becoming the last turnpike in the Dales, its course followed now by the B6265, while the road from Cracoe to Gargrave declined into a country lane.

Ripley to Pateley Bridge

The present B6165 follows the line of the turnpike from Ripley to Burnt Yates. At the north end of Ripley village, tucked into a hedge, a tall stone guide post with indistinct lettering is probably of pre-turnpike days, and is by the side of the old road from the village. There was a tollbar at Scarah but this was later moved to Burnt Yates, near the New Inn (253612). At the western end of Burnt Yates the original route, now a minor road, continued over Hartwith and Brimham Moor, descending past Smelthouses into the Nidd valley at Wilsill. This steep descent was one of the main drawbacks along the road; another was that, by the 1820s, it by-passed the growing industrial villages of Summer Bridge, Dacre Banks and Low Laithe. In 1823 proposals for a new line were considered, resulting in a new Act in 1826 bringing the road along the more southerly course now taken by the B6165, joining the old road at Wilsill (184646). Work was completed in 1828, when the old road ceased to be a turnpike. However, debts on the new road accumulated, while the road deteriorated, and most toll income went to repay creditors. Although the arrival of the Nidderdale railway in 1860-2 reduced toll income even further, the Knaresborough to Pateley Bridge Trust was kept going until 1880, primarily to discharge its debts, but even then the creditors were to receive only 4s 1d in the £1.

Richmond to Lancaster Turnpike

Although it was by no means an early one the turnpike from Richmond to Lancaster was the first, and indeed remained the only, trans-Pennine turnpike within the heart of the Yorkshire Dales. As with many turnpikes, when created it was a stringing together of improved sections of routes already in existence, and an ancient road — much of it a Roman road previously described — that had long been used between the two towns on opposite sides of the Pennines.

In the eighteenth century Richmond was not only an important market centre for a wide variety of goods, but also the centre of a Court of Archdeaconry whose jurisdiction covered a very wide area westwards, beyond the Lancashire border; it also was the seat of a Quarter Sessions. It was, however, by-passed by a number of existing turnpikes. The North Road was about four miles to the east; the Middleton Tyas-Bowes-Brough road to the west, turnpiked in 1743, was four or five miles to the north, thus contributing to Richmond's comparative isolation from main communications. Yet it was the main eastern outlet for lead mined in the northern dales, transported to the ports of Stockton or Yarm.

At the same time Lancaster was growing increasingly important as a west coast port, deeply involved in coastal and overseas trade, especially with Ireland, the Baltic countries, North America and the West Indies. It thus enjoyed a prosperous trade in raw materials as well as manufactured goods.

In June 1751 the Richmond to Lancaster Turnpike Trust was authorised by Act of Parliament; with Alexander Fothergill as Surveyor for the eastern division, from Brompton Lane Ends, on the North Road, to Greenside Gate, on Cam, and subsequently from there to Ingleton bridge. He worked at prodigious speed; within two months tollgates were operating at Redmire, Askrigg, Brackenber and Bainbridge. By January 1756 he reported that the 'Road is Sixty miles in Length, Forty of which have been repaired and made good.' £4,500 had been borrowed at interest by the Trustees, but 'at 24 June 1755 there remains £31.3.5 ¼ ... and the Tolls are not sufficient security for borrowing further Sums of Money.'

Fothergill kept a diary which reveals the extent of his travelling during the building of the road. Although it gives much information about the work organisation, the construction, and the costs, it has remarkably little about those who used the new road. As an example of costs, comparable with those of other turnpikes being built at that time, we read that one Wensleydale man worked sixty-five days in 1764 on repairing the road, received £3 5s 0d — representing a daily rate of 12d (one shilling). A man providing and using a horse and cart earned 2s 6d a day. A note written in 1800 makes a rare revelation of what was carried on the road, which apparently helped to provide Richmond and Wensleydale with 'great quantities of grocery goods, liquor, timber, mahogany and various other

Mile-plaque on Green Bridge, Richmond.

articles brought from Lancaster', while corn and butter were carried in the opposite direction.

In 1795 a deviation from the original route was made, by which the long climb from Bainbridge along the line of the Roman road to Gearstones was eliminated in favour of the present road to Hawes, up Widdale to Newby Head, and down to Gearstones. This eased the gradients considerably as well as ensuring that the maximum height reached was lowered by a significant 500ft. The whole route today is a modern well-surfaced road; the original high-level route from Bainbridge to Gayle Beck is either a stony track, a surfaced road, or a splendid green road, but still shown on an 1816 map as an alternative route.

The road leaves the A6136 (formerly the North Road) at Brompton Lane Ends (225998) where there was a tollhouse, and follows the line of the present B6271 north of the River Swale to Richmond, entering the town along the road called Maison Dieu, then down Frenchgate, which since medieval times was a populous suburb of Richmond outside the town walls, now lined with elegant houses, contemporary with the new road which continued southwards into the north-east corner of the

Holly Hill Turnpike House, Richmond, on the Richmond to Lancaster Turnpike.

Market Place. The exit from this large cobbled area was probably from the opposite corner, where New Road descends steeply to the foot of Bargate. Harman's map of 1724 does not show this, but Jackson's map of 1773 does, so it is likely that this road was made to facilitate access to Green Bridge across the river for the increasing number of horse-drawn vehicles following the making of the turnpike.

Green Bridge was originally a stone structure of four arches with large cutwaters, completely rebuilt by John Carr in 1789. He was principal surveyor of bridges to the North Riding from 1772 to 1803, and his bridge at Richmond (169205) with its three segmental arches is one of his most elegant. A stone in the parapet on the downstream side records distances to Askrigg and Lancaster. This way out of Richmond is now adopted by a minor road, and continues up Sleegill, at the foot of which was one of the original tollhouses, now a cottage. At the top of the hill the road forks right, past Holly Hill house, where a turnpike operated during most of the lifetime of the trust. The single-storey tollhouse survives, next to the Holly Hill Inn (172004).

From there the road continues south-westwards up Waitwith Bank on to open common land, now used by the Army. Jefferys's map shows the turnpike to be unenclosed as far as Halfpenny House, now a farm (127950) but during the making of the turnpike it was an inn, shown as such on the 1854 map.

From Halfpenny House the road follows a straight course south-westwards across Bellerby Moor and Leyburn Moor to Scarth Nick, where it narrows to make a steep descent through woods beneath limestone scars. This part of the old road must have presented problems for horse-drawn vehicles, for the gradient still demands careful driving. A tollhouse stood at the junction (058915) of the old road with that running eastwards to Wensley and Leyburn, shown on Jefferys's map but not on the 1854 OS map. Jefferys also shows milestones on the Leyburn Moor part of the road westwards to Askrigg, but most have since vanished. However, at the southern end of Redmire village (046909) one survives, a low pillar of sandstone, slightly convex on its outer face, but with no decipherable inscription.

Beyond Redmire the road winds steadily westwards, past Swan Farm, which used to be an inn, to Carperby. Half a mile past Carperby a house on the left was formerly the Ballowfield Tollgate, and at a meeting of the trustees in Askrigg in March 1774 sections of the road from Ballowfield to Bow Bridge west of the village, were ordered to be widened, following a survey by Fothergill and his local assistant who checked the width of the road and found a number of places where it was less than the stipulated 7yd. Another old milestone stands by the roadside past Ballowfield (991894).

The former tollhouse at Town Head, Askrigg, is now a private house. In 1762 the gatekeeper collected just over £60 in tolls, his salary being £16. The position of the tollgate seems to have changed from one part of the village to another; what did not change was the position of Brackenber

Gate, near Bow Bridge, a mile west of Askrigg. At Bow Bridge the old road made a loop to the north of the present line, crossing Grange Beck by the medieval bridge which was widened to accommodate the road. The old route can still be seen as a green track crossing the bridge and swinging back past a cottage to rejoin the present route. Brackenber Gate (934909) lay immediately to the west, where the Sedbergh road turns off. This, one of the roads of the Sedbergh Trust, was authorised by Parliament in 1761.

The Richmond to Lancaster road turns south to cross the River Ure by Yore Bridge. When the turnpike was authorised this would have been much narrower than the present structure which was designed and built by John Carr in 1793 at a cost of £884. In Bainbridge the 1751 turnpike crossed the village green from its north-eastern corner to the south-western one, as High Lane, leaving the village near the former Union Workhouse building, now High Hall, and taking the direct line south-westwards by the Cam High Road, on the Roman alignment. This is a surfaced road today for nearly a mile out of the village, but where the modern road turns sharp left the old one continues as a walled straight track, described in Chapter 2. Jefferys marks milestones along the whole of this part of the road, but none has survived the early nineteenth-century enclosures, when they were probably incorporated into walls.

The new road, now followed by the A684 from Bainbridge to Hawes,

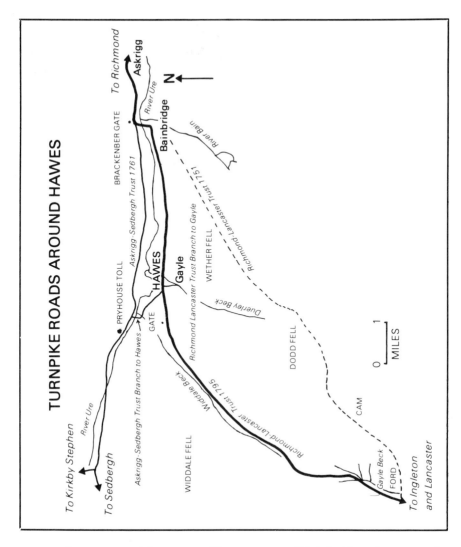

TURNPIKE ROADS AROUND HAWES

was a valley route, with a new tollhouse west of Bainbridge, shown on the 1854 OS map, its site now obscured in road improvements. The road goes through Hawes, and climbs westwards past Gate House on its north side (854897), built as a tollhouse on the new deviation, which became, in the second half of last century, a ropeworks which extended the length of the present garden.

The re-routing of the turnpike through Hawes had a profound effect on the town and the whole of upper Wensleydale. Until 1795 its only communication with the outside world was by packhorse roads. Even the Sedbergh to Askrigg road of 1761 kept a mile to the north. Trade, commerce and the usual run of market functions revitalised the small town; inns flourished, among them the White Hart, which became a posting-house providing accommodation, stabling and conveyances. It may have been at the White Hart that Ruskin stayed in March 1859, describing it glowingly as 'a fine little inn — white home-made bread, fresh trout etc . . . and something really like mountains visible out of the back window. . . .'

From Hawes the road up Widdale takes a gentle gradient to Newby Head where it crosses the watershed and makes an equally well-graded descent to Gayle Beck, picking up the Roman line and the 1751 road near Far Gearstones (785803). One traveller who came this way from Lancaster was the Rev Benjamin Newton, Rector of Wath, near Ripon, who, in 1818 recorded his journey in the family coach drawn by two horses: '. . . after passing over a bridge of a river called the Greta [near Cantsfield, six miles west of Ingleton] soon found ourselves in Yorkshire, the road still continuing very good and much more level than I expected. . . . The whole of the road hence [from Weathercote Cave, near Ribble Head] to within a mile or two of Hawes is through nothing but heath over a very fine road, excepting that it is hilly and uphill till we began to descend towards Hawes.'

Milestones are prominent along the road from Newby Head onwards, and are thought to date from the 1820s, cast iron of triangular section and semi-circular top bearing the name of the parish and the words 'Lancaster and Richmond Road'. An earlier milestone, similar to that at Redmire, is by the roadside north of Newby Head. In 1851 the trustees sought powers to have a tollgate between Newby Head and Gearstones, but free 'to all persons who have paid toll on any other part of the Western district of the road. But persons passing from the Eastern district would again be liable to pay toll.' In the event no such tollhouse was erected.

Although parishes were expected to continue their responsibilities of keeping the road in repair, a Report to Parliament of 1851 stated that although the Trustees (of the Western district, meeting as usual at the Castle Inn, Hornby) had effected 'desirable improvements', they had left the parishes to repair the roads for twenty or thirty years past. In spite of an increase in tolls, receipts fell and clearly the days of the turnpike were numbered. By degrees various stages were closed, and the road disturnpiked by the early 1870s. The whole length of its 1795 alignment survives as an important link between Richmond and Lancaster.

Turnpikes of the Sedbergh Trust
In 1761 a Turnpike Act was passed which led to the gradual improvement of roads radiating from Sedbergh, first to Askrigg, then in 1762 to Kendal and Kirkby Lonsdale, in 1765 to Kirkby Stephen, and in the early nineteenth century, to Dent. A mile west of Sedbergh the Barrett Toll Bar, recently restored as a private house, is at the junction of the Kendal and Kirkby Lonsdale roads which linked to go through the town along Main Street. The Askrigg road leaves the eastern end of Sedbergh by the former Poor House, the line of the present A684, but where this crosses Longstone Fell the original road descended to Garsdale Foot and crossed the River Clough by Danny Bridge (698913). This is now a minor road joining the 1825 deviation two miles to the east of Long Holme (716907).

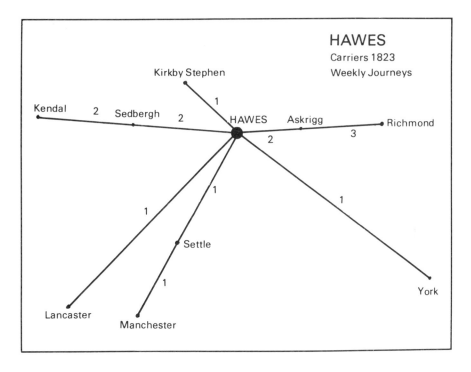

HAWES

Carriers 1823
Weekly Journeys

Kirkby Stephen

Kendal   2   Sedbergh   2   HAWES   Askrigg   3   Richmond

1

2

1

1

1

Settle

1

1

Lancaster

Manchester

York

Cast-iron milestone (about 1825) on the Richmond to Lancaster Turnpike.

Moorcock Inn, Garsdale Head, at the junction of the Sedbergh to Askrigg Turnpike with the Hawes to Kirkby Stephen Road.

New Bridge was built when the new line was adopted. The cottage on the north side of the road near Badger Dub farm track was the Garsdale Toll Bar.

Near Raygill the old road took a more northerly loop (769903), but the 1825 alignment kept closer to the river, the roads joining near Clough Bridge (785918), and continuing the present line to the Moorcock Inn (797927). The inn is not shown on the 1824 map, so presumably it was built very shortly afterwards when the road northwards along Mallerstang was made. The 1809 edition of Cary's map of the Yorkshire turnpike roads marks this place as 'Hawes Junction', the name given, incidentally, seventy years later to the station on the new Settle-Carlisle railway.

The Sedbergh-Askrigg road continued eastwards along the present line to New Bridge (858910), where the old road now carries the minor road to Hardraw and along the northern side of Wensleydale to Brackenber Gate (933909) a mile west of Askrigg. Near New Bridge, by the farm track to Pry House, the former Ellers tollbar has gone. A half-mile west of Brackenber one of the original milestones stands by a wall, but its inscription is no longer legible.

In 1825 the road from Hawes to Kirkby Stephen was improved, with a short extension to Gayle. The present road from the western end of Hawes, through Appersett and across New Bridge to join the Sedbergh turnpike dates from then, following the line of an existing road. A proposed plan of the route shows it leaving the turnpike at a 'Guide Post

Brackenber Gate, Askrigg, on the Sedbergh to Askrigg Turnpike.

on Mossdale Moor', roughly where the Moorcock Inn now stands. An earlier track led from there to Shaw Paddock, formerly an inn (786952), then continuing northwards by How Beck Bridge and Green Bridge to join the old High Way at Hell Gill (786968). The 1825 road took the same line to Shaw Paddock, deviated westwards along the present road, descending into Mallerstang from Aisgill to Thrang Bridge (783005), and then took a new line east of the river through Outhgill and past Dale Foot to Water Gate (777047). B6259 follows this route the whole way and continues it through Nateby to Kirkby Stephen. The only tollbar on the road, now called Gate House, is just south of Castle Cottages between Outhgill and Pendragon Castle. The few mileposts which exist are similar in design, cast iron in triangular section, to those of the Sedbergh-Askrigg Trust (and the Richmond-Lancaster Trust) most of which survive in their 1825 form.

The Sedbergh-Kirkby Stephen Turnpike followed the line now taken by the A683 as far as Rawthey Bridge (713978). The 1765 route took a higher line, followed now by a minor road, past Street Side and Cold Keld, but the 1824 deviation was aligned slightly to the west, rejoining the original just beyond the eighth milestone from Sedbergh. The old toll bar (735010) has gone, but its site is marked by a small plantation. The old road to Kirkby Stephen took a north-easterly alignment through Stennerskeugh (744016) and Flass, is now lost over Black Hill and Pudding Howe Hill, to be picked up as a green track west of the Settle-Carlisle railway (766040), passing Bull Gill, through Wharton Park to Halfpenny House (768071) and Kirkby Stephen. The 1824 line from the former Ravenstonedale Toll Bar is now adopted by the present major road past Tarn House, entering Kirkby Stephen from the south-west.

Other Richmond Roads

It has already been pointed out that, until the creation of the Richmond-Lancaster Turnpike in 1751 Richmond was rather isolated from main highways, although it was the focus of many badgers' and drovers' roads. The important route across Stainmore was turnpiked from Middleton Tyas (near the present Scotch Corner) through Bowes to Brough in 1743-4 and improved in 1770. In that year a branch from near Maiden Castle (868132) to Reeth was authorised, its course now followed by a wild moorland road, by Barras, south-eastwards across Kaber Fell to the coalpits at Taylor Rigg and Tan Hill (896067), continuing down Arkengarthdale to terminate at the Buck Inn at Reeth. The aim of this road was to help the carriage of lead and coal, in which it only partially succeeded, since some gradients were still too steep to accommodate wheeled carts.

This turnpike does not appear on Jefferys's map (1771) but is shown on Tuke's map of 1787, based largely on Jefferys, although it stops midway between Tan Hill and Maiden Castle on Stainmore. Tuke also shows the branch running southwards from Tan Hill to Keld (also a motor road today), and the road westwards from Keld through Birkdale to Kirkby Stephen. On Clarkson's Plan of the Reeth-Tan Hill Turnpike, surveyed for a subsequent renewal of the Act of 1833, buildings at what is now Tan

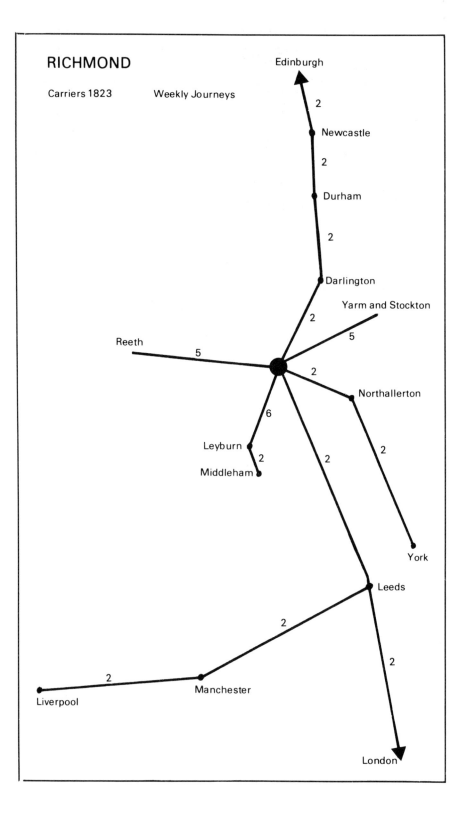

RICHMOND

Carriers 1823   Weekly Journeys

Edinburgh

2

Newcastle

2

Durham

2

Darlington

Yarm and Stockton

2

5

Reeth

5

2

Northallerton

6

2

Leyburn

2

Middleham

2

York

Leeds

2

2

2

Liverpool

Manchester

London

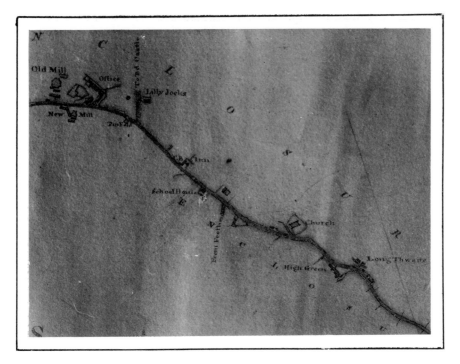

Part of Clarkson's Map of the Tan Hill to Reeth Turnpike, drawn in 1836, showing section in Arkengarthdale. The Old and New Mills were for lead smelting Note 'Lilly Jock's', a drovers' inn by the Stang.

Hill Inn are described as 'Pitt Houses'. Roads to the various coalpits nearby are also shown on this plan, as is 'Lily Jocks' a drovers' inn at Eskeleth (000035) and the only toll-bar on the road, at Punchard (973053), now a private house.

From Reeth the old road to Richmond was used, leaving the village at the bottom of the Green, across Reeth Bridge, rebuilt by Carr in 1773, and at Fremington continuing eastwards by what is now a minor motor road which climbs steeply up by Copperthwaite Allotment and then drops just as steeply again into Marske (104005). Charles Turner, part-owner of the mines and manor of Arkengarthdale, who in the 1760s lived at Clints, near Marske, improved the road through the village, and although the Marske-Downholme bridge had been rebuilt by Carr at the same time, the road to Richmond continued its old, high-level course from Marske, by Richmond Out Moor and High Gingerfield, entering the town at the west by what was the old beast market and 'The Back Ends', now Victoria Road. In spite of the limitations of this and other roads around Swaledale there was in 1823 a regular carriage service from Richmond to most Swaledale villages, and to Darlington, Stockton, Durham, Newcastle, Edinburgh, York, Leeds, Manchester and London. Regular carrier services also operated between Reeth and Hawes, and Muker and Hawes.

In 1836 the Richmond-Reeth turnpike was authorised, primarily to replace the old road through Marske with its steep hills at Reels Head and Clapgate Bank, by a valley route to Reeth where it joined the Reeth-Brough Turnpike at the Buck Inn. This is the present main road. The Swale was crossed by a new bridge at Lownethwaite, with a tollhouse adjoining, and the new road kept to the south side of the valley, linking up at Marske Bridge (114992) with the old road from Marske to Downholme. Continuing along the south side to Stainton Lane End (091974) the turnpike picked up the old occupation road from Downholme through Ellerton to Grinton, crossing the Swale by Grinton bridge, which Carr widened in 1797. Its northern arch shows some late-sixteenth century work, however, and Quarter Sessions accounts make several references to costs of repair. The new road joins the old one at Fremington and follows its course into Reeth. Because of landslips the Richmond-Reeth Turnpike required much maintenance and repair — as it still does — and tolls were charged throughout its life, until the trust ended in 1880. The Lownethwaite tollhouse has gone, but that at Haggs Gill (068975) near Ellerton, survives as a private house. Contemporary with this turnpike was a branch, mainly using an existing highway from near Marske bridge running southwards through Downholme to link with the Richmond-Lancaster road at Halfpenny House.

Skipton-Harrogate
When this road was turnpiked in 1777 it coincided with the enclosure of the Forest of Knaresborough, as a result of which its line in the eastern section from Blubberhouses to High Harrogate (and Knaresborough) simply followed the line set out by the enclosure commissioners. In its western section it took over the Ogilby route described in Chapter 4, and the present A59, a major Trans-Pennine trunk road keeps very much to the turnpike line. Between 1823 and 1827 a deviation was made on Blubberhouses Moor, east of Pace Gate, where the 1777 road took a northerly line between 125550 and 168553, its course now a moor road and a path. On Jefferys's map (1771) this stretch is described as 'Gasgill Causeway' and on Tuke's map (1787) as 'Kexgill Causeway'. Between Blubberhouses and Kettlesing it is named 'Watling Street'. The new line followed the valley of Hall Beck.

In spite of repeated road widenings and improvements several cast-iron milestones survive, probably put up at or soon after the Blubberhouses diversion. There is a much older stone by the north side of the road west of Bolton Bridge, with no legible inscription, and another, showing directions to 'Harrowgate' by the junction with the Ilkley road.

Townships through which the road passed continued to be responsible for repairs in their sections right until the Trust expired in 1876. In January of that year the following allowances were made.

Blubberhouses	£ 28 10s
Fewston	16
Halton	9

Milestone on the Skipton to Knaresborough Turnpikes, probably about 1825.

Bolton	4	
Skipton	2	
Beamsley	1	
Felliscliffe	22	
Hazlewood with Storriths	20	
Bilton	23	
Hampsthwaite	7	10s
Killinghall	13	
Norwood	3	
Great Timble	1	
Total	£150	

Although the various turnpike trusts improved or created many miles of roads in the Yorkshire Dales, mainly between 1751 and 1836, a far greater mileage was never turnpiked at all. Instead, sections of old roads were improved or extended piecemeal as necessity demanded — which was not very often. By comparing successive maps published during the turnpike period and beyond, deductions may be made, although one must not place too much reliance on the maps themselves for information on one, which had been wrong, was often copied on to another.

Jefferys (1771) shows only one road leading northwards from Horton-in-Ribblesdale. This leaves the village by the Crown Hotel, along the minor metalled road of today as far as High Birkwith (800768), which used to be an inn. Beyond that its line is now represented by a farm track to Old Ing (805774), then forward by the stony lane which is now the Pennine Way to Ling Gill bridge, continuing as a green lane to join the Roman road on Cam End (803805). This was the route taken by Edward

Dayes during his *Picturesque Tour in Yorkshire and Derbyshire, 1805*; Horton was described as 'the last village on the upper road to Askrigg'. This clearly implies an alternative route, shown on Tuke's map (1787) and now taken by the B6479, linking with the Richmond-Lancaster road at Ribble Head (766793). The modern map describes this, near Ribble Head, as Gauber Road, then as Ingman Lodge Road, and, farther south, as Selside Shaw Old Lane. Sometime between 1771 and 1787 these old stretches must have been linked, and continued to Horton, crossing the Ribble by a bridge near the Crown Hotel. This bridge is, however, not attributed to Carr, although he was responsible for that over Horton Beck (811721), where a new one has recently been completed. An 1816 reprint of Tuke's map shows the 1795 Widdale line of the turnpike, between Ribble Head and Hawes, downgrading the old road from Settle, via Cam and the Roman road, to a secondary road.

The fifteenth edition of Paterson's 'Roads' (1811) persists in directing travellers along the old road, as part of the way from London to Askrigg, by Halifax, Skipton and Settle, and beyond Horton: 'Old Inge. Three miles farther you encounter the road from Lancaster . . . and turn on the right at the 12th milestone from Settle and just beyond the 26th from Lancaster [Both are marked by Jefferys] . . . Beyond the 28th milestone on Cam Hill, you may turn on the left, through Hawes to Bainbridge, a circuitous route.' This particular point on the Roman road, and the Richmond-Lancaster turnpike, is at Kidhow Gate (830834), where a good green track, now the Pennine Way, runs north-north-east to Ten End (843869) where the long-distance path branches right, leaving the older, alternative route to Hawes descending, steeply at first, then gently, above new afforestation to join the 1795 turnpike road on Birk Rigg (847894). For the last part of its course this route is a stony track between walls 30ft apart.

At the other end of Wensleydale old maps pose different problems. Both Jefferys and Tuke show a road along the south side of the valley from Hawes to West Witton as followed by the present A684, its direct course then indicates it going to Middleham, with a branch crossing Wensley bridge to Leyburn. Smith's map of 1801 also shows this alignment, but the first edition of the OS 6in map, 1856, shows the present line.

Wordsworth travelled through Wensleydale in 1802, on his return to Grasmere from Brompton, near Scarborough, where, as Dorothy wrote, 'on Monday 4th October, my brother William was married to Mary Hutchinson'. Using a chaise they stayed at Leeming Lane, near Bedale, on the Monday, continuing the next day through Bedale to Leyburn for lunch, possibly at the Bolton Arms, and set off for Hawes at 2pm. Dorothy records that they crossed Wensley bridge and continued to 'a long village on the side of a hill'. This must be West Witton, where they changed a horse. Their next stop was Aysgarth, 'where we came to a public house on the side of a hill where we alighted and walked down to see the waterfalls.' The inn was probably the precursor of the present Palmer Flatt Hotel which dates from 1872. Again the horses were changed and the journey continued to Hawes for an overnight stop.

The next day they crossed the Ure a mile west of Hawes, joining the turnpike to Sedbergh. Dorothy noted the hunting-lodge (Rigg House — still there) on the right, but makes no comment on the Ellers Beck tollbar before it. Presumably paying tolls was taken for granted as a necessary concomitant to travel. In Garsdale they noted the public house (Garsdale Hall) near the church which they visited during a walk down Garsdale in 1799. Their journey continued through Sedbergh and Kendal, along turnpikes, and they reached Grasmere at 6pm. It had taken three days to cross England from Scarborough to Grasmere, with long stops for meals and the changing of horses — a good time for a 'pleasure' trip of just over 120 miles.

Paterson's 'Roads' (16th edition of 1822, revised by E. Mogg) is interesting. A route from London to Sedbergh is given, suggesting a line through Wensleydale, via Masham, Jervaulx, East Witton, Cover Bridge, Ulshaw Bridge, Spennithorne, Harmby, Leyburn, Wensley, Redmire, Carperby, Askrigg and Garsdale. Yet his suggested route to Hawes, similar as far as Cover Bridge, stays south of the river, through Middleham, West Witton, Aysgarth and Bainbridge. The problem, as before, is the Middleham-West Witton link. A possible line for this is suggested by a bridleway running westwards across the common land of Middleham Low Moor (muddled but not wholly obscured by racehorse training gallops), crossing the minor road from Wensley to Melmerby at 089872. It continues as the metalled Common Lane to Steeps Head (067875), and makes the steep descent of Moor Bank northwards to West Witton. This route follows a very old road, probably of medieval origin, which linked Middleham Castle with its hunting forest in Bishopdale, referred to in Chapter 5.

The absence of a bridge between Middleham and Leyburn has always made the south-eastern approach to Wensleydale a difficult one. On the site of a ferry an iron suspension bridge, slung between mock medieval towers, was built by public subscription in 1829, but collapsed the following year when a drove of cattle was crossing it. Reopened in 1831 with the Bridge Inn and tollhouse on the south operating until 1856, it was replaced by the present iron girder bridge in 1850.

Swaledale above Reeth had no turnpike roads. Jefferys (1771) and Tuke (1787) show roads on both sides of the river up to Crackpot, and a 1770 estate map of Healaugh Manor, also engraved by Jefferys, shows a 'Wood Bridge' across the River Swale between Low Row and Crackpot (997975); this was rebuilt in stone in 1835. The only road on the old maps then continues on the north side of the valley to Gunnerside, recrossing the river at Ivelet bridge (933978), continuing by the present line to Muker and Keld.

Wharfedale had no turnpike roads above Grassington, but the late eighteenth-century map shows roads on both sides of the valley between there and Kettlewell. Beyond Buckden Jefferys shows roads over Kidstones Pass, one branching into Bishopdale and the other continuing

Middleham Bridge, rebuilt in 1830. The building on the right was a tollhouse.

the old line over the Stake. From Langstrothdale a road is shown between Deepdale and Marsett, but all surface trace of this has now gone except for a few hundred yards near Marsett (903862). The only other route out of the head of Wharfedale continues through Beggarmans (Beckermonds) and Greenfield to Old Ing in Ribblesdale.

The southern road up Littondale is shown, with a continuation beyond Arncliffe on the north side to Litton and Halton Gill, swinging southwards along today's line, by Hesleden to Great Stainforth. Jefferys, however, does show this road coming over Fountains Fell, and marks Silverdale in completely the wrong place. The road across Malham Moor from Arncliffe is clearly depicted, as are most of the roads of the Craven limestone country. Jefferys, Tuke and Smith show the old road from Hawes to Dent, the droving road to Stone House already described. Jefferys has the road (Long Lane) from Clapham to Selside, and also the Kingsdale route from Thornton-in-Craven northwards to Deepdale and Dent. Thus, accepting the limitations of surveying, particularly in the remoter parts of the Yorkshire Dales it can be confidently stated that, two centuries ago, the area was served by a comprehensive network of tracks, with, perhaps, 250 miles of turnpike roads.

These improved roads, linked to the burgeoning turnpike system throughout the north of England, and thus to the major towns and cities, as well as to the capital, encouraged contemporary travellers to visit the area. Early ones came on horseback, later ones used chaises and coaches, and even with the improved roads, most journeys were wisely taken between May and October. From some of their accounts we can obtain glimpses of travelling conditions along the routes they followed.

William Bray visited Derbyshire and Yorkshire in 1777, entered Wensleydale from the south-east, visited Jervaulx and Coverham abbeys, Middleham and Bolton castles. Ruins fascinated early travellers, curiosities like caves intrigued them, natural beauties attracted them, but the wild fells found little favour. Bray was enthusiastic about Aysgarth Falls and the waterfalls above Askrigg, where he probably stayed at the King's Head (now the King's Arms), which had recently been built (1767).

The Hon John Byng also stayed there, in 1792, wrote tetchily about the food and accommodation, appreciatively about Mill Gill and Whitfield Gill. When Edward Dayes stayed there in 1803 he 'received the kindest attention from the landlord and his two daughters'. On his second tour to Scotland in 1772 Thomas Pennant included a visit to the Yorkshire Dales, and commented on the strange limestone scenery around Ingleborough. His account suggests that he travelled from Malham to Settle, by the old road via Stockdale. 'I descended an exceedingly tedious and steep road, having on the right a range of rocky hills with broken precipitous fronts [Great Scar, Settle Scar and Attermire Scar].' It is a pity he did not tell us where he stayed in Settle, where he 'dined at the neatest and most comfortable little inn I ever was at'. Increased trade and traffic through Settle, arising from the new turnpike, had resulted in six inns being established by then— the Black Bull, Talbot, Spread Eagle, Naked Man, Swan and Golden Lion.

The artist Turner paid his first visit to the Dales in 1797, visiting Knaresborough, Fountains Abbey, Richmond, Easby and Barnard Castle. From 1808 he made annual visits for many years, staying with his patron, Walter Fawkes, at Farnley Hall near Otley. During his most important visit, in the wet summer of 1816, he covered 550 miles in three weeks, mainly on horseback but partly on foot. His journey was recently recreated by David Hill, who visited as many as possible of the viewpoints Turner used for his 450 sketches and drawings.

His route followed the east side of Wharfedale to Conistone, the west side to Kettlewell, continuing to Buckden and over the Stake to Semerwater, Bainbridge and Askrigg. He used the turnpike to Carperby, visited Aysgarth Falls, climbed the old packhorse road from West Burton to Morpeth Gate (030878) for a view of Wensleydale and Bishopdale, descended to Temple (034890), forded the river and returned to Aysgarth and Askrigg. Subsequently, Turner rode to Bolton Castle, took the moor road to Grinton, visited Marrick Priory, forded the Swale between there and Ellerton, and took the pre-turnpike track through Downholme and Hudswell to Richmond. From there his route took him out of the Dales northwards to Gilling, Aske and Ravensworth to Rokeby and Greta Bridge.

John Wesley was a regular visitor to the Dales between 1744 and 1788, but his journal makes few references to the routes he travelled, or the state of the roads. He rode on horseback and covered up to 50 miles a day between preaching commitments. In May 1744 he preached at Wensley, Castle Bolton and Redmire, and thirty years later, after visiting Swaledale he wrote, 'We crossed over the enormous mountain into lovely Wensleydale, the largest of all the Dales as well as the most beautiful.' He preached in Wensley, hastened to Richmond where he 'preached in a kind of square', and in the evening he was in Barnard Castle. In 1761 he had an accident with his horse while travelling over Whitaside while on a journey from Askrigg to Low Row. A visit to Pateley Bridge in July 1766 and June

1770 drew his comment: 'It rained as usual all the time.' His visit in 1772, accompanied by his wife, was made in more comfort, for an entry in the Methodist Circuit accounts records the item 'for mending Mr. Wesley's chaise £1.10s.0d.' an indication perhaps, that the roads around Pateley were in need of repair.

Arthur Young published his *Six Month Tour Through the North of England* in 1771, and although his main observations concerned agriculture he does give at the end of his final volume a list of the roads along which he travelled, with comments about their condition. This is the first comparative survey of some of the main roads, including the recently-made turnpikes, as well as many crossroads.

State of the Roads
(from Kirkleatham, via Scorton)

To Richmond	Turnpike	Very good
To Greta Bridge	Turnpike	Very rough and broken
To Bowes	Turnpike	Middling
To Barnard Castle	Turnpike	Good
To Fall of Tees	Cross	Very bad
To Brough	Turnpike	This road runs across Stainmore and is a most excellent one, firm, dry, level and free from loose stones.
To Askrigg	Cross	It runs over the mountains and is fit only for a goat to travel.
To Reeth and Richmond	Cross	Good; owing to the good conduct of Charles Turner, Esq when he lived at Clints.

Young was quite prepared to give praise where due, particularly where it concerned an 'improving' squire or lord of the manor. Thus he is able to say, of part of Lower Wensleydale, 'The roads around Swinton are admirable. [Mr Danby] has either made or greatly improved above 20 miles of roads, a noble example.'

Swinton (215796) is a mile south-west of Masham, which, as we have seen, was for centuries an important market centre on the eastern margin of the Dales. In 1753 an Act was authorised for the creation of a turnpike from Masham to Thirsk; two years later the present stone bridge was built across the river Ure to replace a timber one. In 1800 a number of local gentlemen met at the King's Head, Masham, to consider extending this turnpike south-westwards to Grassington, doubtless looking to the prospect of capturing some of the traffic from the prosperous lead mines there. Such a turnpike would also improve the accessibility of upper Nidderdale, since it would pass through Ramsgill. After many objections it was eventually agreed that it would not be an authorised turnpike but that its cost of construction would be borne by Mr Danby of Swinton and Mr Yorke of Richmond, who owned the estates in Nidderdale.

By 1811, after the land of the proposed route had been surveyed, work was started on the first section from Bouthwaite (124713) to near the Writhen Stone (141747) on Combs Fell, following the ancient monastic route to Intake Gate. From here it branched northwards to the Writhen Stone, a large boulder with no decipherable inscription. By 1813 this section had been completed and today is a rough, steep track for half a mile, the gradient easing to Intake Gate, the stony track continuing, occasionally patched with tarmac, to Writhen Stone. Half a mile beyond Intake Gate a walled lane called Sypeland branches off westwards, an access track made at the Enclosures on Fountains Earth Moor of 1855. This joins the Masham to Lofthouse track near Ouster Bank (121747) which in turn joins the now metalled road from Lofthouse, on Lofthouse Level. A short distance to the north-west along the motor road is an old stoop, the Benjy Guide, on the 'wrong' side of a wall (117754). It may have been moved at the time of the Enclosures, for its present position is neither on a road, nor at a junction, nor on a boundary.

The Masham track at Writhen Stone has a westwards link with the Lofthouse road, and near Black Gutter Bridge it passes Pilsden Cross (128746) a boundary mark mentioned in a charter of 1259, but now insignificantly hidden behind a gatepost. This road crossing Combs Fell and Arnagill Moor was in use in 1810, for in his letter to John Yorke, William Danby suggested it would form the basis of his new road to Bouthwaite. Its eastwards course is very direct, a stony-surfaced track about nine feet wide across heather moor. On Grewelthorpe Moor (172760) a low stumpy cross stands solitary, 70yd from the road, and a short distance to the east the road forks, the northwards branch leading to Ilton (192782) where it becomes a surfaced road to Swinton and Masham, while the eastern branch descends Low Langwith Ridge. At 176762, in the angle between the two roads, and about 20yd from each, is a large boulder, partially on its side, with a cross incised on the upper face. The 1:50,000 OS map marks both it and stump cross referred to, as 'Crosses' in old type. Both stones are on an ancient boundary.

The Grewelthorpe track continues a very straight alignment eastwards, becoming a walled lane, and crosses the valley of Wreaks Beck at a ford (212755), turns and climbs sharply north to the significantly-named Foulgate Nook, and follows Foulgate Nook Lane into Grewelthorpe.

Enclosure Roads
Many miles of new roads were created, contemporary with the turnpikes, when large areas of common land in the Yorkshire Dales were enclosed. Although small amounts of enclosure by private agreement had been going on since the early seventeenth century most of the upland commons enclosures, through Acts of Parliament, were carried out between 1770 and 1830, peaking between 1800 and 1820. Enclosures were done on a parish or township basis, employing professional surveyors to divide up the land among various landowners, a process which often involved a re-drawing of the landscape.

Main roads, including the new turnpikes, usually survived unchanged, and many miles of old roads and tracks remained little changed except that they were given defined edges by the building of walls, usually about 30ft apart. Since the surveyors wherever possible drew field boundaries and new roads with straight alignments, old tracks were sometimes straightened and widened. The width of new roads was often greater then the modern metalled surface down the middle, thus continuing the long-established custom of allowing a traveller to diverge from a track which in places may have become impassable. When drove roads were enclosed they were also kept wide, though not usually straightened, but allowed to follow the land's contours.

With individual parishes having their own Enclosure Awards, space here permits mention of only a few examples. Indeed, the whole subject is worthy of much local research necessitating the study of parish maps on a large scale before and after enclosures, so that comparisons may be made. The OS 6in maps, surveyed for the Dales mainly during the 1850s, are a useful guide to the post-Enclosures pattern of fields and roads, but maps showing the pre-Enclosure landscape are rare, although some exist in the record offices at Northallerton, Wakefield and Leeds.

The Enclosure Award for my own parish of Askrigg was made in 1817 and carried out between 1819 and 1820. Low Straits Lane and High Straits Lane were created to give access from the existing moor road, which climbs northwards towards Muker, to the newly-enclosed fields. Both are named on the map; both are walled, and both end abruptly at the end of the enclosed fields (935923 and 928924) where unenclosed tracks

Dent, near Sedbergh, little-changed in appearance from the late eighteenth century when Adam Sedgwick was born here.

continue to the moorland commons. Another track, running westwards above the top intake wall from Harrock Rigg (947929) on to Whitfield Fell and Askrigg Common, remained unenclosed, but continued to give rights of access for gathering peat or quarrying stone. Retention of the 'peat roads' from villages to their moorland peat commons are a regular feature of the Enclosure Awards, and the name appears repeatedly on large scale maps, together with 'Common Lane', 'Moor Lane', 'Intake Lane' or 'Accommodation Road'.

Dent's Enclosure Award, 1859, was one of the last in the Dales, with the 'Occupation Road' as it is called, a particularly prominent feature. This runs from the Barbondale Road (680863) generally south-eastwards, slowly gaining height, for 5½ miles to Deepdale Head (724824) where it joins the motor road to Kingsdale. For the whole of its length this is rough-surfaced lane more than 30ft wide between stone walls. It probably follows the course of a much older packhorse track and would have served small coal pits and quarries on the northern flanks of Crag. Very steep, stony tracks, worn to holloways in places, branch off (698858) to Flintergill and Dent, and (712846) down Nun House Outrake to Deepdale Foot.

Straightness is not the only clue to Enclosure roads. Right-angled bends, more apparent on large-scale maps then on the ground, where road improvements have ironed out many of these, are significant of the surveyors' work. Enclosure of commons was carried out piecemeal, with little reference between one parish and its neighbour. Thus, one area to be enclosed would have a straight road to a point on the parish boundary where it perhaps met an existing road. An adjoining parish, being enclosed at a different time, might have its road planned to meet the boundary at the same point but would not necessarily be precisely aligned, so that a kink occurred. If the two Enclosure roads were only slightly out of alignment the resultant kink would be small; if they were a lot out one or two right-angled bends would ensue.

A good example occurs on West Witton Moor, in Wensleydale, where the moor road from West Witton to Melmerby crosses the parish boundary (067868) and makes a distinct kink. Reference has already been made to the sharp bend on Hollins Lane nearby (092874) where Hollins Lane meets the common land of Middleham Low Moor. Another example is on Scosthrop Moor, west of Kirkby Malham (866617), and again at Grains Bridge half a mile to the east.

Continuing road widenings and improvements have largely obliterated the road network implanted somewhat geometrically upon scores of parishes throughout the Yorkshire Dales. That in turn supplemented but rarely altered the lines of the turnpikes, and underlying it all is the older system of roads and tracks that had evolved over a thousand years or more. The resulting palimpsest of routes is a superimposition of the journey needs of fifty generations of dalesfolk. Today they are used for work and pleasure by more people, in or out of vehicles, than at any time in their history. Yet only a century ago, say between the 1870s when the

An enclosure road of 1859 in Dentdale.

railways entered the area, and the beginning of the motor age thirty years later, Dales' roads were probably quieter than they had been for centuries. Much yet needs to be found out about our roads and tracks. This survey has tried to show something of the part they have played in the history of the Yorkshire Dales landscape and its people.

Bibliography

Abbreviations

YAJ Yorkshire Archaeological Journal
NYCRO North Yorkshire County Record Office
   For the map references given in this book the prefix letters are as follows:
SD where the *first* figure of the reference is 5, 6, 7, 8 or 9, and the fourth figure of
the reference is 4, 5, 6, 7, 8 or 9.
SE where the *first* figure of the reference is 0, 1, 2, 3, and the fourth figure of the
reference is 4, 5, 6, 7, 8, 9.
NY where the first figure of the reference is 6, 7, 8, 9, and the fourth figure of the
reference is 1, 2, 0.
NZ where the first figure of the reference is 0, 1, 2 and the fourth figure of the
reference is 0, 1, 2.
Thus, Hubberholme church is SD 926783, and Linton church is SE 005633. In
order to obtain the correct 2½in (1:25,000) map, take the prefix letters and the
first and fourth numbers, so that Hubberholme is on SD97 and Linton on SE06.

General Books
Dodd, A.E. and E.M., *Peakland Roads and Trackways* (1980)
Hartley, M. and Ingilby, J., *The Yorkshire Dales* (1956)
   A Dales Heritage (1982)
Hindle, B.P., *Roads and Trackways of the Lake District* (1984)
Jervoise, E., *The Ancient Bridges of the North of England* (1931)
Muir, R., *The Shell Guide to Reading the Landscape* (1981)
Raistrick, A., *The Pennine Dales* (1968)
   Old Yorkshire Dales (1967)
   Green Roads in the Mid-Pennines (1978)
Speakman, C., *The Yorkshire Dales Anthology* (1981)
Taylor, C., *The Roads and Tracks of Britain* (1979)

Chapter 1: Prehistoric Trackways
Victoria County Histories for Yorkshire and Westmorland.
King, A., *Early Pennine Settlement* (1970)
Raistrick, A., *Prehistoric Yorkshire* (1965)

Chapter 2: Roman Roads

Margary, I., *Roman Roads in Britain* (1967)

Pearson, F.R., *Roman Yorkshire* (1936)

Raistrick, A., 'Roman Remains and Roads in West Yorkshire', *YAJ* 31 (1933) 214-23.

Villy, F., 'The Bainbridge-Ilkley Roman Road', *Bradford Ant*, **8**, 203 and **9**, 46.

Chapter 3: The Dark and Middle Ages

Hindle, B.P., *Medieval Roads* (1982)

Fieldhouse, R. and Jennings, B., (editors), *A History of Richmond and Swaledale* (1978)

Jennings, B. (editor), *A History of Nidderdale* (1983)

Jusserand, J.J., *English Wayfaring Life in the Middle Ages* (1888, 2nd edition 1909)

Kershaw, I., *Bolton Priory: The Economy of a Northern Monastery* (1973)

Lancaster, W.T. (editor), *Abstracts of the Charters and other Documents in the Chartulary of the Cistercian Abbey of Fountains* (1915)

McCutcheon, K.L., 'Yorkshire Markets and Fairs to the end of the eighteenth century', *Thoresby Soc*, **39** (1940) 1-186.

Platt, C., *The Monastic Grange in Medieval England* (1964)

Raistrick, A., 'Role of the Cistercian Monasteries in the History of the Wool Trade in England', *Journal Wool Educ Soc* (1953). (Reprint of a talk)
Malham and Malham Moor (1971)

Whitaker, T.D., *History of Craven* (1812)
History of Richmondshire (1822)

Chapter 4: Tudor and Stuart Times

Camden, W., *Britannica* (1590)

Crofts, J., *Packhorse, Waggon and Post* (1967)

Edwards, R., *The Itinerary of King Richard III 1483-5* (Richard III Society, 1983)

Leland, J., *Itinerary* (1546)

Morris, C. (editor), *The Journeys of Celia Fiennes* (1947 and 1983)

Ogilby, J., *Britannia* (1675)

Williamson, G.C., *Lady Anne Clifford* (1922)

YAJ, Various Quarter Sessions Records.

Chapter 5: Packhorse Ways and Trade Routes

Bonser, K.J., *The Drovers* (1970)

Brayshaw, T. and Robinson, R.M., *A History of the Ancient Parish of Giggleswick* (1932)

Brigg, J.J., 'Customary Milestones' *YAJ*, Vol XXX

Brooks, S.D., *A History of Grassington* (1969)

Cooper, E., *A History of Swaledale* (1973)

Defoe, D., *A Tour Through the Whole Island of Great Britain* (1724-6), (Penguin, 1971)

Head, B., 'Stoops to be set up in Crosse Highways', *Yorks Life*, **34**, No 11 (1980)

Hey, D., *Packmen, Carriers and Packhorse Roads* (1980)

Houghton, F.W., *Upper Wharfedale* (1980)

Raistrick, A., 'Badger Ways', *Dalesman*, Vol 3, (1946)
The Wharton Mines in Swaledale, (NYCRO Publication No 31, 1982)
The Lead Industry of Wensleydale and Swaledale (2 Volumes, 1975)

Lead Mining in the mid-Pennines (1973)
Turton, R.B., 'Some Old West Riding Milestones', YAJ, Vols XXII and XXIII
'Warburton's Journal', YAJ, Vol XV (1900), P61.

Chapter 6: Drove Roads
Bonser, K.J., *The Drovers* (1970)
Raistrick, A., *Old Yorkshire Dales* (1970)

Chapter 7: Turnpike Roads
Albert, W., *The Turnpike Road System of England, 1663-1840* (1972)
Boulton, D. (editor), *Adam Sedgwick: Dent* (1984)
Bray, W., *Sketch of a Tour into Derbyshire and Yorkshire* (1777)
Brigg, J.J., *The King's Highway in Craven* (1927)
Byng, Hon John, *The Torrington Diaries, III 1792* (1934)
Cary's Travelling Companion, 1787-98 (1968)
Cunliffe-Lister, S., *Days of Yore* (1978)
Dayes, E., *A Picturesque Tour in Yorkshire and Derbyshire* (1805)
Fieldhouse, R. and Jennings, B. (editors), *History of Richmond and Swaledale* (1978)
Grainge, W., *Nidderdale* (1859)
Harker, B.J., *Rambles in Upper Wharfedale* (1869)
Hartley, M. and Ingilby, J., *The Old Hand-Knitters of the Dales* (1951)
Hill, D., *In Turner's Footsteps* (1984)
Housman, J., *A Descriptive Tour and Guide to the Lakes, Caves and Mountains and other Natural Curiosities in Cumberland, Westmorland, Lancashire and Part of the West Riding of Yorkshire* (1800)
Howson, W., *An Illustrated Guide to the Curiosities in the environs of Malham* (1786)
Hurtley, T., *A Concise Account of some Curiosities in the environs of Malham* (1786)
Jennings, B. (editor), *A History of Harrogate and Knaresborough* (1975)
A History of Nidderdale (1983)
Marshall, W., *Rural Economy in Yorkshire, Vol II* (1788)
Mogg, E. (editor), *Paterson's Roads*, 18th edition (1822)
Moorman, M. (editor), *Dorothy Wordsworth's Journal 1800-03* (1971)
Pennant, T., *A Tour from Downing to Alston Moor* (1773)
Pocock, R., *Journal* (1751)
Raistrick, A., *Old Yorkshire Dales* (1967)
Speight, H., *Romantic Richmondshire* (1897)
The Craven and North-West Yorkshire Highlands (1892)
Thompson, M.M., *Mallerstang* (1965)
Thompson, W., *An Illustrated Guide to Sedbergh, Garsdale and Dent* (1894)
Wenham, L.P. (editor), 'The Diary and Papers of Alexander Fothergill, the surveyor of the Yorkshire portion of the Richmond-Lancaster road, 1751-1775' NYCRO (1985)
Wesley, J., Journal (1770)
Willan, T.S., *An Eighteenth Century Shopkeeper: Abraham Dent of Kirkby Stephen* (1970)
Young, A., *A Six Months Tour through the North of England* (1771)
Directories for 1822, 1823, 1827 and 1837.
Minute books, accounts and plans of various Turnpike Trusts, in the County Record Offices.

Index

.